Jesus and History

How We Know His Life and Claims

Dr. Steven Waterhouse

Westcliff Press
P.O. Box 1521, Amarillo TX 79105

**Library of Congress
Cataloging-in-Publication Data**

Waterhouse, Steven W.
   Jesus and History; How We Know His Life and
Claims/Steven W. Waterhouse

282p. 23cm.
   Includes Biblical References
   ISBN 0-9774051-7-6

   1. Bible. N.T. Gospels – Evidences, Index,
       Glossary –
   2. Bible. N.T. Gospels – Criticism,
       interpretation, etc.
   3. Jesus Christ – Historicity

   BS 2555.2
   226

Cover photograph by the author. These artifacts
remain over the 1st Century foundation of the
synagogue of Capernaum. Jesus taught at this site.

About The Author

Dr. Steven Waterhouse has served as the Pastor of Westcliff Bible Church in Amarillo, Texas, since 1985. He has degrees from Dallas Theological Seminary (D.Min.); Capital Bible Seminary, Lanham, MD (Th.M. in Hebrew and Greek); Spring Arbor University in Michigan (B.A. Social Science); and Cornerstone University in Grand Rapids, Michigan.

Information about this book and others written by Dr. Waterhouse can be accessed at his web site: **www.webtheology.com**

Other Books By Steven Waterhouse

A Biblical Look at Unborn Children

Papias and Matthew: Papias and His Elder John

Not By Bread Alone; An Outlined Guide to Bible Doctrine

*Strength For His People; A Ministry For the
Families of the Mentally Ill*

Blessed Assurance; A Defense of the Doctrine of Eternal Security

*What Must I Do To Be Saved? The Bible's Definition of Saving
Faith*

Life's Tough Questions

Holy Matrimony; The Image of God in the Family

Depression Recovery According to the Bible

Books available on amazon.com or www.webtheology.com
**All e-book files available for free download
at www.webtheology.com**

Third Printing 2020, Second Printing 2017, First Printing 2009,
Copyright 2009 by Steven W. Waterhouse

Westcliff Press, P.O. Box 1521, Amarillo TX 79105
1-806-359-6362 email: westcliff@amaonline.com
web site: www.webtheology.com

ISBN: 0-9704051-7-6
Library of Congress Catalog Card Number 2009926703

Scripture taken from the New American Standard Bible,
Copyright The Lockman Foundation 1960, 1962, 1963, 1968,
1971, 1972, 1973, 1975, 1977, 1995

Note: Minor variations exist because the NASB undergoes
periodic refinement.

Preface

Motivation for this work came from our son. While I have long tried to stay current with reading New Testament scholarship, I had no plans to write this book. Nathan, a soldier in the U.S. Army, explained he would not have the opportunity to read the 100 books that I did, and then asked me to evaluate the complex topic for him. That was sufficient incentive to write this research. We hope that others who want a simple introduction to the history of Jesus will also benefit from this book.

Some of the admitted literary flaws (such as repetition) result from the assumption most readers would be intelligent beginners but not professional historians. Note the many fine reference materials in the bibliography. They represent international scholars from many denominations. Those who want to pursue deeper reading can identify the experts. We should be encouraged that after 2,000 years the life of Jesus remains of deep interest across the world. The subject cannot be made into easy reading but will repay serious students and direct honor to the Lord Jesus Christ.

Jesus and History

How We Know His Life and Claims

Chapter 1

The Historical Reliability of the Gospels

The latest round in the relentless attack upon the Bible directs criticism at the reliability of the Gospel accounts. Liberals claim the Gospel records were written long after the time of Christ by those who did not have eyewitness information about the life of Christ. Skeptics deny that the words attributed to Christ give Jesus' actual sermons or conversations. They claim early Christians made up stories and teachings to persuade people to join the church. In this radical view, Jesus Himself never made the grandiose claims that were attributed to Him by early Christians. This study intends to condense and simplify the argument for the reliability of the Gospels, especially the facts given on the life of Christ. Its goal is not a thorough analysis of all issues but an introduction in the hopes the reader will consult the full treatments in the fine works given in the bibliography. Some of the greatest attacks on the Bible are in our time. Some of the greatest Bible research on this and other more theological issues is also being done in our time.

Why Four Gospels?

Evidence for the life of Christ is strengthened by having four accounts with minor variations. If there were only one Gospel, then skeptics would charge only one account has no support. On the other hand, if the four accounts were virtually identical, then skeptics would charge there was a conspiracy. With four Gospels that give variations, we have four witnesses to the life of Christ not just one. No one can claim any collusion. Thus, the divergences (not contradictions) in the Gospels actually strengthen their credibility.

Even scholars who do not work with the premise of biblical infallibility point out a number of criteria for its general trustworthiness. When two or three (usually the synoptics, i.e. Matthew, Mark and Luke) and especially when all four accounts give the same event, this gives increased confidence in its historicity. A list of such "multiple attestations" gives the main events in the life of Christ.

1

Other criteria by which historians judge reliability include historical cohesion, embarrassment, and dissimilarity. Historical cohesion refers to the Gospels fitting the culture, geography and known history of the time (see Chapters 9-12). Embarrassment means that embarrassing accounts are not likely to be fiction. The failures of disciples, e.g., Peter's flaws or accounts involving women as witnesses, would not be contrived by those making up stories. Regarding the life of Christ, his baptism by John would not be fictional, as no one would contrive that Jesus would need baptism. It must have happened.

Dissimilarity refers to actions that do not conform to societal expectations. Therefore, they too, must have happened. Jesus was constantly associating with outcasts and those in sin. This feature is likely to be true given the culture of His time. Also, the term *Son of Man* occurs in the Lord's sermons but not in the New Testament epistles. Thus, it clearly originates with Jesus and is not a reading of early church doctrine back into the Gospel accounts.

The existence of four Gospels with variations enhances rather than diminishes credibility. A second consideration is the evidence that the Gospels were all written in the first century A.D. It is not possible to maintain they originated in later generations.

The Late Range for Composition: Before A.D. 100

Quotations in the writing of the early church fathers plus the earliest papyrus fragments require dates for the Gospels within the possible lifetimes of the eyewitnesses. A third consideration for an early date is the attachment of titles in the early manuscripts.

Gospel Quotes in Early Church

Immediately following the close of the New Testament era Christian authors began writing books and sermons. Among the earliest authors and dates for composition we find: Clement of Rome (A.D. 69-70 or 95-96), Ignatius, Bishop of Antioch, (A.D. 107), Polycarp, Bishop of Smyrna, (about A.D. 110) and the *Didache* (A.D. 90-110, *Didache* is Greek for "the teaching").[1] Scholars detect what appear to be quotes from the Gospels within these materials.[2] Since the words and ideas from the Gospels are already within these early writings, the Gospels themselves (or minimally the early written and/or oral sources) must have been composed even earlier. Fairness demands that the time frame for the Gospels or gospel material be placed around A.D. 95-100 **at the latest possible date.**

An Early Papyrus Fragment of John

In the 19th century Bible critics savaged the integrity of the Scriptures (which partially explains the 20th Century!).[3] Liberals argued the Gospel of John was written as late as A.D. 170 and that it contains nothing of historical worth. Neither the events of Jesus' life nor the quotes of His words could be trusted. It has been said that the discovery of papyrus 52 consigned over two tons of liberal books to the trash heap. Papyrus 52 is a small scrap containing only John 18:31-33, 37-38. It is now in the John Rylands Library in Manchester, England. After its discovery in Egypt it had been neglected. Scholars date it in a range of A.D. 100-130. Daniel Wallace from Dallas Theological Seminary contends for a date around A.D. 100 and mentions the Papyrus Egerton 2 material as drawing on the synoptics and John at a similar early date. [4]

If the Gospel of John was circulating in Egypt around A.D. 100, it was composed still earlier. Furthermore, recent scholars argue for John's great accuracy in matters of history, geography, and culture.[5]

Early allusions to the Gospels or their sources and early fragments point to the dates of the originals within the first century. While the Gospels do not formally identify their authors, several leading European scholars argue that the titles "According to Matthew, According to Mark, According to Luke, According to John" were attached (often with a tag to the scroll) as soon as the Gospels began to circulate. Martin Hengel (Tubingen, Germany) and Bo Reicke (Basel, Switzerland) argue that the traditional authors were attached to the Gospels by A.D. 100.[6] The probable early dates for the traditional title give one point in favor of 1st century composition. In addition, the uniformity of tradition and choice for authors argue that the early church made accurate conclusions.

Liberals may argue Matthew did not write Matthew, Mark did not write Mark, Luke did not write Luke and John did not write John. However, whenever the early manuscripts do attach any title, it is always Matthew, Mark, Luke and John. Likewise, when church fathers attribute a Gospel to an author, they are uniformly Matthew, Mark, Luke and John. If such attributions are contrived or mistakes, why is there no disagreement in the record? The uniform tradition is best explained by concluding it is accurate. Furthermore, in the case of the synoptics, why would the early church attribute them to non-apostles and non-eyewitnesses such as Mark and Luke unless this were factually true? Why not just exaggerate and boldly claim Peter and Paul as authors? Likewise, the attribution of the first Gospel to the relatively obscure Matthew (a formerly hated tax collector) would not have been invented only to bolster the books' authority. Unless Matthew was known to be the actual author, the claim would have better publicity impact if attributed to a more prominent apostle.[7]

Probable Gospel allusions from early church authors, early papyrus fragments and considerations about traditional attributions on authorship (early titles, uniform and obscure claims for authors) tend toward a 1st century date of composition. A survey of New Testament scholarship from those in traditionally liberal circles still yields dates for the Gospels within the lifespan of those who witnessed Christ's life.

Martin Hengel (Tubingen) dates Mark at 69-70, Luke at 75-85, Matthew at 90-100, and the "editing" of John at 100-110. Raymond Brown (Catholic, Union Seminary in New York City) concludes Mark's date around 68-73, Matthew at 80-90, Luke at about 85, and John at 80-90. John Bowker (Cambridge) concludes the time for Mark at 65-70, Luke at 80, and Matthew at 85-90. He says the latest date for John would be 100 but believes it could be much earlier. Bruce Metzger (Presbyterian, Princeton) feels it reasonable to date Mark in the 50's, Luke at about 61, Matthew around 70, and John "toward the close of the First Century."[8]

The lines of evidence to this point force a conclusion that the Gospels were written within the first century. However, so far we have only established the latest dates permissible. Evidence from church history, and internal clues within the Gospels indicate more reasonable dates for composition lie in the late 50's through the 60's. It is best to consider each Gospel separately, and then come to an overall conclusion.

Internal clues within the Gospel of Matthew also support a connection back to the Apostle. While Mark 2:14 and Luke 5:27-28 refer to the calling of Levi, Matthew 9:9 calls him by his other name, Matthew. Only in the first Gospel apostolic list do we learn Matthew's profession. He is "Matthew the tax collector" only in Matthew 10:3. Also, there are more frequent references to money in Matthew than the other Gospel writers including units of money (drachma, stater, talents) and a reference to bankers in 25:27. In the Lord's Prayer Luke gives a valid understanding of "forgive us our sins" (Luke 11:4). Matthew uses the original meaning of forgiveness "forgive us our **debts**" (Matthew 6:12). All this points in some way to Matthew the tax man.

Solid evidence exists for the present Gospel of Matthew to be related back to the document written by the Apostle Matthew in Aramaic. While Greek Matthew does not seem to be a direct translation, it may be Matthew himself used his own previous work as a draft source for writing the Gospel of Matthew in Greek.

Others conclude a Matthean disciple perhaps under his supervision (or even after his death) incorporated Matthew's Aramaic sources and added material from the Gospel of Mark. Since Matthew was either the supervisor or main source, he was credited as the author. Daniel Wallace prefers Matthew as being directly involved in writing the Greek text either as author or supervisor of the final content.[12] The Apostle Matthew is the authority behind the Gospel of Matthew, probably as the actual author or at least as the main source for the book's unique material.[13]

Previous information has shown the latest possible dates for Matthew in the 80's or 90's (see pp. 2-4). However, more probable dates for the synoptic gospels are in the 60's with the Gospel that is viewed as being composed first (either Matthew or Mark) being in the late 50's.[14]

Matthew: **Date and Place of Composition**

Both internal clues within Matthew and comments from early church history point to composition no later than the 60's. Internal evidence concerns the issue of whether Matthew was written before or after the destruction of the Temple and the city of Jerusalem in A.D. 70.

Some of the teaching in Matthew assumes the existence of the Temple and the operation of the Jewish worship system. Matthew 5:23-24 tells the reader to leave the altar to be reconciled with a brother. Matthew 17:24-27 refers to payment of the Temple tax. There are also references which criticize and warn against Sadducees (3:7, 16:1-4, 16:5-12, 22:23-33). In addition, Jesus' prediction about the end-time destruction of the city parallels the destruction by the Romans in A.D. 70. One of the main warnings tells his listeners to " . . . flee to the mountains" (Matthew 24:16).

Those who date Matthew after A.D. 70 believe the preceding points only reflect the author quoting the previous teaching of Jesus and give no indication of time for the book's composition. They also conclude comments in Matthew 22:6-7 mean the city has already been destroyed. (It is better to take Matthew 22:7 as another veiled prediction of the future burning of the city.)

In response we must ask why retain so much material (and/or even more why invent fiction) about Temple practices and warnings about the Sadducee priesthood after a date of their destruction and cessation? The rationale of retaining this material is difficult to explain after A.D. 70. Why choose to stress such topics after a date when there are no more Temple rituals and no more Sadducees?

Predictions about the city's destruction primarily refer to a future fulfillment in the end-times. However, no doubt a parallel was intended with the destruction of Jerusalem by the Romans in A.D. 70 (see especially Luke 19:43-44, 21:20-24). It is unlikely anyone writing after the destruction of the city would emphasize the warning to flee the city. It would have been too late!

The predictions are never inaccurate because the actual subject is an end-time destruction just before the coming of the Son of Man. However, no one writing after A.D. 70 would fabricate Jesus' prediction this way unless the Lord had indeed made the prophecy in advance of the Roman destruction. He told them to pray their flight

The Synoptic Problem

The "synoptic problem" need not overlap with the issues of the historical reliability or even the inerrancy of Scripture. Neither does "problem" necessarily refer to the essential authorship of the synoptic gospels (i.e. Matthew, Mark, and Luke).

Instead, "problem" refers to the issue of whether the authors of the synoptics used each other as research or source material. Did a later Gospel author use or copy from a previous book? This issue or "problem" arises from observing that Matthew, Mark and Luke often follow a similar order and even phraseology in their narrative. Bock gives a short explanation in *Studying the Historical Jesus*, pp. 163-179. A chart on page 169 shows 609 of a total of 622 verses in Mark have parallels in Matthew (a 90% overlap) while over one-half of Markan material shows up in Luke. "Only 30 verses of Mark lack a parallel in Matthew or Luke."[19]

Did Matthew and Luke follow (even sometimes copy) from Mark? Did Mark use Matthew and Luke? Which Gospel came first? Was there any literary dependence with each other?

It may be that the ultimate position should be "nobody knows the answer." The synoptic problem need not involve problems with traditional authorship or infallibility. Ultimately, I remain open as to the final solution. However, let us consider the alternatives before giving up. There are basically four views:

▶ 1. Independence

The Gospel writers did not use each other at all. Probably the dominant view among lay people (and perhaps pastors) is that the Gospel authors wrote without knowledge or use of each other. The similar order of events and even wording could be explained by the inspiration of the Holy Spirit and by the order of events in the life of Christ.

Proponents of the independence view include: Robert L. Thomas and F. David Farnell (The Master's Seminary, CA.),

Thomas Edgar (Capital Seminary, Lanham, MD), and Eta Linneman (former teacher at Philipps University, Marburg, Germany).[20]

▶ 2. The Augustinian Order (Matthew, Mark, and Luke)

The difference between the independence view and the Augustinian view is that with this second view the Gospel authors did know and use each other. Augustine (345-430), Bishop of Hippo in North Africa from 396, concluded the Gospels were written in the order Matthew, Mark, Luke, John. The order in our Bibles today reflects this view (see *The Jesus Crisis* pp. 54ff.). Modern advocates of the traditional order (with literary dependence on each other) include B.C. Butler and John Wenham.[21]

▶ 3. The Two Gospel View (Matthew, Luke and Mark)

One early church father expressed this order. Clement of Alexandria (A.D. 150-215) believed the Gospels with genealogies were written first (see p. 21). Following this order, Matthew and Luke precede Mark.

Sometimes this view is called the Griesbach hypothesis for a German scholar (1745-1812). However, contemporary advocates prefer calling this the "Two Gospel" View.

Each of the first three positions has the advantage of following church tradition that Matthew must come first in order. ". . . there is the evidence of the church fathers that Matthew was first."[22] Whether Mark was viewed second or Luke as second (Clement of Alexandria), this poses a problem for the dominant view in New Testament scholarship: Marcan Priority. Marcan priority has often been viewed as a settled conclusion. However, advocates of the other views have been zealous to win back the argument for Matthean not Marcan priority

Recent scholars who contend for literary dependence in the order of Matthew, Luke, and Mark include: William Farmer (Southern Methodist University and University of Dallas with many books published by Mercer); Bernard Orchard (Ealing Abbey London, Catholic), John Niemela (Chafer Seminary, Albuquerque); David Alan Black (Southeastern Baptist Seminary, Wake Forest, NC); Alan McNicol (Austin Graduate School of Theology); David Peabody (Nebraska Wesleyan); Lamar Cope (Carroll College, Wisconsin); and David Dungan (University of Tennessee-Knoxville).[23]

▶ 4. Marcan Priority: Mark was written first then Matthew and Luke

While church tradition places Matthew first in order, most contemporary scholars believe Mark was the first written Gospel. They conclude that similar order of content and phrases establish some kind of literary dependence. The next point in the argument concerns the order of dependence. If Matthew and Luke used Mark as a source, then they would be adding information about Jesus (e.g. the Lord's Prayer or the Sermon on the Mount material). If Mark used Matthew or Luke, he would be deleting material (crossing out the Lord's Prayer or the Sermon on the Mount!) in order to condense. Therefore, given literary dependence of some kind, most choose Marcan priority. Matthew and Luke supplemented Mark's research. Mark did not condense or delete such important historical or doctrinal truths.

While many in the past who advocated Marcan priority have been very liberal, it need not follow those with this position are skeptical of the historical reliability or even inerrancy of the New Testament. Daniel Wallace and Darrell Bock accept inerrancy and Marcan priority.[24]

The two-source variety of Marcan priority argues that Matthew and Luke not only used Mark but also a "Q" document (German for *quelle* or source). "Q" is a hypothetical document consisting of material common to Matthew and Luke but not found in Mark.

B.H. Streeter (Oxford) argued for the 4-source variety of Marcan priority. He assumed that not only did Matthew and Luke use Mark and "Q" but also material unique to Matthew or material unique to Luke which had been previously written. These four sources are then labeled: Mark, Q, M, and L.

Personal Evaluation:

It is possible to hold to the traditional authorship and reliability (even inerrancy) of the Gospels and advocate any of the views on the synoptic problem. Church history should not be discounted. The church fathers were closer to the time of composition than are we. They also had access to more books and sermons that are lost to us, as well as, oral traditions. They claim Matthew wrote first.

They did not have instant communication or computers to do literary analysis. While the independence view may be correct as the Holy Spirit could have controlled the order and phrases, strictly literary analysis favors some sort of dependence.

Indeed, it is easier to envision Matthew and Luke adding material to the Gospel of Mark. Mark is not likely to have copied from Matthew and Luke and deleted so much important material. Yet, are we not possibly thinking in a box? What if Mark is not only a literary work but also a transcript of Peter's oral presentations? Furthermore, if Peter was loosely using a previous written Matthew, then the order and even phrases in the life of Christ would be preached in a similar pattern to Matthew. Yet, in oral presentations some topics are deleted while others are given extemporaneous additional comments. A partial "sermon transcript" view of the Gospel of Mark could explain why some topics are deleted in Mark while others have even more extended detail than Matthew or Luke. Writing as one who has done public speaking for decades, I know it is possible to follow a written sermon text but delete some point and add extra facts to other topics based upon audience need or reaction. A purely literary analysis favors Marcan priority, but was the Gospel of Mark only written in a library or was it also a revised sermon transcript?

David Alan Black lists patristic evidence in *Why Four Gospels?* (pp. 37-42 with comments pp. 42-47). Consult him and

Bernard Orchard for a more complete study. Here we need only consider Clement of Alexandria's comments that Mark is a record of Peter's public sermons.

> Clement of Alexandria (ca. 150-215; *Adumbrationes in epistolas canonicas* on 1 Peter 5:13): 'Mark, the follower of Peter, while Peter was publicly preaching the gospel at Rome in the presence of some of Caesar's knights and uttering many testimonies about Christ, on their asking him to let them have a record of the things that had been said, wrote the gospel that is called the Gospel of Mark from the things said by Peter'... [25]

This quote need not be taken as infallible. It does, however, provide caution not to think only in terms of strict literary analysis of the Gospels. If Mark is primarily sermon transcripts, it could follow Matthew with deletions in some areas and elaborations in others.

I prefer not to be completely certain on the synoptic question. The issue is worthy of research but not hostility between the various camps.[26] On purely literary grounds, there seems to be dependence with a reasonable conclusion that Matthew and Luke expand a previously written Mark (as opposed to Mark deleting Matthew). Yet, there are other possible explanations. Most important to me is the uniform church tradition that Matthew is the first Gospel. The stalemate could be resolved by positing the earlier material by Matthew in Aramaic (proto-Matthew, no later than the 50's) with the Gospel of Mark being the first Gospel to be written in Greek in a final edition (then comes our Matthew in Greek and Luke or as a minority believe Luke then Matthew, see endnotes 45 and 84). This would have the advantage of following the priority of Matthew in church history but also explaining the literary details that slightly support Marcan priority. Here the original Aramaic source of Matthew would be the first Gospel but still allow for some use of Mark in Matthew's final Greek form.

The Gospel we conclude was written first should be dated no later than the 50's with the remaining synoptics no later than the 60's (John could be the 60's or 90's). Further tentative refinements will be given as this study progresses.

Conclusions on Matthew

The Apostle Matthew was the authority source and probable author (or supervisor) of the Gospel of Matthew. It is to be dated no later than the 60's with the Aramaic (proto-Matthew) probably being composed in the 50's. It likely arose from the Jerusalem church with an interest in Antioch, Syria. (See Blomberg *Rethinking the Synoptic Problem* pp. 30-31, 35; and *The Historical Reliability of the Gospels* pp. 206-208. Blomberg seems to also believe in a "proto-Matthew.") Now we study the authorship and time for the Gospel of Mark.

Chapter Two
The Gospel of Matthew

Chapter 3

The Gospel of Mark

Critics imply or boldly assert the early Christians were involved either in a cover-up or in delusional publicity hype when it comes to the life of Jesus. The Christians may have asserted apostolic authorship to New Testament books only to give them credence. However, in the case of the synoptics, why would they select Matthew as a false author? He would otherwise be among the most obscure of the apostles, another "Jude the Lesser."

Even more telling against any false attribution of authorship is the wide and unanimous conclusion that Mark wrote the second Gospel. The tradition is also that Peter is the authority and eyewitness behind the book. Why then not just label it the "Gospel according to Peter?" The early church was careful with the facts and not given to hype or imagination. Mark and only Mark was credited as author. This is true not only in quotes from church history but also in the titles attached to the second Gospel. When a title is given, it is always "Mark".[27]

Mark and Peter

In the previous chapter we quoted Papias, Bishop of Hieropolis, concerning Matthew. That quote comes in a larger context concerning Mark. Some date Papias' writings from 90-110. Others slightly later. Papias wrote about information he received from "the Elder." The following chapter on John will argue that this "Elder" is the Apostle John. Even if we posit another "John the Elder" who was not John Zebedee, this information still comes from an eyewitness disciple of Jesus. The complete quote identifies Mark as the author of the Gospel based upon Peter's memories and speeches. This quote comes from Eusebius' *Ecclesiastical History* 3.39.15-16 and follows the translation of David Alan Black:

This too the Elder [*ho presbyteros*] used to say: Mark, having become the recorder [*hermeneutos*] of Peter, indeed wrote accurately albeit not in order whatever he [Peter] remembered of

19

the things either said or done by the Lord. For he had neither heard the Lord nor was a follower of him, but later, as I said, of Peter, who used to deliver his teachings [*didaskalias*] in the form of short stories [*chreias*], but not making as it were a literary composition of the Lord's sayings, so that Mark did not err at all when he wrote down certain things just as he [Peter] recalled them. For he had but one intention: not to leave out anything he had heard, nor to falsify anything in them.[28]

Papias following the Elder John (The Apostle) claims Mark as the author based upon Peter's authority and information. Church history is uniform in this conclusion. Additional quotes do show geographical diversity in the opinion Mark wrote the Gospel and was Peter's attendant. Papias was from what we now call Turkey.

Irenaeus from Lyon in Gaul (France) has been quoted above about Matthew. He lived about A.D. 115/130-200 and wrote about A.D. 180. His information continues from the subject of Matthew to the subject of Mark. We follow Ellis in his English translation.

"What [the apostles] first preached, they later delivered to us in writing . . . Matthew . . . also produced a written Gospel among the Hebrews in their own dialect; Peter and Paul, however, were in Rome preaching the gospel and founding the church. After their departure [*exodon*], Mark, the disciple and interpreter of Peter, also delivered to us in writing, the things that were then being preached by Peter."[29]

In addition to comments from Turkey and France, the early church fathers from Rome linked the writings of Mark with Peter. The first quote comes from a prologue to an Old Latin Bible dating about 160-180. Then we quote Justin Martyr A.D. 100-165 and finally the Muratorian Canon which is a list of New Testament books made for the church in Rome (A.D. 140-155).[30]

"Mark . . . who is called stumpfingered . . . was the interpreter of Peter. After the death of Peter himself, he transcribed [*descripsit*] this Gospel in [various] places in Italy."[31]

Justin Martyr called the written Gospel "Peter's Memoirs" in *Dialogue with Trypho* 106. 9-10.[32] While the Muratorian Canon is fragmentary at the beginning, it does give this line immediately before writing about the third Gospel. Of the second Gospel it says, ". . . at these, however, he was present and so he set them down."[33] This information shows the second Gospel was a transcript or notes from some greater figure (presumably another support for Mark being Peter's assistant).

Finally, from Egypt and North Africa church tradition also claims Mark as the author and ties him to Peter. Tertullian (Carthage) 160-225 in *Against Marcion* 4.2.1-2 *calls* Mark and Luke "apostolic men," that is, assistants to the apostles.[34] Clement of Alexandria gives at least three quotes concerning Mark as the author and Peter as the authority for the second Gospel. Regarding order, Clement wrote "those Gospels containing genealogies [Matthew and Luke] were written first." Here is a more complete quote regarding the authorship of Mark with the two additional quotes:[35]

"Those Gospels containing the genealogies were written first, but the Gospel according to Mark had this design ... After Peter had publicly preached the Word in Rome . . . many who were present exhorted Mark (as one who had long followed Peter and who remembered the things that had been said) to write up the things that had been said and, after he did it, to distribute the Gospel among those who asked him. Peter, having learned of this [proposal], neither strongly forbade nor promoted it." (Clement of Alexandria cited in Eusebius, *Ecclesiastical History* 6.14.5.ff.)

"[Peter's hearers at Rome persuaded Mark] and thus became the cause of the Scripture called the Gospel according to Mark. And they say the Apostle, when he knew what had been done (since it was revealed to him by the Spirit), was pleased with the men's zeal and ratified the writing for reading in the churches." (Clement of Alexandria, *Outlines* 6., cited by Eusebius, HE 2.15.1.)

In commenting on 1 Peter 5:13 in *Outlines* Clement also said this regarding the composition of Mark:

"While Peter was publicly preaching the gospel at Rome before some of Caesar's knights . . . [and] was requested by them that they might be able to commit to memory what was being spoken, Mark, the follower of Peter, wrote (*scripsit*) from the things that were spoken by Peter the Gospel that is called according to Mark."

The church fathers need not be regarded as infallible. However, critics who charge exaggeration or forgery must provide evidence rather than pure assertion. Such evidence as does exist from extensive and diverse geographical sources is that the otherwise secondary character Mark wrote the Gospel of Mark and that he was Peter's attendant.

Readers may notice the above quotes can be taken as conflicting over the precise date (did Mark write before or after Peter's death?) and location (Rome implied but perhaps as we shall see Caesarea and Jerusalem were the main places of research). The church fathers can be reconciled with each other on these matters of date and place. For the present, however, we stress that they all clearly and uniformly trace the written Gospel back to Mark and tie Mark to Peter.

The New Testament itself does not identify the author but does associate Mark with Peter (in 1 Peter 5:13 "Babylon" probably refers to Rome, Acts 12:12). Mark's mother probably owned the "Upper Room!" Perhaps Acts 13:5 where Luke calls John Mark a "helper" identifies him as one of the authors Luke consulted before writing Luke. Luke 1:1-2 has the same Greek term "servants of the Word."

Internal Clues as to Eyewitnesses/Petrine Authority behind the Gospel of Mark

Papias and Irenaeus are perhaps the strongest authority for Marcan authorship and Peter's supervision. However, even if we only had the Gospel of Mark itself, there would still be literary clues back to Peter and even more general clues that the information was based on eyewitness testimony.

The book begins and ends with Simon Peter. After introducing Jesus Christ, the Son of God (1:1) and John the Baptist as announcing the Lord's coming, Mark 1:16 begins the calling of Simon. Mark 16:7 closes the Peter *inclusio* with ". . . go and tell His disciples and Peter . . ."

Another hint at Peter's influence is the way the book portrays Peter as deficient. One would presumably think the early church would delete such unflattering references to its hero. It is far less likely for an unassisted writer to "deflate" Peter than for Peter himself to be the ultimate guide and to have given blessing to say such things as "... he [Peter] did not know what to say (Mark 9:6)."[36]

Other subtle references tending to express Peter's humility (and thus his influence over the writing of Mark) include the observation that Mark 8 does not include the Lord's comments about using Peter to build the Church (unlike Matthew 16:18 and indirectly John 21:4-19). Mark also tends to focus on Peter in subtle ways (1:36-38, 8:29, 9:5-6, 14:37-38). Mark 1:36 refers to "Peter and those around him."

Literary scholars have argued that the outline for Mark follows the outline of Peter's sermon in Acts 10:34-43 (C.H. Dodd in 1932).[37] More impressive is Cuthbert Turner, (1928) who did a "point of view" or "focalization" research on Mark. Turner argued that the author of Mark has often written "they" changing from an original "we." Matthew and Luke often substitute, "Jesus" did this or that or "He" acted. Yet, the Marcan parallel text uses "they." Because the author was not an eyewitness, he would change the eyewitnesses sources' viewpoint from "we" did such and such to "they did such and such." Bauckham counts 21 such examples and believes they tend to be texts associated with Peter.[38] He also argues for a greater usage of the names "Simon" and "Peter" in Mark than either Matthew or Luke (Mark a ratio of one reference to Peter per 432 words, in Matthew the ratio is one to 654, in Luke the ratio is one to 670).[39]

Internal clues within the book alone would not be sufficient to prove conclusively that Peter is Mark's authority in writing. Yet, the material is quite consistent with that position and gives it a secondary support.

Date for the Composition of Mark

Several lines of argument point to a likely date no later than the A.D. 60's and perhaps the 50's. External quotes from the Church Fathers, internal clues within Mark's text, and conclusions on the synoptic problem are the main factors in dating the Gospel of Mark.

The quotes that link the Gospel to Mark and Mark to Peter have been given above and need not be repeated in full. They uniformly associate Mark to Peter. Peter is likely to have died in Rome about A.D. 65.[40] Did Mark finish his book before or after Peter's death? Irenaeus *AH*, 3.1.1. said, "After their [Peter and Paul] departure, Mark, the disciple and interpreter of Peter, also delivered to us in writing the things that were then being preached by Peter . . ." The word translated "departure" is *exodon*. It could mean Mark wrote after Peter died or after Peter **departed** Rome for more missionary work. In addition, the word "delivered" could mean Mark distributed more copies. It need not refer to the time of composition. The same is true with the Anti-Marcionite Prologue. When it says Mark transcribed (Latin *descripsit*) this Gospel in Italy, this could mean he made copies to distribute after Peter's death rather than he first wrote his book after Peter's death.[41] Papias, Justin Martyr, and Tertullian give the above comments that help with authorship. However, they did not help any further with dating the book (other than the limits of Mark's lifespan).

Clement of Alexandria does date the composition of Mark within Peter's lifetime (see above quotes on pp. 21-22). He claims Peter "neither strongly forbade nor promoted" the idea of writing, and that after composition Peter "was pleased" and "ratified the writing for reading in the churches." Thus, Clement believed Mark was written before Peter's death. Papias seems to imply a transcript approach which favors composition within Peter's life. In addition, Irenaeus can be interpreted and reconciled as saying Mark wrote after Peter's **departure (not death)**. Then his full paragraph makes more sense because it also says that Mark delivered "the things that were **then being preached** by Peter" (i.e., both composition and distribution within Peter's lifetime).

The church fathers can be understood as contradictory on the date of Mark's book (Clement as before Peter's death, Irenaeus after Peter's exodus, i.e. death). Nevertheless, they can also be harmonized with a slight edge to Mark being dated before Peter's death (before A.D. 65). If not, then the book is shortly after.

Additional issues include the date for Mark relative to the Temple's destruction and views on the synoptic problem. Above we argued that Matthew was written before the Jerusalem Temple was destroyed in A.D. 70 (see pp. 9-10). Mark 13:18 says, "Pray that it may not happen in winter." While Jesus could give this hypothetical warning in prediction of events future to his days, anyone writing after A.D. 70 would omit the potential problem with the reference to "winter." The Romans destroyed the Temple in August! Additional internal clues for an early date will be given below. They could be indications of an early composition but at the least show the sources and information from which Mark drew are very early.

Views on the synoptic problem also relate to the date for Mark's composition. As will be discussed in following sections, the book of Acts ends before Paul's trial in Rome with no mention of the Temple's destruction or the deaths of Peter and Paul in A.D. 65-70. In fact, Acts does not even mention the death of James, the Lord's half-brother, which happened in A.D. 62 (even Josephus mentions this, *Antiquities*, 20.197ff.). Therefore, the Book of Acts is best dated before A.D. 62 and the Gospel of Luke in A.D. 60-61. While synoptic similarities might be explained by other ways, it is more probable that Luke used Mark. If so, Mark probably dates into the 50's and must be dated no later than the 60's. The sources for the Gospel of Mark are likely even earlier (see pp. 30ff. below).

The Place of Composition: Rome?

Many trace the Gospel of Mark back to Rome. As Mark was Peter's assistant and Peter probably died in Rome, this seems reasonable.

The book has several Latin terms in it (*speculatora*, "executioner" in 6:27, *quadrans* in 12:42; a coin that Wallace on www.bible.org says only circulated in the West, *sextarinus* in Mark

7:4, *centurio*, 15:39, 44-45, as examples for a total of 10 Latinisms).[42] Also, Mark explains Jewish words, customs, and names for gentiles (3:17, 5:41, 7:3-4, 11, 5:41, 10:46).

The above quotes from the church fathers do indeed associate Mark's work with Rome. However, they can be taken to mean only the idea for writing Peter's speeches came from the Romans or that the book was later distributed or publicized in Rome. The Anti-Marcionite Prologue says Mark "transcribed **or transmitted**" his book in Rome.[43] Irenaeus can also be understood to refer to the **transmission** of the written Gospel in Rome.[44] Therefore, the information from the church fathers allows for a composition in Rome, but technically only requires a Roman appeal that something be eventually written which later was distributed there. Also, Latin influence in the text of Mark might also fit some of the work being done in Caesarea, the Roman capital of Judea.

In addition to a Latin influence, Mark has more Aramaic than Matthew (the Gospel for the Jews!) as will be discussed below (see p. 30). While Peter himself would be a mobile source of information, other clues in Mark point to an origin within Israel. One could limit composition to Rome or believe the finishing touches have a Roman slant. However, it may be better to think Mark also gathered information from Israel (especially on visits to Jerusalem) while based with Peter in Caesarea. Maybe some of the written work took place there, and then was later distributed (or finalized) in Rome. This is the view of both Ellis (Southwestern Baptist) and Reicke (Basel). They further believe Mark and Luke collaborated on their Gospels and that this joint work explains some shared themes. Ellis based on Galatians 2:9 believes the pillars of the Church (Peter, James and John) plus Paul were the ultimate origin of the four Gospels (Peter with the church in Caesarea led to the Gospel of Mark, Paul also in prison in Caesarea led to the Gospel of Luke, James and Matthew presided over the church in Jerusalem and also led to the production of Matthew, John left Jerusalem before A.D. 70 and finished his Gospel in Ephesus). These conclusions can not be treated now, but they are important. The overlap between Matthew, Mark, and Luke focused on Caesarea (and Jerusalem) could explain many features of the synoptic Gospels being similar. In the present context, we will only pause to consider whether the Gospel of Mark might also have origins in Caesarea in addition to distribution (or even final editing) in Rome.

The Place of Composition: Research in Israel, Writing in Caesarea or Rome?

While Peter as Mark's main source of information would be constantly on the move, below we will discuss the probability that Mark's other sources were in Israel. Did Mark research some of his Gospel in Jerusalem and Caesarea, and then do the actual writing in Rome? Did he finish the Gospel of Mark in Caesarea (for the Romans there), and then also distribute it further in Rome? Was there a preliminary written Gospel of Mark in Caesarea with a final revision in Rome? Can various drafts explain two endings for the book?

Any of these is possible, but I do believe that some of the work for the Gospel of Mark must have occurred in Judea. In other words, it was not all done in Rome. Furthermore, a good explanation for the overlap in the Gospels would involve Mark writing some of it in Caesarea and sharing the material with Luke who was in attendance upon Paul in prison there (see Acts 20-26). Thus, at least some of the Gospel of Mark was written in Judea (Caesarea) before Mark went with Peter to Rome where he distributed or finished the Gospel of Mark.

Peter obviously had ties back to Galilee, the Jerusalem church (Acts 12 and 15) and Caesarea (Acts 10). Mark's mother probably owned the Upper Room in Jerusalem (cf. Acts 1:13, 12:12). Evidence presented below for Aramaisms within Mark, evidences for early material, eyewitness accounts, additional possible sources for Mark such as Bartimaeus, and even the possibility of written material on the Passion Week even before the composition of Mark 8-16 make one think that the Gospel of Mark originated in Israel even if it also had ties to Rome. Origins in both the Jerusalem church but also Caesarea could explain the Latinisms as Caesarea was the Roman capital of Judea with Cornelius and Peter key figures in the church there.

The provenance of the prison epistles perhaps overlaps with the writing of both Mark and Luke. Colossians, Ephesians and Philemon were likely written from the same place. If it was Rome, then Mark and Luke were together in Rome (Colossians 4:10, 14; Philemon 24).

27

If these prison epistles were sent from Caesarea, then Mark and Luke were probably together in Caesarea. We will present evidence for these positions in the next chapter on the Gospel of Luke. Nearly all scholars take the position that these letters were written from Rome. Reicke and Ellis prefer a contrary view. If the prison epistles could be proven to come from Caesarea, then Mark, Luke, (and even Matthew) would have been close to each other both in location and the dates at which they wrote their Gospels.[45]

Ellis believes the idea for Mark to write materials based on Peter's speeches did originate in Rome while Peter preached there in A.D. 53-54. Then Peter returned to Israel where Mark researched and wrote the Gospel of Mark in Caesarea around A.D. 55-58 (thus, explaining Latinisms). Finally, Peter returned to Rome for additional ministry and martyrdom about A.D. 65. During this ministry and after Peter's death the Gospel of Mark was distributed in Rome. This theory explains both a connection to Israel (especially Caesarea) and Rome in the background to Mark's Gospel.[46] While no one can be certain, this reconstruction has much to commend it both as explanation for the provenance of the Gospel of Mark and the synoptic problem. Regardless of the place for the prison epistles, evidence for the sources in Mark is alone sufficient to link this Gospel back to Israel in some way. Materials for the Gospel, whether oral traditions and/or written, pre-date Peter's ministry in Rome.

An old Latin prologue to Mark (A.D. 100-200) says, "But after the demise of Peter, taking this gospel that he had composed he [Mark] journeyed to Egypt, and being ordained the first bishop of Alexandria he founded the church there . . . ."[47] Eusebius also links Mark to Egypt after Peter's martyrdom. Eusebius says, "Now they say that this Mark was the first to be sent to Egypt to preach the gospel that he had also committed to writing, and was the first to establish churches in Alexandria itself"[48] (Eusebius, *Ecclesiastical History* 2.16.1). Black (following Farmer) suggests that the additions to Mark 16:9-20 may have been added by Mark in Egypt after he had read Matthew or Luke.[49]

Hints in Mark for Early Dates and Origin in Israel

In addition to previous literary arguments that Peter was the main source behind Mark, several features point either to an early date and/or an ultimate origin in Israel. Each of these features might be given other explanations but cumulatively they support traditional conclusions and even establish that Mark's information comes from data far earlier than latest possible time of final composition (A.D. 60's).

Marcan Details and Aramaic Expressions

Phrases in Mark give details, specific times, and emotions. Opponents would argue these may only indicate creative writing skills on the part of an author who supplements the facts. Thus, by itself such style would not prove early and eyewitness sources to a resistant critic. Yet, if we come to these observations after having considered and accepted the evidence for Petrine and other early sources, these facts give additional secondary supports to an early dating for the Gospel of Mark. They fit and add to the direction that the stronger evidence already supports.

While in a boat during a storm, Jesus slept on a "cushion" Mark 4:38 (a sandbag used for ballast?). At the multiplication of the bread the grass was "green" (Mark 6:39). They sat in "groups" (the Greek is "garden beds") of "hundreds and fifties." Mark's sources observed such details. Five times Jesus looked around the circle to gauge reactions (Mark 3:5, 34, 5:32, 10:23, 11:11.) Luke mentions this "look" only once; Matthew, not at all. Mark's sources observed the details of the events.

When Jesus viewed the masses, He was "moved with pity" (Mark 1:41). He looked upon those who criticized healing on the Sabbath with "anger" (Mark 3:5) and was "indignant" at the disciples for not allowing children to come for His blessing (Mark 10:14). Mark's sources observed Jesus' emotions. Mark's text also gives time and place notations: "that evening, at sun-down" (Mark 1:32-33), ". . . it was already late" (Mark 11:11), "they passed by in the morning" (11:20).[50]

Reference has been made above to Latinisms within Mark. Yet, there are also many Aramaic expressions. "Mark contains the highest incidence of Aramaic words preserved in Greek transliterations: for example, *Boanerges* (3:17), *talitha koum* (5:41), *corban* (7:11), *ephphatha* (7:34), and *Abba* (14:36)."[51] Bauckham cited Hengel (Tubingen) and Casey (Cambridge University Press) to argue for Aramaic influence.

> "The author of Mark seems to have been bilingual competent in both Greek and Aramaic, a characteristic that suggests a Palestinian, and most plausibly a Jerusalem Jew. Martin Hengel points to the many Aramaic terms that have been preserved in the Gospel. 'I do not know any other work in Greek which has so many Aramaic or Hebrew words and formulae in so narrow a space.' More recently Maruice Casey has argued that substantial parts, at least, of this Gospel were translated from Aramaic." [52]

Indications of eyewitness details and Aramaisms fit and secondarily support an early date and Jewish origin for the Gospel of Mark. This would also be compatible with Peter as the authority behind the book and a composition in Rome (as Peter was an eyewitness whose main language was Aramaic). However, additional considerations from the text indicate Mark had other sources beyond Peter and that the information in his book comes from Israel. Thus, Mark must be dated no later that the 60's, although many facts indicate still earlier sources. The book was distributed in Rome, and Mark perhaps finalized his collection of information there. However, it is probable that initial composition took place within Israel (Caesarea would best explain Latin terms).

Sources and Date Indications in Mark

The Gospel of Mark mentions Jesus' trial before the high priest but does not give his name (Mark 14:53ff.). Matthew 26:3, 57 and John 18:13, 14, 24, 28 refer to the trial before Caiaphas and Luke 3:1-2 mentions him as the priest in Jesus' time. A possible explanation for Mark's omission is that Mark's material comes from the time when Caiaphas was still high priest (before A.D. 37).[53] Another important contrast is that sometimes characters who remain anonymous in Mark are named in the other Gospels. This feature could have arisen from an effort to protect these people from the dangers of prosecution. From the viewpoint of the authorities, these events may have still been unsolved crimes.[54] Assuming "protective anonymity" was in the mind of the author, the date for the book would be very early and would point to origins in Israel. Perhaps Caiaphas was still the high priest and those unnamed were all still alive and in the vicinity. Mark says, "one of those who stood by" cut off the ear of a "slave" of the high priest (Mark 14:47). In Mark's text it is not even clear the assailant is a follower of Jesus (as in Matthew 26:51, Luke 22:50). John names both Peter and Malchus (John 18:10). The Gospel of Mark was probably written while there was still danger. There are several other possible examples. In Mark 11:1 "two of His disciples" were sent to find a young donkey for Palm Sunday. "Two of His disciples" were sent to prepare the Upper Room for the Passover (Mark 14:12-16, probably Mark's own family residence, compare Acts 1:13, 12:12). "There came a woman" to anoint Jesus' feet (Mark 14:3). She would be remembered forever in the whole world (14:9), but strangely she is not named within Mark's text!

Matthew and Luke also protect the identity of the owner of the Palm Sunday donkey and the Upper Room. Most would conclude they follow Mark. By contrast, John names the woman who anointed Jesus. She was Mary, brother to Lazarus (John 12:3).[55] By the time (or from the place) John wrote, it was no longer dangerous to "blow the cover" of those who might otherwise still be prosecuted. At an earlier time and place closer to Jerusalem unnamed characters in Mark may not be safely named. Absences of names liable to danger indicate an early date and location within Israel for the origin of Mark's Gospel. Next, likely informants other than Peter also point to early sources from Israel not just Peter in Rome.

Only Mark includes the young man who flees the Garden of Gethsemane naked (Mark 14:51-52). It is not necessary for our purposes to debate his identity. Many believe it was Mark himself. Some think Lazarus who had followed Jesus in the Palm Sunday procession (John 12:9-11) may be the participant in this event. We only need consider that this young man is probably an early witness in addition to Peter (another case of protective anonymity?). He follows after Jesus when the others have fled. Thus, whatever his identity, he

31

probably shows Peter was not Mark's only source of information. There are possible indications of others.[56] These may include: Bartimaeus, Alexander, Rufus, and the women standing by the cross.

Jesus healed numerous people. Only three or four are ever named (Bartimaeus, Lazarus, Jairus, father of the girl raised from the dead, and probably Simon the Leper). One reasonable conclusion is that those specifically named became Christians and continued to retell their stories (see following material on oral traditions in Chapter Seven). Thus, it is likely that Bartimaeus and Jairus were sources for the writing of Mark in addition to Peter. The same is true for Mary Magdalene (not a case of healing but exorcism). Many others who were healed or delivered either never became Christians or did not give public testimonials in early Jewish churches (guardians of the traditions).

While not examples of healings, it is likely that Joseph of Arimethea, Simon of Cyrene, and the group of ladies viewing the cross (Mark 15:40) are additional eyewitnesses who informed Mark. Most interesting are those named in Mark but unnamed in the other Gospels. Despite charges that stories about Jesus became increasingly specific as wild exaggerations and hype arose over time, literary analysis shows the reverse. "In no case does an unnamed character in Mark gain a new name in Matthew or Luke .... The material common to the three Synoptic Gospels therefore shows an unambiguous tendency toward the elimination of names ..." [57]

The best explanation of people who were named in Mark but unnamed in Matthew and Luke is that Mark goes back to an earlier time and place. At the time and place Mark was written, people knew or at least remembered Bartimaeus (Mark 10:46), Alexander (Mark 15:21), Rufus (Mark 15:21), and Salome (Mark 15:40). Luke also mentions Jairus by name (Mark 5:22; Luke 8:41), but Matthew deletes his name from the story (Matthew 9:18-26). Such observations likely indicate an early date and information coming not only from Peter in Rome but others in **Jewish** churches.[58]

A final consideration for the early sources for Mark involve whether the story of the Passion Week was already in written form before it was in the Gospels. Rudolph Pesch of Munich makes a case that the material in Mark 8-16 arises from previously written sources and that his work on Mark has "demonstrated its origin in the early Jerusalem Church and determined that it dates back to the year A.D. 37 as *terminus ante quem.*" [59]

Bauckham (St. Andrews) quotes Gerd Theissen (Heidelberg) as dating Mark's Passion Week material to A.D. 40-50. "He [Theissen] argues that various features of Mark's passion narrative reflect the situation of the Jerusalem church in or around the decade 40-50 C.E." [60] In *The Historical Jesus* Gerd Theissen writes of his own research in the third person. "Stimulated by this observation [i.e. Pesch's work], in 1989 G. Theissen systematically collected all 'indications of familiarity' in the passion tradition . . . . They indicated the probability that the narrator pre-supposes that those whom he addresses have prior knowledge of persons and events . . . the traditions in the passion narrative might already have been formulated in the first generation in Jerusalem." [61]

Summary of the Gospel of Mark

Evidence for Mark's authorship based on Peter's authority comes from both external church history and internal clues within the text. Mark can conclusively be taken as the author with a likely date in the 60's (before the Temple's destruction).

If Mark is regarded as the first written Gospel and/or if one believes the prison epistles were written from Caesarea, then the Gospel of Mark should be dated no later than the 50's (likely the early 50's).

Finally, the facts in the immediately preceding section point in the direction of the origins of Mark at an even earlier date and from within Israel (Caesarea?) even if the final editing occurred in Rome. The view that generations of hype and stories about Jesus were read back into the Gospels is a myth. Mark was written within the lifetimes of eyewitnesses.

Chapter Four
The Gospel of Luke

Chapter 4

The Gospel of Luke

Authorship: External Evidence

Whenever an early manuscript of Luke has a title attached, it is attributed to the name Luke. No alternative name is ever given. Reicke, Hengel, and Wallace believe the traditional titles were in place between A.D. 100 to 125.[62]

Quotations from the early church fathers attributing authorship to Luke arise from a later date as compared to Matthew and Mark. Nevertheless, as with the titles, they uniformly give Luke as the author. There were no known doubts or alternative candidates. With no evidence to the contrary, we should yield to the information that does exist. It is hard to see how the book was associated with Luke if untrue, or how Luke's name came to displace another without a trace of disagreement. After all, if it were not for the authorship of Luke – Acts, Luke would be a very obscure selection. He is only mentioned in lists of names (Colossians 4:14; Philemon 24, 2 Timothy 4:11). Why falsely attribute a book to such a minor character who was not even an eyewitness to the life of Christ?

The Muratorian Canon gives Luke as the author adding he was Paul's companion and a doctor. The Anti-Marcionite Prologue attributes the book to Luke adding he was a doctor from Antioch, wrote the book in Achaia (Greece), and died at the age of 84. Irenaeus also gives Luke as the author.

"The third book of the gospel is according to Luke. Luke the physician, when Paul had taken him with him after the ascension of Christ, as one skilled in writing, wrote from a report in his own name, though he did not himself see the Lord in the flesh." Muratorian Canon, Rome, A.D. 170-180[63]

"Luke was a native of Syrian Antioch, a physician by profession, a disciple of the apostles. Later he accompanied Paul until the latter's martyrdom, serving the Lord without distraction

. . . So then, after two gospels had already been written – Matthew's in Judea and Mark's in Italy – Luke wrote this gospel in the region of Achaia . . ." Anti-Marcionite Prologue, A.D. 150-180[64]

"Luke also, the companion of Paul, recording in a book the Gospel preached by him." Irenaeus, (Lyon, France), A.D. 170-180.[65]

Irenaeus' brief comments indicate there was no need to debate authorship in his day. Tertullian (*Against Marcion* 4.2.2, 4.5.3), Clement of Alexandria (*Stromateis* 1.21) and Eusebius (*Ecclesiastical History* 3.4.2) support Lucan authorship. Justin Martyr (about A.D. 155) wrote that this gospel was a "memoir of Jesus" written by a follower of Paul (*Dialogue with Trypho* 103.19).

Authorship: Internal Evidence

The Gospel of Luke and the Acts of the Apostles are companion volumes (Luke 1:1-4; cf. Acts 1:1). The author's presence in traveling with Paul can be traced by following the first person plural, "we." The anonymous author was with Paul in Acts 16:10-17, 20:5 - 21:18, and 27:1- 28:16. By a process of elimination, we can delete all of Paul's traveling companions who are named within this section (Silas, Timothy, Sopater, Aristarcus, Secundus, Gaius, Tychicus, Trophimus). In fact, all co-workers named within the book of Acts could be eliminated (Mark, Silas, Barnabas).

Since the "we" sections have the author with Paul in Rome (Acts 28) scholars often make a list of traveling companions named in the epistles, especially the prison epistles (Ephesians, Philipians, Colossians and Philemon). The list includes: Epaphras, Epaphroditus, Timothy, Tychicus, Aristarchus, Mark, Jesus called Justus, Demas and Luke. If we first eliminate all those specifically named within Acts, then next we delete Mark who wrote another Gospel and Demas the traitor (2 Timothy 4:10) the revised list becomes: Epaphras, Epaphroditus, Jesus called Justus, and Luke. Of these remaining four only Luke has any merit as a candidate for author.

Using lists of traveling companions from the prison epistles to identify the author of Luke seems to have more strength if those epistles were written from Rome as in Acts 28 when Paul and the author were in Rome together. However, the same line of reasoning might even be valid if the prison epistles were written from Paul's imprisonment in Caesarea. Paul's traveling companion who ended with him in Rome obviously started the voyage from Caesarea (Acts 27:1).[66] In general if a complete list of Paul's associates were made and then those names within Acts were deleted, we would end with the internal evidence also pointing to Luke.

In 1882 W.K. Hobart wrote the book *The Medical Language of St. Luke.* He argued that the author was a doctor. In 1926 H.J. Cadbury disputed that medical terms in Luke/Acts proved the author was a physician. He found many of the same terms among educated authors who were not doctors. Today most would agree that the language was written by a well-educated author (such as a doctor). Still, what are we to make of a comparison of Mark 5:26 with Luke 8:43? The Mark account says the women spent all her money on physicians and only became worse. The third Gospel omits the slam on money-grubbing quacks. Does this indicate the author was a doctor?

Given both external evidence from the titles to manuscripts and also quotes from the early church and internal clues among Paul's associates, there is every reason to conclude Luke wrote the third Gospel. If the early Christians were making up stories about authorship, they hardly would have picked Luke. Such evidence as does exist is universally in favor of Lucan authorship with no one else ever named as a possibility.

Eyewitness Sources

Since the Gospels themselves do not name an author, it would not be any embarrassment to biblical authority if we could not identify the author. Some Christians prefer to remain neutral as to authorship for a Gospel. Yet, they still assert the material is based on eyewitness testimony and is reliable.[67] The introductory paragraph to the Gospel of Luke emphasizes that the author carefully researched those with first hand knowledge of the life of Christ (Luke 1:1-4). His sources "from the beginning were eyewitnesses and servants of the Word" (1:2). He conclusion is that Luke should be dated no later than the early 60's. Additional conclusions must be held tentatively.

The Provenance of Luke

Suggestions for the place of Luke's composition range from Antioch, Syria to Cesaerea to Achaia, Greece (as in the Muratorian Canon) to Rome (just before the writing of Acts, which some view as a trial brief defending Paul and Christianity). While no one knows for certain, I personally believe Luke at least researched the life of Christ during Paul's imprisonment in Caesarea (A.D. 58-60). Since the "we" passages in Acts (Acts 21:8, 16-17) show Luke came to Jerusalem with "the disciples of Caesarea," and then drops out of the narrative until "we" sailed from Caesarea (27:1), it seems logical that Luke spent his time in Israel researching the life of Christ (as in Luke 1:1-4). Ellis believes Luke at least "assembled materials for his Gospel in A.D. 58-60" while Paul was imprisoned in Caesarea.[72] European scholars, F. Blass and M.E. Boismard, contend a first draft of Luke was written in "Palestine at the time of Paul's Caesarean imprisonment" and a second, "Western draft later from Rome." This is used to explain the longer "Western" readings in the textual tradition in Luke-Acts.[73] Regardless of whether there were Eastern (Alexandrian) and Western drafts to Luke, it is likely Luke researched his book in the East (A.D. 58-60). "Thus, he was in possession of most if not all the materials used to write his Gospel . . . prior to his voyage to Rome . . . Whether he began to write in Palestine in A.D. 58-60, whether he took the materials or had them sent to Rome and wrote there in A.D. 61-63 . . . are open questions." [74]

The case for Luke beginning his work while Paul was in prison in Caesarea seems reasonable. Whether he wrote the Gospel of Luke in Israel can not be proven. Furthermore, progress towards the provenance of Luke (and toward a better understanding of the synoptic problem) would be made if we knew for certain the provenance of Paul's prison epistles.

The Prison Epistles

Since Luke and Mark were in contact with Paul as he wrote the prison epistles (Colossians. 4:10, 14; Philemon 24), knowledge of their provenance could help explain literary similarities between Mark and Luke. It would also help with precise dates for these two Gospels. Mark and Luke were together with Paul when he wrote these prison epistles. Can we make any conclusions about the origins of the Gospel of Mark and the Gospel of Luke by consideration of the prison epistles?

Most conclude the prison epistles were written from Rome. This is so common in our circles no one realizes there may be an alternative.

Wallace argues that the prison epistles were written from Rome.[75] In Rome Paul was under house arrest with relatively free mobility (Acts 28:30). It would be easy for runaway slave Onesimus to visit Paul in a Roman prison. In Philemon 22 Paul asks that Philemon prepare lodging for him after his release from prison. Most conclude it is unlikely this would be the Caesarean imprisonment as in Caesarea Paul had appealed to Caesar in Rome. Thus, he could not expect an early release from Caesarea to visit Philemon. There would have been a mandatory trial in Rome.

The book of Acts does not portray Paul under mistreatment in the Caesarean prison. Could he not have had visitors there, as well as, Rome? Also, Paul's trial in Caesarea was held only after two years of inactivity on his case (Acts 24:27). Perhaps during this time Paul felt release was certain. Only later did he appeal to Caesar.

Both Reicke and Ellis contend that the prison epistles (Ephesians, Colossians and Philemon) were written from Caesarea.[76] Further, this allows for contact between Mark and Luke explaining verbal similarities and common order in these two Gospels.

Reicke believes that the word "now" in Philemon 9, "now a prisoner," indicates a brand new condition in the apostle's life.[77] Paul's first extended imprisonment was in Caesarea. Reicke believes personal contract between Luke and Mark in Caesarea can explain some of the literary similarities between Mark and Luke.

"This offers a possible explanation for the structural analogies between the Gospels of Mark and Luke as emerging from a concrete personal situation . . . . No literary theory is able to explain these structural analogies in combination with stylistic differences so well as a reference to a personal contact of the evangelists [i.e., Mark and Luke]."[78]

Reicke also concluded the Gospel of Luke was written from Caesarea. "When in the summer of A.D. 58 he came to Caesarea again to work as a collaborator of the imprisoned Paul (Philemon 24 . . .), Luke was enabled to interview Philip [Reicke referenced Acts 21:8, 16-17 in his preceding sentence] and his people more thoroughly. It thus seems probable that Luke composed his Gospel in Caesarea, merging material that he shared with Mark and tradition units that he gathered with Hellenists in Jerusalem and Philip in Caesarea."[79]

Much of Ellis' views have been given in the immediately preceding section.[80] Ellis believes Luke researched Luke-Acts while in Caesarea/Jerusalem/Israel in general. He is unsure whether Luke began to write in Palestine and finished in Rome or wrote totally in Palestine or Rome. However, Ellis insists that evidence "strongly favors" that Ephesians, Colossians, and Philemon were written from Caesarea not Rome.[81]

In Philemon 22 Paul asks Philemon to "prepare me a lodging." Paul wanted to go to Spain (Romans 15:24). This travel plan fits a departure from Caesarea, then to Colossae, then west to Rome and Spain. A trip from Rome to Spain via Colossae is more unlikely.

Secondly, the name Onesimus is not found in Ephesians. Starting from Rome, the runaway slave would first come to Ephesus with no introduction. However, starting from Caesarea, Onesimus and the letter carrier would arrive at Colossae and visit Philemon. This makes any introduction to the Ephesians quite unnecessary.

Thirdly, several of Paul's associates mentioned in the prison letters are the same attendants who traveled with him with a collection for the poor in Jerusalem (Aristarchus, Luke, Timothy, Tychicus).

Perhaps this indicates they were still with Paul after his arrest in the Jerusalem Temple and subsequent transfer to prison in Caesarea.[82]

Finally, an earthquake leveled Laodicea in A.D. 60. Silence on this event in a letter also intended for beloved Laodicea (Col. 2:1, 4:13, 15-16) favors an earlier date written from Caesarea, late 50's.[83]

That Luke researched the Gospel of Luke while Paul was in prison in Caesarea is not totally dependent upon a Caesarean provenance for the prison epistles. One can simply believe Luke was in contact with Mark and Peter at this time because Mark and Peter were also in the area (Acts 10-12). Using texts from the prison epistles linking Mark and Luke is not absolutely essential to the argument.

However, if the case for Caesarea being the provenance of the prison epistles is accepted, then the belief the Gospel of Luke started in Caesarea (or Jerusalem, or at least Israel) is even stronger.

Overlap between the synoptics may be partially explained by contact between the authors (especially between Mark and Luke). Furthermore, we may date the Gospel of Mark to the 50's with Luke making a draft around 58-60, regardless of whether the final was in Caesarea or elsewhere.

That Mark and Luke collaborated while Paul was in prison in Caesarea is an attractive theory made even stronger by Reicke's and Ellis' arguments. Yet, contact between these two authors could still be maintained without a Caesarean provenance for the prison epistles and either way would nicely explain biblical data and literary observations of the similarities between the synoptics.[84]

Conclusions on the Gospel of Luke

Both external (titles attached to manuscripts and quotes from early church fathers) and internal (the "we" passages) evidence support the conclusion that Luke, the physician, was the author of Luke and Acts. He was a careful researcher and author (Luke 1:1-4) as can be judged by the book of Acts (see pp. 153-156) and the general historical reliability of the Gospel of Luke (see Chapters 9-12).

The Gospel of Luke should be dated no later than A.D. 60 or 61 based upon the observation that the book of Acts ends all historical references at about A.D. 62 (no trial for Paul, no execution of the Lord's brother, James). This boxes in a date for Luke even if one remains neutral on its provenance.

If we assume that Luke was composed somewhere in the "West" (i.e. not in Israel), then we are likely back to the same date, i.e. A.D. 60-61. If Luke had not yet written before that voyage to Rome, then he likely wrote (or finalized) the Gospel of Luke after that voyage but before Paul's trial. This also leads to a dateline in A.D. 60 or 61 in Rome, regardless of any conclusion on the provenance of the prison epistles. Those who adopt a Roman origin for these prison epistles may see some collaboration between Mark and Luke in Rome. However, even without such joint work, if Luke wrote after departure from Caesarea, then Rome in A.D. 60-61 is likely.

However, it seems likely that Luke at least consulted his many witnesses (Luke 1:1-4) some time during Paul's imprisonment in Caesarea. Thus, at least research and maybe even some or all composition should be dated A.D. 58-60 within Israel (Caesarea given Luke's gentile viewpoint). This possibility allows for finishing literary touches elsewhere such as Rome but begins the process earlier and in Israel.

One could maintain this view without a stance on the Caesarean origin of the prison epistles. However, it is strengthened by the theory that Paul wrote Ephesians, Colossians, and Philemon from Caesarea with Mark and Luke associating together at this juncture (Colossians 4:10, 14; Philemon 24). Perhaps they consulted on writing ministry, and Mark shared his written work with Luke. Such a theory goes a long way toward explaining the known data, especially common order and wording but also variations among individual authors.

The specific data may be slightly uncertain. However, there can be confidence that Luke was an excellent historian, and the book dates to within the lifespan of the eyewitnesses he consulted.

Chapter 5

The Gospel of John

The Gospel of John claims to be from an eyewitness source. John 1:14 says, "we saw His glory . . ."[85] This statement means more than a purely mental comprehension of Jesus' glory and should be compared to the assertion of eyewitness experience in 1 John 1:1. Also, John 19:35 traces the contents of the Gospel back to one who witnessed the crucifixion. "And he who has seen has testified, and this testimony is true, and he knows that he is telling the truth, so that you also may believe." Finally, John 21:24 identifies the author (or at the very least the source and authority for the book) with the often mentioned "beloved disciple." "This is the disciple who is testifying of these things **and wrote these things**, and we know his testimony as true." Some regard "wrote these things" as "caused to have them written." In other words, the eyewitness is the source of information for the book that was composed by another. Then the phrase "we know that his testimony is true" is regarded as the endorsement of the final editors or elders in the home church. This could be possible if other data demanded it, but on the face of the reading the eyewitness disciple is the author. Can he be identified?

The Author of the Fourth Gospel

Daniel Wallace in www.bible.org traces the title "according to John" back to "the beginning of the second century" (see also Hengel p. 48ff. and Reicke p.150). No one else is ever identified as the author. If "John" were not the author, how did this attribution to him arise so early and without disagreement? Wallace also argues that textual considerations point to Johannine authorship being attested at a very early period.[86]

Church tradition asserts "John" wrote the Gospel. Some believe this is a mistake. Others assert the author's name was indeed John, but he was a different John from the Apostle John, the son of Zebedee.

45

Lazarus as the Beloved Disciple

Several evangelical scholars conclude church history mistakenly identified the Apostle John as the author of the Gospel of John. As with all four Gospels, the author is not directly identified in the text.

David A. DeSilva (Ashland Theological Seminary) says, "Lazarus may or may not have been the Beloved Disciple, but internal evidence points to him more plausibly than to the Son of Zebedee . . ." [87] Ben Witherington III (Asbury Seminary) is perhaps the strongest adherent of the view that the beloved disciple is Lazarus. Most references to the beloved disciple occur after the reference of Jesus' great love for Lazarus (John 11:3, 5, 36 then following 13:23, 19:26, 20:2, 21:7, 20). Also, if Lazarus were the author, then the rumor that he would not die is more understandable (21:23).

Witherington cites textual research on Papias Fragment 10.17 that the Apostle John was martyred and can be ruled out as the author of the Gospel of John. Evidently, some dispute this conclusion on the text of Papias' fragments.[88] Furthermore, Wallace asserts that even an early martyrdom of John would not rule out the Apostle as the author if (as Wallace argues) the Gospel was written in the 60's.[89]

It is possible that the unnamed disciple in John 1:38-40 indirectly refers to the author long before any references to Jesus loving Lazarus in Chapter 11. Confusion over the author not dying before the Second Coming is just as likely for John as for Lazarus. Finally, Lazarus is named within the text whereas the Apostle John is not. This seems to rule out Lazarus as the author. It is better to conclude that the early church fathers did not get it all wrong in attributing the Gospel to John. What about the view that a different John is the author?

The "Elder" John and the Apostle John

A long list of scholars concludes the author of John is the Apostle John (Bock, Wallace, Barnett, Ellis, Blomberg, Westcott, Leon Morris, Homer Kent, Guthrie, Henry Thiessen to name a few).

However, some, especially in Europe, argue that there were two "Johns" in the early church. Martin Hengel (Tubingen, Germany), Richard Bauckham (St. Andrews, UK), C.K. Barrett (Durham, UK), and Joseph Ratzinger (Pope Benedict XVI) contend the author of the Gospel of John is the Elder John to be distinguished from the Apostle John. Most with this view believe this Elder John was also an eyewitness to Jesus' life and gives a reliable account of His life and teachings. Those who advocate two early Johns interpret a quote from Papias as listing two early Christians named John.

Papias: One John or Two?

Papias reflecting back upon an earlier time in his life (Bauckham dates it to A.D. 80) gives a list of sources of his information.[90]

"And again, if anyone came who had been a follower of the Elders, I used to inquire about the sayings of the Elders – what Andrew or Peter, or Philip, or Thomas, or James, or John, or Matthew, or any other of the Lord's disciples said (*eipen*) and what Aristion and the Elder John, the Disciples of the Lord say (*legousin*). For I did not think that I could get so much profit from the contents of books as from the utterances of a living and abiding, voice" (Papias, quoted by Eusebius, *Church History* 3.39.4).

One interpretation of this text is that Papias in his past talked with followers of the elders who used to listen to the apostles. By this understanding, three spiritual generations were involved: followers, then elders, then the list of apostles. Evidently two who listened to the Apostles and had seen the Lord were still alive: Aristion and the Elder John. By this interpretation the first John mentioned was the Apostle John but the second was a different John called the Elder John.

However, it is equally possible to understand that both references to John are to the same person. Perhaps the apostles are the elders. Also, the change in tense may separate the living from the dead. Regarding the first group of names, Papias refers to what these leaders had taught in the past with all but John having died. Two who witnessed the Lord's life were still speaking: Aristion and the Elder

John. Those who adhere to apostolic authorship of 2nd and 3rd John have no problem equating the Elder John with the Apostle John. Elder could be a title of honor referring to a long service, meaning simply "The Veteran John."[91]

The first view distinguishing two Johns can not be excluded, but neither can it be proven. After quoting Papias, Eusebius himself distinguishes two Johns. However, Eusebius disliked premillenialism and, therefore, wanted to find another author for Revelation not the Apostle John. Papias himself may have equated the Apostle John with the Elder John (as Peter is both Apostle and elder in 1 Peter 1:1 and 5:1). ". . . he referred to the witness of John twice just because this disciple had survived the apostolic generation, so that he represented early traditions and recent communications in one person."[92]

Carson and Moo strongly insist that Papias only intends one John and that "the Elders" are the apostles as far as Papias defines them.[93] They also note that Ireneaus claims Papias knew the Apostle John (see also Guthrie).[94] If Papias knew the Apostle John, then it is more likely that we should interpret his above quote with fewer spiritual generations (i.e., the Elders are the Apostles not just apostolic followers) and that the Elder John who spoke in the present tense is best taken to refer to the Apostle John who was still living. In the next section we argue that Ireneaus' references to John are to the Apostle. Regarding Papias, therefore, Ireneaus says he was taught by the Apostle John personally. "And these things are borne witness to in writing by Papias, the hearer of John, and a companion of Polycarp . . . (*Against Heresies*, 5.33.4)." Others who give good arguments insisting Papias has only one John in mind include: Orchard, Zahn and Gundry.[95]

It must be remembered that whatever Papias intended to say, this quote does not touch upon the subject of authorship. Even if one concludes there were two Johns, this is a far removal from evidence that the obscure John wrote one of the Gospels. At best this vague quote may be used to show the existence of another John. This does not prove that this shadowy figure wrote a Gospel.

Ireneaus and the Author of John

Ireneaus, the Bishop of Lyon, in Gaul (modern France) lived about A.D. 125-200. (His birth is given dates ranging from 115-130.) He wrote *Against Heresies* in approximately A.D. 180. Most understand him to be teaching the Apostle John wrote the Gospel of John. Often those who attribute the book to another Elder John will conclude Irenaeus confused the two "Johns." They would interpret his statements as references to the Apostle John but believe he made a mistake. By contrast Richard Bauckham argues that Irenaeus intended to be understood as saying the Elder John, not the Apostle, was the author.[96]

Ireneaus connects the fourth Gospel to John in *Against Heresies* 3.1.1. "Afterwards, John, the disciple of the Lord, who also had leaned upon His breast did himself publish a Gospel during his residence at Ephesus in Asia." [97] Here the book is attributed to "John the disciple."

Yet, in *Against Heresies* 1.9.2-3 Irenaeus makes references to doctrines from the Gospel of John and twice calls the author "the apostle." "... the apostle ...." further declares, 'And the Word was made flesh and dwelt among us.' "[98] Thus, Ireneaus attributes John 1:14 to the Apostle John. In 3.3.4 Ireneaus refers to the disciple John fleeing a bath-house because the heretic Cerinthus was inside. A few sentences later John, the only possible apostolic name in the context, is ranked with the apostles.[99] Also, in 3.5.1 Ireneaus refers to "those apostles who did also write the Gospel" and then seems to refer to John 14:6, "... our Lord Jesus Christ is the truth and that no lie is in Him." [100]

Several other quotes from Ireneaus could be taken to refer to the Apostle John as the author. In *Against Heresies* 2.22.5 "the Gospel" seems to refer to the written Gospel. Ireneaus' writing continues with references to "Asia" and "the disciple of the Lord" and . . . "the other apostles also . . ."[101] This alone may not prove John is the Apostle John, but Irenaeus had already labeled him as such above (1.9.2-3). This tips the balance in favor of thinking this later sentence also intends to rank the author and disciple John with the apostles. Eusebius quotes Ireneaus' *"Letter to Victor"* with similar phraseology. ". . . John the disciple of our Lord and the other apostles with whom he had associated" (Eusebius, *Ecclesiastical History*, 5.24.16).[102]

John, called twice "the disciple of the Lord," is the author of the Gospel in 3.11.9. Then Irenaeus quotes John 1:1.[103]

It is true that the title "apostle" may be used in a non-technical sense and go beyond "The Twelve." The Bible does so when it calls Barnabas an apostle in Acts 14:14. Bauckham finds references in Irenaeus of Paul, Barnabas, John the Baptist, and probably the "Seventy others" (Luke 10:1) being called apostles.

Someone like the Elder John might be called an apostle. However, possibility must give way to probability on this matter. Apostle likely refers to an apostle unless there is some information to the contrary. This is even more true when the name "John" is attached.

Given the stature of John the Apostle, how could Irenaeus call the author of the Gospel the Apostle John and expect readers to understand a different John without explanatory language? How could he best refer to the Apostle John except by calling him an apostle as in 1.9.2-3? The traditional view, that Ireneaus referred to the Apostle John as the author is the best understanding of his words.

Ireneaus is perhaps the most important source for the background to the Gospel of John. Irenaeus was a disciple of Polycarp who in turn knew John personally. Thus, Ireneaus is only one spiritual generation from John by way of Polycarp. While writing in A.D. 180, his facts go even further back in time linked to John himself.

In his *Letters to Florinus* Irenaeus tells of his youth.

"For, while I was yet a boy, I saw thee [Florinus] in lower Asia with Polycarp . . . I have a more vivid recollection of what occurred at that time than of recent events . . . so that I can even describe the place where the blessed Polycarp used to sit and discourse . . . also how he would speak of his familiar intercourse with John and with the rest of those who had seen the

Lord and how he would call their words to remembrance . . . .

These things, through God's mercy which was upon me, I listened to attentively, and treasured them up not on paper, but in my heart, and I am continually, by God's grace, revolving these things accurately in my mind."[104] (*Ante-Nicene Fathers* 1.568)

It is best to take Irenaeus as referring to the Apostle John when he uses the name "John" with the term "apostle" and uses the disciple of the Lord interchangeably. Those who believe the Elder John refers to another than the Apostle John usually think Ireneaus made a mistake. However, the above quote shows Ireneaus was quite certain of the facts he had learned in his youth.[105]   Also, we should give attention to one of Ireneaus' disciples, Hippolytus (A.D. 170-235). While students can come to different conclusions from their teachers, it would be easier to explain Hippolytus followed Irenaeus' view that John the Apostle wrote the Gospel. Likely, he got this conclusion from Irenaeus as opposed to changing his teacher's views. This adds some support that interpreting Ireneaus' references to the author of the Gospel as the Apostle John is the correct understanding of Ireneaus' intent.[106]

Other External Evidence of the Authorship of John

Ireneaus is considered the most important source of information on the authorship of the Gospel of John because of his ties to Polycarp and Polycarp's to John himself. Other early church writings ascribe the book to John (never Lazarus or anyone else).

The Anti-Marcionite Prologues can be dated to the time even before Ireneaus (about 175-180). Its introduction to Luke also mentions John and calls the author the "apostle." "Later still, the Apostle John, one of the twelve, wrote the Apocalypse on the island of Patmos, and then the Gospel in Asia." [107] The introduction before the Gospel of John says, "The Gospel of John was published and given to the churches by John while he was still in the body, as Papias of Hierapolis, John's dear disciple has related in his five exoteric, that is his last, books. He wrote down the gospel accurately at John's dictation."[108]

F.F. Bruce comments that the word "exoteric" was changed in transmission from the book title by Papias: *Exegesis of the Dominical Oracles.* Thus, "exoteric" was likely "exegesis." Also, regarding Papias being John's secretary, Bruce says it is possible for Ireneaus said that Papias knew John (see endnote 102 and Eusebius, HE 3.39.1). However, in Greek it would be easy to go from "they" wrote to "he" wrote. "They," originally meaning John's associates or the churches in Asia Minor around Ephesus. [109]

Therefore, the Anti-Marcionite Prologue probably supports the better understanding of Ireneaus that the Apostle John wrote the Gospel. Bock also lists Tertullian (Carthage, c. 155-240) and Clement of Alexandria (c.150-211/216) as advocating apostolic authorship of the Gospel of John.[110] Guthrie agrees and adds Origen.[111]

Several other church fathers give the author's name as John without specifically mentioning "the Apostle." Presumably John was so familiar that the name referred to him alone, but those in modern times who are inclined to see another John could dispute this. Theophilus, the 7th Bishop of Antioch wrote *To Autolycus* no later than A.D. 181. He says, ". . . hence the holy writings teach us, and all the spirit-bearing [inspired] men, one of whom John says, 'In the beginning was the Word and the Word was with God.' "[112] The Muratorian Canon, likewise, gives John as the author of the fourth Gospel. The list may be dated near the end of the second century.[113] "The fourth Gospel is by John, one of the disciples. When his fellow-disciples and bishops encouraged him, John said, 'Fast along with me three days from today, and whatever may be revealed to each, let us relate it to one another.' The same night it was revealed to Andrew, one of the Apostles, that John in his own name should write down everything and that they should all revise it."[114] Most scholars think the material about Andrew helping John write is "an elaboration on the tradition."[115] Still, the Muratorian Canon as with all church tradition or early New Testament manuscripts gives the name "John" whenever any one is named as the author of the final Gospel. This would be a fine point to move to a conclusion about the external evidence, but first we should comment about Richard Bauckham's argument that Polycrates, Bishop of Ephesus, intends that another John, not the Apostle, is the author of the Gospel. This would be important as the Gospel of John has ties to Ephesus.

Polycrates on John

Polycrates was born no later than A.D. 130 in the vicinity of Ephesus. An extract of his writings exists within Eusebius HE 5.24.2-7. and HE 3.31. Polycrates as Bishop of Ephesus wrote to Victor the Bishop of Rome concerning the proper date for Easter observance. In the letter Polycrates says he is the eighth Bishop in Ephesus. The previous seven were relatives. He mentions Philip had been buried in Hierapolis with two of his virgin daughters who were prophets (see Acts 21:8-9). However, a third daughter "lived in the Holy Spirit" and "rests in Ephesus." This means she was a prophetess and likely we are to assume one of Polycrates' ancestors. Then Polycrates also says John has "fallen asleep in Ephesus." Polycrates' real point was that the Ephesian church had powerful authorities in its past. They celebrated Easter as a Christian Passover on Nisan 14 whether it fell on a Sunday or not.

Bauckham observes that Polycrates said this about John: ". . . John also, he who leaned back on the Lord's breast, who was a priest, wearing the priestly frontlet (*to petalon*), both witness (*martys*) and teacher. He has fallen asleep at Ephesus . . . . These all observed the fourteenth day for the Paschal according to the Gospel . . ."[116] (Eusebius *HE* 5.24).

Bauckham contends that wearing the breastplate refers to substituting for the Jewish High Priest. If the High Priest were incapacitated from his duties, another might officiate. If it is true the author of John wore the High Priest's vestments, then the author must be the "Elder John" not the Apostle John who as a fisherman was definitely not in line to wear the holy breastplate of the High Priest. Bauckham thinks Polycrates equated the author of John's Gospel with the priestly John mentioned in Acts 4:6, "And Annas the high priest was there, and Caiaphas, and John and Alexander, and all who were of high-priestly descent." While Polycrates would have made a mistake identifying the Gospel author with this priest named John, this mistake is taken by Bauckham as a hint that Polycrates did not believe the Apostle John wrote the Gospel. The author must have been the "Elder

John," or Polycrates would have never made this mistake about substituting for the high priest.

Guthrie wrote that Polycrates' term the "gospel" need not be the written Gospel.[117] However, it seems best to take the reference to the written Gospel of John.

Regarding the Apostle John as a priest, many scholars believe this is quite possible. John 18:15 teaches that the author was "known to the high priest." Also, there is the possibility that the Apostle John and Jesus were cousins (explaining why John would be Mary's guardian, John 19:26-27). Salome may be the mother of the sons of Zebedee (Matthew 27:56, Mark 15:40) and may also be equated with Mary's sister also at the scene of the cross (John 19:25). If true, then John and Jesus were cousins. Another cousin, John the Baptist, was definitely from a priestly line like his parents (Zecharias and Elizabeth, see Luke 1:5, 36). Thus, it is possible that the Apostle John was of a priestly family.

From this the tradition may have come the exaggeration that he performed the services of the high priest in the Temple. This mistake is actually easier than believing Polycrates equated the author of John with the priestly John mentioned in Acts 4:6. This John was unsaved and in opposition to Christianity. How could Polycrates have equated this non-apostle John with the author of the Gospel? The John who wrote the Gospel was next to the Lord at the Last Supper, present at the cross, the guardian of Mary, and a witness to the empty tomb. It is unlikely Polycrates could have identified him with the high priestly but non-Christian John in Acts 4:6. It is more likely that the story about the Apostle John being from a priestly line got blown up to having the Apostle John officiating in the Temple. An exaggeration about the Apostle John substituting in the Temple is an easier explanation of Polycrates' words than concluding he wrote that the non-apostolic (but also non-Christian John) in Acts 4:6 should be identified with the author of John.

54

Conclusions on External Evidence for Authorship of John

The view that another John, "Elder John," wrote the Gospel of John may be useful as a fallback position if on other grounds we could definitely prove that the Apostle John could not be the author. Those who hold this position still believe the author was an eyewitness who gives a reliable account about the life of Christ. If hypothetically some clear evidence would surface that proved the Apostle John was martyred very early, then the Elder John theory would have more of a basis.

However, the evidence that does exist favors the traditional view of the Apostle John being the author. There are three basic choices regarding Irenaeus' comments. First, he intended to write of the Apostle John and was correct. Next, he intended to write of the Apostle John but was wrong. Third, he intended to claim "The Elder John" as the author, but most have misunderstood him down through the centuries.

Chances are good Ireneaus knew the truth. He seems confident of the facts he learned in his youth. His contacts go back to an early time of being a student of Polycarp who was a student of John. Not only is it probable Irenaeus had his facts straight, it is most improbable he intended to refer to a different John by using the title "apostle" with the name "John." Since Ireneaus equates "apostle" and "disciple" in other texts, the fair conclusion is that he intends John to be identified as the Apostle John even in the passages where he calls him a disciple. While it may be possible that he used the term apostle in a loose sense, it would take much stronger evidence to overturn the traditional view that John equals to Apostle John. If we do not limit ourselves to what might be remotely possible, all the evidence that does exist points in the direction that Irenaeus meant the Apostle John and that he was in a position to know. Other quotes from the church fathers either clearly support this conclusion or are compatible with it. Furthermore, the internal clues within the text of John reinforce traditional authorship by the Apostle John.

Internal Evidence on the Authorship of John

John 1:14, 19:35, and 21:24 are best taken to mean the author was an eyewitness of Jesus. John 21:24 identifies the "disciple" as the one who "wrote these things." While it is possible this means "caused to write" (claiming the disciple is the witness and source of information for the Gospel but not the author), this view "does involve a rather broad interpretation of the sense of *graphas* ["having written"] of John XX1.24, in the sense of writing by means of another . . . It would not be out of keeping with the external evidence **provided the apostle himself was assigned the main responsibility in the production of the Gospel.**" [118]

The disciple or beloved disciple is mentioned clearly in John 13:23, 19:26, 20:2, 21:7, 20 and probably intended in John 1:35-40 and 18:15-16. Lazarus is named in the book and, therefore, makes an unlikely author, especially since church tradition uniformly names "John" as the author. Within the Gospel of John, John the Baptist is simply called "John" but never John the Baptist (e.g. John 1:19, 26, 28, 32, 35; 3:23, 24-27). Evidently, the author has no concern the readers will confuse this John with another John. If we suppose for the sake of argument the author is an obscure "John," it is difficult to explain why he deletes all references to the Apostle John or has no concern the name "John" alone, without the description of "the Baptist" will be taken as the Apostle John. Deletions of any direct reference to the Apostle John and lack of concern that "John" alone would cause identity confusion with the Apostle, is best explained by the author expecting the readers to identify the writer with the Apostle John. This explains the name "John" never being used of the Apostle in the text. The readers may assume that another named John refers to "John the Baptist" not the author. If an obscure Elder John were the author, there would be no need to delete references to the Apostle John. It would be more needful to identify John as the Baptist so first time readers would not think the name John alone refers to the Apostle.

References to the "disciple whom Jesus' loved" point to the Apostle John not some obscure Elder John whose very existence may be possible but can be disputed. John 13:23 says this disciple was reclining on the dining couch next to Jesus at the Last Supper. One could theorize others beyond the Twelve participated in this meal. While this can not be definitely ruled out, the synoptics stress the apostles as the participants in the Last Supper. The evidence that does exist favors the Apostle John not an obscure John. Here are the synoptic accounts:

Now when evening came, Jesus was reclining at the table **with the twelve disciples** (Matthew 26:20).

When it was evening He came **with the twelve** (Mark 14:17).

When the hour had come, He reclined at the table, and **the apostles with him** (Luke 22:14).

The evidence that does exist strongly favors the Apostle John as having the place of honor at the Last Supper. Furthermore, the beloved disciple in the text of the book is often paired with Peter. Given that Peter was one of the pillars of the church, his counterpart is best not taken to be an obscure John. Peter and this beloved disciple are close to Jesus at the Last Supper (John 13:23-24), "running mates" to the empty tomb (John 20:2-3), and "fishing partners," after the resurrection (John 21:7, 20).

The inner three in the synoptics are Peter, James, and John. They alone were present with Jesus at the raising of Jairus' daughter (Mark 5:37), the Transfiguration (Mark 9:2), and the Garden of Gethsemane (Mark 14:33). If we must identify the beloved disciple, a choice among these inner three is better than choosing an obscure John whose existence can be disputed. Among the inner three Peter can be ruled out as he is paired with the disciple. The Apostle James was beheaded too early to be the author (Acts 12:2). The Apostle John is easily the best candidate as one being especially close to Jesus. Furthermore, Peter and John are paired as close co-workers within Acts (e.g. Acts 3:1, 11; 4:19). In Acts 4:20 Peter and the Apostle John tell the Temple officials they "cannot stop speaking about what we have seen and heard." The phrase "seen and heard" from the Apostle John sounds much like the author of John 3:32 and 1 John 1:3. Reasoning from the beloved disciple's pairing with Peter and the Apostle John's pairing with Peter in Acts, plus identifying the beloved disciple as within the inner three; internal clues favor the Apostle John as the author.

In John 19:26-27 Jesus on the cross entrusts the care of His mother Mary to the beloved disciple. "His mother's sister" (John 19:25) could be identified as "Salome" (Mark 15:40), "the mother of the sons of Zebedee" (Matthew 27:56). If this woman is the same, Jesus and the Apostle John were cousins. Jesus' half brothers did not believe in Him until after the resurrection (cf. John 7:5; 1 Cor. 15:7; James 1:1; Jude 1). It is more likely the Apostle John became Mary's caretaker as opposed to an unknown "John" whose existence depends upon a debatable interpretation of Papias.

The beloved disciple of John 21:7 and 20 went fishing with the group listed in John 21:2: "Simon Peter, and Thomas called Didymus, and Nathanel of Cana in Galilee, and the sons of Zebedee, and two others of His disciples . . ." Peter, Thomas, and Nathanel may be ruled out as they are all named in the book and/or contrasted with the beloved disciple. The choice is between "two others" or the "sons of Zebedee." It will be conceded that the beloved disciple could theoretically be among "two others." Yet, the sons of Zebedee (including the Apostle John) were fishing partners with Peter and his brother Andrew (Luke 5:10).

Internal clues within the text of John yield the same conclusion as does the evidence from the church fathers. The view that an unknown Elder John is the author might be made to fit the evidence if on other conclusive grounds the Apostle John could be clearly ruled out as an author. Those who maintain this view usually believe this Elder John was also an eyewitness. While not a matter of heresy, Ireneaus is best taken to support the apostolic authorship of John. It is highly probable that the beloved disciple was the Apostle John within the circle of the inner three, that the Apostles were the main participants in places of honor at the Last Supper, that the Apostle John is the beloved disciple paired with Peter, and that the Apostle John became Mary's guardian. The reason the author of the Gospel never mentioned the Apostle John (or his brother James) and has no concern that readers would identify "John" with the Apostle John not the Baptist is that the author assumed everyone understood the Apostle John was the one writing the book. Would anyone else except the older and respected Apostle John dare compare himself to Peter favorably or label himself as the beloved disciple?

Date and Place of Composition

Critical scholars in the 19th century often dated the Gospel of John "to the mid- or even to the late second century."[119] Whatever the final decision regarding the date, the book should not be placed after A.D. 100. The earliest fragment of any New Testament book is John 18:31-37, 37-38 called p[52]. It "is to be dated as early as 100 C.E., and the Papyrus Egerton 2, which is to be dated at about the same time, draws on both John and the Synoptics for its material."[120] If the Gospel of John circulated in Egypt (the location where p[52] was found), in A.D. 100-125, then the original book was penned even earlier. These fragments have ruled out critical views on a very late date for John's Gospel. Also, some scholars find "early patristic *hints*" to quotes from John in the writings of "Ignatius, Justin, and Tatian."[121] Ignatius, the Bishop of Antioch, is the earliest possible quote as he wrote in approximately A.D. 107-108. Barnett compares Ignatius' *Letter to the Philadelphians* 7.1 to John 3:8,[122] "For it [the Spirit] knoweth whence it comes and whether it goeth" (Philadelphians 7.1). Regarding Justin's use of the Gospel of John, Guthrie thinks it is probable. "Certainly the theological ideas of Justin would seem to find roots in the Gospel and in one or two places it is highly probable that Justin directly cites it."[123]

The early manuscripts especially rule out the critical view that John was written in the second century. Most believe the choice comes down to the A.D. 90's or A.D. 60's.

John 5:2 says, "Now there **is** in Jerusalem by the sheep gate a pool, which is called in Hebrew Bethesda, having five porticos." Note John does not write, "There **was** a pool having five porches" but "There **is** a pool having five porches." The pool in question was destroyed when the Romans destroyed Jerusalem in A.D. 70.[124] The reference to the pool still existing and the non-use of the Gospels of Matthew, Mark, and Luke by the Gospel of John could indicate that John was also written before the destruction of Jerusalem in A.D. 70. Since the synoptics were written no later than the A.D. 60's, it seems very unlikely that John would not be aware of them if he wrote as late as the

A.D. 90's. Thus, the initial writings of the Gospel of John could possibly be traced back to a time in the 60's. If so, it could still be true John wrote the last of the four Gospels, but not long after Matthew, Mark and Luke.[125] If the Gospel was entirely composed in the 60's, a date before A.D. 66 is best. In A.D. 66 war broke out between Judea and Rome. The absence of any prediction about the Temple's destruction within the text of John would be easier to explain by a pre-A.D. 66 date. A minority of scholars date John to the 60's. However, most follow strong church tradition that John was very old when he wrote the Gospel and that its origins may be traced back to Ephesus in Roman "Asia."

Irenaeus in *Against Heresies* 3.1.1 says that John wrote "afterwards" compared to Matthew, Mark, and Luke and also that John "did himself publish a Gospel during this residence at Ephesus in Asia." Also, *Against Heresies* 2.22.5 places elderly John in Asia and says, "And he remained among them up to the times of Trajan" (i.e., at least A. D. 98). The Anti-Marcionite Prologue to John also says that John wrote the Gospel in "Asia."[126]

It is possible to merge internal clues with church tradition. Perhaps John began to compose the Gospel while still in Jerusalem before the city's destruction, but he finished the book after a move to Ephesus.[127] We could also take the view that most of the book (perhaps all but Chapter 21 explaining his old age) was written before leaving Jerusalem, but that John did move to Ephsesus and lived to an old age continuing to publish, teach, and distribute his Gospel. Some combination of a tie to both Jerusalem and Ephesus and to both the A.D. 60's until the A.D. 90's seems likely. Any later date beyond this may be ruled out.

Chapter 6

Conclusions on the Four Gospels

All the evidence that exists regarding the written Gospels points to the involvement of the traditional authors and a composition date no later than the A.D. 60's for the synoptics. Matthew was likely the author of an Aramaic source that later became the material for the unique content within our canonical Greek Matthew. Either Matthew himself reworked the material or a disciple (under his supervision). The Gospel of Matthew by one of these means is rooted in the Apostle Matthew and was finished before the Temple's destruction in A.D. 70.

Strong external evidence confirms Mark wrote the Gospel of Mark as Peter's assistant. The book was also written before the Temple's destruction with many indications of even earlier sources.

Whenever any name is attached to the third Gospel, it is Luke. Acts does not mention the death of James the Lord's brother (A.D. 62) nor the destruction of the Temple (A.D. 70). The book's main characters, Peter and Paul, are still alive with Paul under house arrest in Rome around A.D. 62. The Gospel of Luke must precede the writing of Acts. This pushes its date to no later than the early 60's.

Finally, all lines of church history indicate the Gospel of John was written by "John." The author was an eyewitness who participated in the Last Supper, observed the cross, ran to the empty tomb, and fished with Jesus. Those who adhere to "the Elder John" as the author usually still accept that he was an eyewitness. However, there is no reason to overthrow the traditional view that the author was the Apostle John. Some of the material probably dates from the A.D. 60's with a final composition in the A.D. 90's in Ephesus.

We can be more definitive that the Gospels are tied to Matthew, Mark, Luke, and John and that the synoptics date no later than the 60's. Neither Matthew (a tax collector and otherwise obscure apostle) nor non-apostles Mark and Luke would have been selected as the Gospel authors, had there not been the strength of evidence to support the traditional view during the earliest period and among those who would be in a position to know the facts. [128]

More narrow conclusions as to dates and places may not rise to the definitive category but can be held as reasonable. The early church held that Matthew was the first Gospel and that it was written in Hebrew (Aramaic). Yet, literary details, while not absolute, tip the balance in favor of Marcan priority. One plausible hypothesis is that Aramaic material by the Apostle Matthew came first, followed by the full Gospel of Mark, then in less certain order our Greek Matthew, then Luke according to most scholars, (but it could also have been Luke then Matthew, see endnotes 45 and 84). Reasoning that Luke must have been written around A.D. 60 or 61, this likely pushes Mark and our hypothetical Matthean source into the 50's.

If we reason that Luke probably researched the life of Christ while Paul was imprisoned in Caesarea in A.D. 58-60, then even more clearly Luke was written in the late 50's with proto-Matthew in the early 50's and Mark in the early to mid-50's. The Greek Matthew probably precedes Luke.

Therefore, the synoptics must be no later than the 60's, but it is even more probable they came no later than the 50's if we reason that Luke must precede Acts and that church tradition and literary observation mean an Aramaic source for Matthew and the Gospel of Mark must be even earlier than Luke.

One final step could admittedly be an error but would likely explain the similarities between Matthew, Mark, and Luke. If the prison epistles (Ephesians, Colossians, and Philemon) were written from Caesarea around A.D. 60 or 61, then it is even more probable that Luke wrote his Gospel in A.D. 58-60 and that Luke and Mark shared material (compare Philemon 24, Colossians 4:10,14). A Caesarean provenance of the epistles is not essential to the opinion that the Gospel of Luke dates from the late 50's (with proto-Matthew and Mark still earlier), but it would make that case more credible. The synoptics are no later than the 60's but a case can be put forward for the 50's.

A reasonable guess can be given for the place of origin for each written Gospel, but definitive answers are not possible. Matthew probably arises from the Jerusalem Church with some interest also in Antioch, Syria (see Matthew 4:24). Mark has both Aramaic words and Latinisms. Aramaic can be explained either as originating from a location in Israel or Peter's influence perhaps even in Rome. Yet, because of the many indications of early sources for Mark, a good choice as to its origin would also be Israel, but it was directed at the Roman world with probable links to Caesarea and even more strongly to Rome.

Luke may have consulted his many "eyewitnesses" (Luke 1:1-4) while Paul was in prison in Caesarea. Thus, it is also possible he wrote some or all of the Gospel in Israel, but finished or distributed the Gospel in areas west of Israel. He went with Paul on the trip to Rome.

Following church tradition the Gospel of John was likely finished or distributed widely in Ephesus. Yet, it too has hints of original material in Jerusalem before the destruction of the Temple (see John 5:2).

Because the Gospels do not actually name an author or give a date, errors in the traditional conclusions about authorship would not affect the Bible's accuracy or authority. Even if the traditional authors were not Matthew, Mark, Luke and John, the books still date within the lifetimes of the eyewitnesses of Jesus and the authors still assert their writings go back to accurate sources from the beginning (Luke 1:1-4; Acts 1:21-23, 10:36-42; John 15:26-27, 19:35, 21:24, probably also Mark 10:46, 15:21, 40, 43; Luke 8:3, 10:38ff.).

This book is not just about the authors and dates for the Gospels. Our topic is the history of Jesus. Therefore, we conclude the Gospels were written within living memory of Jesus. They were based upon still earlier and reliable witnesses. The evidence points to the traditional authors with no good reason to find fault with the Gospels going back to Matthew, Mark, Luke and John. Still, we now continue research on the history of Jesus by moving to a time period that could be called the "Generation Gap". Given that the Gospels were written no later than the 60's, it is possible to prove that details about the life, claims, and teaching of Jesus arise from a time even earlier than the

A.D. 50's or 60's. The next two chapters show that various details about Jesus can be proven to have come from the A.D. 30's to the A.D. 50's (closer to the time of Jesus than the times for the composition of the Gospels). While it is vital to research the dates for **composition** of the Gospels, the facts and **information** in these books obviously comes from a still earlier period.

Chapter 7

Jesus and Gospel History from A.D. 30 – A.D. 60

The four Gospels can be traced back to their traditional authors (Matthew, Mark, Luke, and John) with probable dates in the 50's and at the latest the A.D. 60's. With authors of such honesty who were writing at a time well within living memory, one can have confidence the Gospels record the actions and teachings of the Lord Jesus Christ.

Yet, it is possible and helpful to establish that the roots of the information about Jesus go back to times earlier than the date for the composition of the Gospels. The date for the Lord's crucifixion and resurrection could be April, A.D. 30. Yet detailed arguments point to April 3 and April 5, A.D. 33. Scholars advocating this precise time include: Harold W. Hoehner (Dallas Seminary), Earle E. Ellis (Southwestern Baptist Seminary Ft. Worth), Paul Maier (Lutheran, Western Michigan University), Darrell Bock (Dallas Seminary) and Paul Barnett (Anglican, Regent College, Canada and Macquerie University, Australia).[129]

The time gap between the events and the final form of the Gospels is best viewed as only about 25-30 years. Given the integrity of these authors and dates of composition within the lifetimes of the participants, one can trust their writings. Furthermore, it is possible to counter skeptics with evidence that material about the historical Jesus comes from an even earlier time.

Oral Tradition and the Early Church

Modern habits are to record information in print. We can misunderstand and fail to appreciate the ability of ancient peoples (and even now some contemporary cultures) to transmit materials carefully. We tend to think of the game involving the whispering of a message to the first person in a circle. By the time the message passes from person to person in the circle, it comes out the end garbled and distorted.

A transfer of this silly game into a parallel of information regarded as **holy** in a context of **matters of life and death** is a foolish mistake. Those with a flippant attitude toward Judeo-Christian culture could make this mistake, but sacred traditions were more important within Jewish culture and to the first Christians.

Transmission of Written Traditions

While one can not prove oral transmissions and written transmissions were identical, scribal practices among Jewish peoples do reveal an attitude about strict transmission of religious truths. The Massoretic scribes worked from A.D. 500-950. Comparisons of their work to the earlier Dead Sea Scrolls (in the case of Isaiah, 1QIsa[a] dates to 125 B.C.) show great faithfulness in written transmission.[130] Jewish scribes exercised great care in handing on written tradition to following generations.

> "In making copies of Hebrew manuscripts which are the precious heritage of the Church today, the Jewish scribes exercised the greatest possible care, even to the point of superstition – counting, not only the words but every letter, noting how many times each particular letter occurred, and destroying at once the sheet on which a mistake was detected, in their anxiety to avoid the introduction of the least error into the sacred Scriptures, which they prized so highly and held in such reverent awe. Moreover, each new copy had to be made from an approved manuscript, written with a special kind of ink, upon sheets made from a "clean" animal. The writers also had to pronounce aloud each word before writing it, and on no account was a single word to be written from memory. They were to reverently wipe their pen before writing the name of God in any form, and to wash their whole body before writing "Jehovah," lest that holy name should be tainted even in the writing. The new copy was then carefully examined with the original almost immediately: and it is said that if only one incorrect letter were discovered the whole copy was rejected! It is recorded how one reverent rabbi solemnly warned a scribe thus: "Take heed how thou doest thy work, for thy work is the work of heaven, lest thou drop or add a letter of the manuscript, and so become a destroyer of the world!"[131]

Transmission of Oral Traditions in Judaism

Oral transmission of religious information in Jewish circles also seems to have been quite controlled. While one could object information about these practices within Judaism comes from a later time, or that the early church was distinct from Judaism, still Jewish practices must be a closer parallel than a modern party game. Rabbi Saul of Tarsus, later the Christian Apostle Paul, uses language of Christian traditions that parallel the rabbinic transmission of knowledge to students.

1 Corinthians 11:23, "For I *received* from the Lord that which I also *delivered* to you" . . . and 1 Corinthians 15:1-3 ". . . you *received* . . . " (v. 1) and ". . . I *delivered* to you . . ." (v. 3) speak in the rabbinic language of a rabbi "delivering" and a student "receiving" a tradition. Other verses indicate a process of oral transmission of Jesus' teaching within the early church. Sometimes Jesus' teaching on subjects was known by oral tradition without ever being recorded in the four Gospels (e.g., Acts 20:35 on giving and 1 Cor. 7:10 on divorce). E. Earle Ellis in *The Making of the New Testament Documents* argues for extensive use of pre-formed traditions within the New Testament. He also believes several additional phrases and words in the New Testament give clues that the biblical material derives from pre-formed traditions (see endnote 172). Ellis gives estimates for the percentage of pre-formed materials within each New Testament document.

Birger Gerhardsson (Sweden) devoted his academic career to studies of oral traditions within Judaism.

"His ground breaking doctoral dissertation … drew a parallel … between the way in which rabbis taught their disciples and the way Jesus taught his disciples. That way involved memorization of the master's teaching. If the rabbinic disciples handed on their master's tradition with great care, how much more the disciples of Jesus would have done so with what he taught them."[132]

After the above quote from Hagner's forward to Gerhardsson's book, Hagner quoted Gerhardsson himself giving his thesis:

67

"The implication is that the words and works of Jesus were stamped on the memories of those disciples. Remembering the attitude of Jewish disciples to their master, it is unrealistic to suppose that forgetfulness and the exercise of a pious imagination had too much hand in transforming authentic memories beyond all recognition in the course of a few short decades."[133]

Bauckham (St. Andrews, UK) summarizes Gerhardsson's views this way:

"In 1961 the Swedish scholar Birger Gerhardsson published his book *Memory and Manuscript*, in which he developed the insights of his teacher Harald Riesenfeld and proposed a radical alternative to form criticism's understanding of the oral transmission of Jesus tradition. He provided a major study of oral transmission in rabbinic Judaism and argued that early Christianity must have adopted the same methods and practices. Thus, unlike the form critics, he provided a particular model of oral tradition as practiced in a specific historical context and presented it as the nearest available parallel to the Jesus tradition. The disciples of rabbis were expected to memorize their master's teaching, and importance was attached to preserving the exact words. Mnemonic techniques and other controls were used to minimize deviation from the version learned. The emphasis on Jesus' teaching of his disciples throughout the Gospels indicates that he would have expected them to memorize his teaching. In the early Jerusalem church the Twelve would have functioned as a kind of rabbinate formulating, controlling, and passing on the Jesus tradition. Thus the tradition would have been preserved much more carefully and faithfully than the form critics envisaged."[134]

An alternative to a strict rabbinic model of oral transmission in the early church has been suggested by Kenneth Bailey. Bailey worked for more than 30 years in the Middle East and has extensive experience observing oral tradition in village life.[135]

Within Moslem and Eastern Orthodox Christian circles, forms of story telling exist which may be called formal controlled tradition and also informal controlled tradition. By formal controlled tradition Bailey refers to a formal teacher supervising the memory and strict recitation by a chosen student. This still occurs in the Middle East in both Christian and Moslem circles. Large amounts of material are required to be learned by memory (e.g., in Luke 9:44 Jesus commands, "let these words sink down into your ears . . .").

Yet, by an informal controlled method the story telling is not limited to a special teacher and student. Other knowledgeable people may retell the story. However, the group controls the process to preserve the accuracy of the information.

"The basic flow of the story and its conclusion had to remain the same. The names could not be changed. The summary punch-line was inviolable . . . The story-teller had a certain amount of freedom to tell the story in his own way as long as the central thrust of the story was not changed."[136]

Bailey's model for oral transmission if applied to the Gospels could explain variations between the synoptics with the essential facts remaining the same. One might introduce the story either with "Jesus said" or "He said" allowing variation but without essential changes. The Swedish school of thought following Gerhardsson argues for a tighter more controlled oral transmission. Bailey followed by N.T. Wright (Bishop of Durham) and James Dunn (University of Durham) adopted Bailey's model.

In a brilliant book, Richard Bauckham adds to the picture a **control by the original eyewitnesses** of the events over the oral retelling of their stories.[137] It would, for example, be hard to envision the oral retelling of a story in the early church that did not begin with the original participants themselves retelling what Jesus had done for them. Bartimaeus, for example, would tell his own story of Jesus healing his blindness. In years to follow, the eyewitness participants would be present to affirm and attest (or correct) any retelling of stories about Jesus by group members.

While introductory material or even the order may have variations, this limited degree of flexibility did not cancel a foundational control. Any variation in the retelling of a story was guarded and stabilized by the apostolic and often eyewitness guardians of the tradition. Variations may involve word selection, style and even arrangement, but not name changes or the morphing of the account into a different account of the facts or the underlying lesson.

Thus, the analogy of the game in which a message is distorted in the transmission has nothing to do with the oral transmission of the life of Christ events. The story was told in public with guardians of the truth, often the apostles and the still living participants, controlling the information.

This might allow for minor variations in phraseology (one of the explanations for variations in the synoptics) but not the morphing of one story into a completely different story. The apostles and elders of the early church could and would have supervised oral teachings until written in the New Testament documents. It is also likely preliminary **written** materials were available to supplement oral retelling of the stories about Jesus (see p. 33 and endnotes 59 and 61). Jewish culture used oral ways to transmit information but also obviously honored books.

Regardless of the precise method of oral transmission, the early church would have had no problem passing on the cherished memories of Jesus from A.D. 30 to the time of the written Gospels.

"Those who passed on the traditions about Jesus were, on the contrary, trained by culture to memorize and recount with considerable accuracy. Moreover, if Birger Gerhardsson's connection of early Christianity with Jewish rabbinic traditions holds any water, then some of those who passed on the sayings of Jesus had been specifically trained to do this with exemplary precision . . . . not only were there recognized leaders, those who had walked with Jesus and been inundated with his teachings, but also the whole community acted together to provide a place for the telling of stories about Jesus and for weighing these stories by community memory . . . . the early Christians believed

Jesus was uniquely special as a teacher, and they believed his words were authoritative and life-giving. Thus, they had strong motivation to remember and accurately pass on what he had said . . ."[138]

Although Price's words concern oral traditions in the transmission of the Old Testament, they are surely even more true of the short period of transmission between the life of Christ and the written Gospels.

". . . Some have asked how long an oral tradition can be and still be considered reliable in its rendering of past events. In other words, how soon does historical information have to be written down in order to preserve it accurately? In answer, there is no reason to doubt the accuracy of the oral tradition that preserved and passed on the biblical text. As one Copenhagen scholar, Paul Hoffmann, has pointed out, 'Not granting the generations of a thousand years [ago] the ability to understand anything about themselves on the basis of their own reality is [not] worth calling wisdom.' Although our society depends on recorded information for knowledge, for most of history, and particularly in the Middle East, less-literate cultures depend on oral transmission of knowledge. They were able to manage huge bodies of text. Even today, Muslim clerics and Eastern Orthodox clergy still memorize hundreds of pages of sacred texts."[139]

Carson (Trinity Evangelical Divinity School) and Moo (Wheaton College Graduate School) conclude that Birger Gerhardsson's rabbinic model of oral transmission would not have been an exact parallel in the early church but that memory and accurate oral transmission of information would have been true of both Judaism and the early church, as well as, "the Greco-Roman world at large."

". . . many form critics are guilty of underestimating the degree to which first-century Jews would have been able to remember and transmit accurately by word of mouth what Jesus had said and done. The so-called Scandinavian School, represented particularly in the work of Birger Gerhardsson, looked to key authoritative figures in the early church as the transmitters of the

71

gospel tradition and argued that the process would have been akin to the transmission of the rabbinic traditions, in which both written materials and careful memorization would have played key roles. Criticism that this particular approach assumes a similarity between the scholastic setting of the rabbis and the more popular setting of early Christianity is warranted. But the importance of memorization in first-century Jewish society is undeniable, and we are justified in thinking that this provides a sufficient basis for the careful and accurate oral transmission of gospel material. Recent study of eyewitness testimony in the Greco-Roman world at large also generally confirms the value and accuracy of such testimony. And when we add to these points the very real possibility that the words and actions of Jesus were being written down from the beginning, we have every reason to think that the early Christians were both able and willing to hand down accurately the deeds and words of Jesus." [140]

Given the relatively short time between the life of Christ and the final written Gospels, the early Christians could and would have passed on correct information about the events and teachings of Jesus. Oral transmission in such a culture can be regarded as accurate tradition.

While the first generation of Christians understood the claims of Jesus even better with the passing of time, a number of features in the Gospels prove that the church did not invent claims about Jesus that were later read back into the life of Christ in the written Gospels.

Claims of Christ Proven to Pre-date the Written Gospels

The title "The Son of Man" does not occur in the epistles. Other than the account of the story about Stephen in Acts 7:56, the New Testament church did not call Jesus "The Son of Man." [141]

Yet, "The Son of Man" is among Jesus' favorite titles that He employs of Himself. He uses this title of Himself 14 times in Mark alone. Clearly, the early church was not reading this title back into the life of Christ narratives in the Gospels. It must originate with Jesus.

This in turn means that Jesus Himself claimed to be the Messianic world ruler mentioned in Daniel 7:13-14 and Psalm 110:1. When Jesus used the title "The Son of Man" at His trial before the Sanhedrin, it was the Lord's way of giving an affirmative response as to whether He claimed to be, ". . . the Christ, the **Son of God**" (Matthew 26:63-66; also Mark 14:61-64; Luke 22:67-71). Caiaphas tore his robes, and all present regarded the claim to be "The Son of Man" as blasphemy. It equated Jesus saying He is the Son of God. A full understanding of "The Son of Man" involves God the Father giving Jesus eternal and world-wide power as in Daniel 7. The Son of Man sitting on "the right hand of power" refers to David's prediction in Psalm 110:1 that the Messiah would sit beside God's throne as co-ruler. This prediction is introduced by the phrase, "The LORD says to My Lord [David's Lord]: 'Sit on my right hand.' " Thus, God the Father calls the Messiah David's "Lord" (Hebrew *Adonai*). Jesus Himself used Psalm 110:1 to claim that the Messiah was more than a human descendent of King David. He is also David's Lord (a hint of deity, see Matthew 22: 41-46; Mark 12:35-37; Luke 20:41-44). Jesus also tied "The Son of Man" title with the privileges of deity in Mark 2:7, 10-11, 28.

Jesus' favorite self-description is a title that claims to be the Messiah, co-ruler with God in heaven, The Son of God, and One with the powers of deity. Again for emphasis, at His trial Jesus used this response as agreement that He claimed to be the **Son of God** (Matthew 26:63-64; Mark 14:61-62; and Luke 22:69-70). Since the rest of the New Testament does not use this title, it can not be asserted that the early Christians placed Jesus' claim back into the lips of Jesus. He Himself during His own life and ministry claimed to be the Master, Messiah, and God's Son.

Next, there are only two references in the epistles to the Aramaic word *Abba* meaning "father" or even more intimate "daddy." Twice Paul says believers (only because of their relationship with Christ) may address the Heavenly Father as Abba (Romans 8:15; Galatians 4:6). Since this is an Aramaic word and used infrequently, its origin should not be traced back to popularity in the early church.

Jesus first made the claim (then regarded as odd, inappropriate, or close to blasphemy) that God was His own "daddy." Only because of a believer's relationship to Christ as Savior may we call God our "Abba." The term itself originates with Jesus.

Thus, the claim that Jesus regarded God the Father as His own "daddy" is not an example of early Christians reading their theology back into the teaching of Jesus. Pope Benedict XVI (following Joachim Jeremias Lutheran, University of Gottingen, Germany) correctly traces Jesus' claim to be God's Son to the Aramaic original of calling God His Abba, i.e. beloved and intimate Father. Jesus' claim was a claim to unity with God unlike any other. This Aramaic word (see Mark 14:36) points to an early form original with Jesus Himself.

"The term 'the Son' thus goes hand in hand with the simple appellation 'Father' that the Evangelist Mark has preserved for us in its original Aramaic form in his account of the scene on the Mount of Olives: 'Abba.' Joachim Jeremias has devoted a number of in-depth studies to demonstrating the uniqueness of this form of address that Jesus used for God, since it implied an intimacy that was impossible in the world of his time. It expresses the 'unicity' of the 'Son.' Paul tells us that Jesus' gift of participation in his Spirit of Sonship empowers Christians to say 'Abba, Father' (Rom. 8:15; Gal. 4:6). Paul makes it clear that this new form of Christian prayer is possible only through Jesus, through the only-begotten Son. The term 'Son,' along with its correlate 'Father (Abba),' gives us a true glimpse into the inner being of Jesus – indeed, into the inner being of God himself. Jesus' prayer is the true origin of the term 'the Son.' It has no prehistory, just as the Son himself is 'new,' even though Moses and the Prophets prefigure him. The attempt has been made to use post-biblical literature – for example, the Odes of Solomon (dating from the second century A.D.) — as a source for constructing a pre-Christian, 'Gnostic' prehistory of this term, and to argue that John draws upon that tradition. If we respect the possibilities and limits of the historical method at all, this attempt makes no sense. We have to reckon with the originality of Jesus. Only he is 'The Son.' "[142]

In addition to the title "The Son of Man" and the term "Abba," the Parable of the Tenants provides a third example of Jesus' claim to be God's Son which can be proven to originate with Jesus Himself and can not be fiction placed back on Jesus' lips. In Mark 12:1-12 (also Matthew 21:33-46 and Luke 20:9-19) Jesus refers to a rented vineyard. The landowner keeps sending servants to collect the rent. Since the tenants refuse payment, finally the owner sends his "beloved Son" (Mark 12:6; Luke 20:13). The worthless tenants kill the son with the result of certain punishment by the landowner. The scribes and chief priests knew Jesus' parable threatened them with God's punishment (Matthew 21:45; Mark 12:12; Luke 20:19). This made sense because Isaiah 5 compared Israel to a vineyard. Jesus had also quoted Psalm 118:22, "The stone which the builders rejected, this became the chief cornerstone."

Thus, by this familiar phrase, (used every Passover) Jesus claimed to be the King of Israel who would reign by God's blessing despite any opposition. Even more startling, He was telling His enemies that He is God's "beloved Son." He predicted they would kill Him and then face God's wrath.

Craig A. Evans (Acadia Divinity College, Nova Scotia) makes a forceful argument that this parable makes no sense from a critical perspective. It can not be fairly viewed as a later church teaching written back into the life of Christ. The parable is clearly based upon a Jewish background. The vineyard is Israel, and the evil tenants were the religious establishment who would reject Jesus. After countering alternative interpretations, Evans insists the parable makes no sense in a gentile or church setting. In must have originated with Jesus Himself in a controversy with Jewish leaders, but then so too is Jesus' claim to be God's "beloved Son."

> "All attempts to interpret the parable as a creation not of Jesus but of the church suffer shipwreck on the rock of the parable's basic story line: the focus is not on the identity of the vineyard – it is Israel, and that is presupposed and remains constant – the focus is on the conflict between those who care for the vineyard and the owner of the vineyard, whom the tenant farmers do not respect and will not obey. This is the only plausible

75

interpretation of the parable, and it is the meaning that is consistent with its context in the New Testament gospels."[143]

Jesus' claims to His own identity can be shown to pre-date the time of the composition of the written Gospels. They are not the imagination of the early church read back into artificial Jesus' stories. This is also true of the events that are recorded of Him.

Events in the Life of Christ Proven to Pre-date the Composition of the Written Gospels

Craig A. Evans also shows the way on this subject. Historians have developed criteria by which literature may be screened for historicity. His list includes: historical coherence (a statement fits the known historical setting), multiple attestation (the sayings or actions appear in more than one source such as Mark and the material common to Matthew and Luke), embarrassment (something embarrassing is not likely to be fiction), dissimilarity (teachings that are different than the early church must have originated with Jesus Himself, e.g. "The Son of Man" claim as explained above), Semitisms (Hebrew or Aramaic terms), and Palestinian background (accurate geography, topography or customs), and finally coherence (consistency with what Jesus is known to have said or done by the above criteria).[144]

By such criteria Evans (following E. P. Sanders) presents the following as the basic facts in the history of Jesus:

1. Jesus was baptized by John the Baptist. **2**. Jesus was a Galiliean who preached and healed. **3**. Jesus called disciples and spoke of there being twelve. **4**. Jesus confined his activity to Israel. **5**. Jesus engaged in a controversy about the temple. **6**. Jesus was crucified outside Jerusalem by the Roman authorities. **7**. After his death Jesus' followers continued as an identifiable movement. **8**. At least some Jews persecuted at least parts of the new movement (Gal. 1:13, 23; Phil. 3:6), and it appears that this persecution endured at least to a time near the end of Paul's career (2 Cor. 11:24; Gal. 5:11, 6:12; see Mt. 23:34, 10:17).

Evans' citation of Sanders ends here, but then he adds four more facts insisting that all who are fair with the historical data should concede these points as true and as based upon critical scholarship's own standards of analysis (we will continue the list with numbers though Evans has written in paragraph form):

9. "Jesus was viewed by the public as a prophet" (Mk 6:4; Lk 7:16, 39). **10.** ". . . he spoke often of the Kingdom of God" (Mk 1:15; Lk 6:20). **11.** " . . . his temple controversy involved criticism of the ruling priests" (Mk 11:15-12:12). **12.** " . . . the Romans crucified him as 'king of the Jews' " (Mk 15:26).[145]

After insisting that critics who follow their own criteria for authenticity must agree with the above points on the life of Christ, Evans wrote an entire chapter arguing Jesus must have then been a miracle worker (Chapter 7, "Diminished Deeds" in *Fabricating Jesus*).

The standard of embarrassment makes perfect sense. Details that are likely to have been embarrassing should not be placed in the fictional category. An example would be Peter's denial of Christ. Given Peter's leadership in the early church, his failure should be judged to have been historical. No one would have written a make believe story that is so potentially embarrassing (even damaging) to Peter's legacy. Other examples of embarrassments might include that the disciples often were dense in understanding Jesus' teaching or that women were the first to witness the empty tomb. Evan's own point is that applying the rather sensible criteria of embarrassment consistently (not selectively) establishes that His claim to be the Messiah, His ministry as an exorcist, and His healings must also be judged to be known facts about the historical Jesus.

In Mark 3:21 Jesus' relatives want to take custody of Jesus claiming He had gone crazy. This embarrassing idea was not invented as fiction by the early church. It must be judged as factual. Yet, the reason for the family reaction was that Jesus was beginning His ministry of casting out demons. Thus, Jesus' reputation as an exorcist must also be judged as historically true. In the very next verse, Mark 3:22, the authorities concede Jesus' power; however they claim that Satan, not God, was His power source.

By consistently using the historical-critical criteria of embarrassing details being factual, we should at least believe Jesus was widely regarded as a powerful exorcist. Yet, this in turn supports the validity of His reputation as a healer and miracle worker. He would not have been regarded as having power over Satan unless the public also accepted Him as a healer of those He delivered. As will be explained in Chapter 12, the New Testament makes the claim that even Jesus' enemies admitted His miracles. They concede His power but claim Satan was the source of power (in addition to Mark 3:22 see also Matthew 12:22ff.; Luke 11:15ff.; John 7:20, 8:48, 52, 11:47-50).

Jesus' reputation as an exorcist and thus a healer sometimes goes beyond the New Testament records. The Jewish Talmud in Sanhedrin (43a) says that Jesus was killed for practicing sorcery.[146] Also, a rather strange document from ancient Egypt counseled that pagans should invoke the name of Jesus in order to combat demons (like the Jewish exorcists in Acts 19:13-20). Published by the University of Chicago, part of this text reads, "After placing the patient opposite you, conjure as follows, 'I conjure you by the God of the Hebrews, Jesus . . . .' "[147] The principle of embarrassment (applied to Mark 3:21-22) leads to the conclusion that it is an historical fact Jesus was well known for an exorcist ministry, and this overlaps with a reputation as a miracle worker and healer.

The principle of multiple attestation to a seemingly non-miraculous claim also ends with Jesus' ability to come across as displaying God's supernatural powers. The most liberal of Bible critics assume Jesus was a great teacher. Among His favorite topics was the Kingdom of God. Yet, the claim to bring the Kingdom of God can not be divorced from the claim to destroy the kingdom of Satan. This brings us right back to supernatural powers. Skeptics will often agree Jesus was a great human teacher. However, the great masses did not listen to Him because of His rhetorical skills. They came because of His reputation for powers. Following Evans throughout this topic, we again quote from his *Fabricating Jesus*: ". . . crowds followed Jesus not so much because he was a great teacher but because of his reputation as a powerful healer. The crowds grew because this reputation seems to be well founded. An ineffective healer would have had difficulty sustaining an enthusiastic following."[148] Being a great leader and teacher on the Kingdom of God involved, in the people's minds, the ability to overthrow the kingdom of Satan. If Jesus taught that He brought the Kingdom of God (historically, He must have taught this!), then He also acted in a way to gain a reputation for power over Satan. Jesus Himself made this connection in Matthew 10:1, 7-8 and Mark 3:13-15 where the authority to teach the Kingdom of God is tied to demonstrating power over Satan. In Luke 11:20 Jesus insists it was His power over Satan that proved "the Kingdom of God has come. . . ." His reference to the "finger of God" points back to Exodus 8:18-19 where Egyptian sorcerers had to concede the supernatural powers of God had been proven to overcome the occult.[149] Almost everyone acknowledges Jesus claimed to bring the Kingdom of God, but this in turn supports that His reputation for being a miracle worker with power over Satan is also historical truth.

People at the time of Jesus would not have listened to Jesus' claim to usher in the Kingdom of God without corresponding actions to destroy Satan by clear evidence of powers. Evans linked Jesus' language in Mark 3:26 to the expectation of His time found in the *Testament of Moses,* a "fictional work scholars are pretty sure was written in Palestine right around A.D. 30, at about the same time Jesus was at the height of his ministry."[150] *The Testament of Moses* says, "And then [God's] kingdom will appear in his whole creation and the Devil will have an end, and sorrow will be led away with him" (10:1).

The culture of Jesus' time associated the coming of God's Kingdom with the destruction of Satan's kingdom. Thus, in order to claim He brought the Kingdom of God, Jesus would also have had to demonstrate powers sufficient to support a reputation that He could overcome Satan.

Before we move on from a summary of Evans' argument that historical-critical analysis of the text still supports Jesus' miracles, we must return to the principle of embarrassment regarding John the Baptist. In Matthew 11:2-6 (also Luke 7:18-23) John the Baptist expressed his doubt as to whether Jesus is really the Messiah after all. If Jesus is the Christ, then why is his main promoter in prison under threat of death?

Evans reasons this event must have historically occurred. "The criterion of embarrassment strongly supports the authenticity of this exchange. Why would an early Christian invent a story about John the 'forerunner' expressing doubt about Jesus?"[151]

An even more important conclusion follows. If John the Baptist's doubt must be judged as authentic by the criteria of embarrassment, then Jesus' reply must also be accepted as authentic history. Jesus allays John's doubt by evidence that He is a miracle worker fulfilling the Messianic predictions from the book of Isaiah. "Go and report to John what you see: the blind receive their sight and the lame walk, lepers are cleansed, and the deaf hear, and the dead are raised up, and the poor have the gospel preached unto them. And blessed is he who takes no offense at me" (Matthew 11: 4b-6). Various phrases in Jesus' reply point back to Isaiah (Evans lists Isaiah 26:19, 35:5-6, and 61:1 as underlying Jesus' reply to John).[152]

Evans also teaches that Jesus' reply must be judged as true not only by the criteria of embarrassment but also by the criteria of coherence with cultural expectations. A scroll from Qumran's Cave 4 shows that anyone claiming to be the Messiah would need to have convinced the people he could fulfill these predictions from Isaiah.

[...For hea]vens and earth shall listen to his Messiah . . . . For he will honor the pious upon the th[ro]ne of the eternal kingdom, setting prisoners free, opening the eyes of the blind, raising up those who are bo[wed down] . . . . and the Lord shall do glorious things which have not been done, just as he said. For he will heal the injured, he shall make alive the dead, he shall proclaim good news to the afflicted . . . " 4Q521, fragments 2+4[153]

Consistent and fair application of objective criteria for the historicity of a document still leads to a Jesus who attracted masses of people not just by ethical teaching but by a reputation for bringing in the Kingdom of God by overpowering evil with signs and by convincing others He fulfilled both Old Testament predictions of the Messiah and the expectations of His time period of what the Messiah would do.

It is not plausible to hold that Jesus was only a teacher who preached on the Kingdom of God without feats demonstrating power over the kingdom of evil or that people in Jesus' time would take His Messianic claims seriously without fulfilling the pervasive expectations of Messianic powers.

The subject of miracles will be covered again from the angle of an explanation for the rise of the Christian movement in Chapter 12. The method in this present treatment has only been to summarize Craig A. Evans' work by showing that the accepted criteria of historical analysis applied consistently still point to a supernatural Jesus making Messianic claims. The early church did not create a miracle-working Messianic claimant by placing fictional events back into an earlier time of one who had only been a teacher of ethics. His claims to bring in the Kingdom of God were rather based upon a reputation for having also controlled the kingdom of Satan by supernatural powers. Likewise, other teachings and events in the life of Christ can be shown to have originated with Jesus not the early church. Earlier we noted the title "The Son of Man" can not be a projection of church doctrine back into the life of Christ (see pp. 72, 73). The epistles never use that title and Acts only once (Acts 7:56). The assumption that the early church made up stories that were projected back into the life of Christ is furthermore contradicted by Bauckham's observation that names in the Gospel accounts seem to have been deleted not added over time.

Names as Evidence the Church Did Not Create the Jesus' Stories in the Gospels

A liberal assumption is that the real life of Jesus has been obscured by wild stories told about Him in the early church. These were then imposed back into the time of Jesus. However, Bauckham (with the assumption of Marcan priority, which this book has tentatively followed) has researched the names in the Gospels (and also the earlier writings of the church fathers). Contrary to the addition of names over time as Bible critics assume, the evidence shows the opposite. As time passed, the original eyewitnesses passed on and were unfamiliar to the readers. Therefore, the names were deleted in the retelling. This trend refutes liberal German scholar Rudolf Bultmann on the idea that contrived stories about Jesus were attributed to Him by the imaginative early Christians. For full treatment, please consult Richard Bauckham.[154] We will quote the gist of Bauckham's work:

> "The material common to the three synoptic Gospels therefore shows an unambiguous tendency toward the elimination of names, which refutes Bultmann's argument . . . . It was a common Jewish practice, in retelling or commenting on the biblical narratives, to give names to characters not named in Scripture . . . . So it would not have been surprising to find Christians doing the same with the Gospel narratives from an early date. But the evidence suggests that this did not happen. Certainly there is no ground for postulating that it occurred in the transmission of the Gospel traditions behind and in the Synoptic Gospels.[155]

The evidence from the Gospel literature is that Jesus Himself claimed to be the Messiah and had a reputation for powers over Satan. The early church did not make up additional stories and add them back into writings on the life of Christ. The habits of oral transmission explained earlier were more than sufficient to guarantee faithful transmission of information from the time of Christ's life (A.D. 30, more probably A.D. 33) to the time of the written Gospel accounts (likely no later than the A.D. 60's and probably at least the A.D. 50's). Finally, in this chapter concerning the period between Jesus' early ministry and the composition of the written Gospels we must consider the factor of human memory.

Memories about Jesus

Memory is a tricky phenomenon. Sometimes we can not remember where we placed a book we read last week, but we remember many details about the situation in which we first learned of the terror attacks on 9/11/2001.

What is likely to be forgotten or confused? What is likely to be remembered with accuracy for many years? Psychological research has been done in areas of recollective memory.

Usually this has not been applied to the topic of memories about Jesus. Richard Bauckham certainly has done so. His work gives no encouragement to a critical view that witnesses to Jesus' life are likely to have forgotten what really happened or what Jesus really said in the period between Jesus' life (A.D. 30 or 33) and the writing of the Gospel texts (probably A.D. 50's or 60's). Yet, before any summary of Bauckham's chapter on "Eyewitness Memory," it is best to consider the intent of the Gospel authors regarding their recording of Jesus.

One major evangelical response to the liberal Jesus Seminar was the book *Jesus Under Fire*. Darrell Bock's contribution was Chapter 3, *"The Words of Jesus in the Gospels: Live, Jive, or Memorex?"*

Bock argues that the Gospel authors did not always write the *ipissima-verba* ("his very words") of Jesus' teaching, but they did write Jesus' *ipissima vox* ("his very voice, i.e. the presence of his teaching summarized").[156] Given that Jesus' original sermons were likely in Aramaic and much longer than written Gospel summaries (even the Sermon on the Mount only takes 5 minutes to read), it must be true that the Gospel authors are intending to give accurate summaries of His teaching. In Matthew, Mark, Luke, and John we have accurate but abbreviated reports of Jesus' speeches. Sometimes exact quotes are included (especially memorable "zingers"), but other times the writer selects, reorders, deletes, and condenses Jesus' words. The basic content remains and the gist or main point is included, but original sermons that were hours in length are reduced to the essential but true elements. Bock illustrates by showing the different orders in the account of the devil tempting Jesus. Matthew 4:5-7 gives the second appeal as jumping from the Temple. Then the final temptation is the offer of the kingdoms of the world in Matthew 4:8-9. Luke's order switches the temptations with the kingdoms being offered second and the final enticement being jumping from the pinnacle (Luke 4:9-12). There are other examples of the freedom to reorder material yet without fabrication or falsification of detail.[157] Variations also occur in quotations. Bock's examples are from Peter's confession of faith in Matthew 16, Mark 8, and Luke 9.[158]

"Who do people say the Son of Man is?" (Matthew 16:13).

"Who do people say that I am?" (Mark 8:27).

"Who do crowds say I am?"(Mark 8:27).

"You are the Christ, the Son of the living God" (Matthew 16:16).

"You are the Christ" (Mark 8:29).

"The Christ of God" (Luke 9:20).

These are examples of verbal variation but with the same messages, the same historical truths, and the same theology. One can agree with the conclusion the Gospels intend to present historical reports on the teaching of Jesus but not to have verbatim quotes of His extensive teaching. Words have been altered in the transition from Aramaic to Greek but Jesus' teaching has been preserved.

> "It is texts like these that cause interpreters to distinguish between *ipissima verba* ("the exact words" [of Jesus]) and *ipissima vox* ("the exact voice" [of Jesus]). One can present history accurately whether one quotes or summarizes teaching, or even mixes the two together. To have accurate summaries of Jesus' teaching is just as historical as to have his actual words; they are just two different perspectives to give us the same thing. All that is required is that the summaries be trustworthy – a factor made likely not only by the character of the writers and the nature of their religious convictions, but also by the presence of opponents and eyewitnesses who one way or the other could challenge a fabricated report."[159]

The preceding consideration of the intent of Gospel historical reporting has been included in the sub-topic of memories about Jesus for an obvious reason. It is far easier to contend the eyewitnesses of Jesus could remember the essential truths and events of Jesus' life than verbatim quotations of long sermons. Jesus told the eyewitnesses that the Holy Spirit would help them to remember (see John 14:26 and 15:26-27). However, even without consideration of the endowment of supernatural ability, one can point out to skeptics that human memory can recall the types of material we observe in the Gospels. Even without aid from God, it was well within the capacity of human recall to give accurate, historical reports on Jesus' life and His most important teachings. The time between Jesus' life and the written Gospels was too short for His followers to forget.

Bauckham's review of psychological studies on memory show that the events in the life of Christ meet the known criteria for accurate recollection. **Jesus had the sort of life not easy to forget.** While we often complain about forgetfulness, it is true, "we also know from human experience that for most everyday purposes memory is reliable enough. Human society could not be sustained otherwise. And we know, if we reflect on it, that memories can survive with a considerable degree of accuracy over a long period."[160]

The more unusual and emotional the event, the more likely we can recall it accurately. Routine and forgettable go hand-in-hand. The sort of events and teaching in the life of Christ were hardly routine.

Before applying psychological studies to memories of Jesus, Bauckham illustrates with a grisly murder case in Norfolk, England in 1901. Newspapers and court reports detail the trial. At the time a ten-year-old boy was not a part of the proceedings, but he had lived in the same village. Seventy-three years later this man gave an interview and the subject turned to the murder in the past. Regarding the night the body (hanging by a cord over a cliff) was discovered, he could recall numerous facts all later verified by old court and newspaper documents. In addition, he added still more details to the story that had not surfaced at the time. Even after 73 years a murder scene was very much memorable. Unexpected events tend to be remembered. Humdrum routine events tend to be forgotten.

One hundred years ago my grandfather, Remmert Herwich (Raymond in America) was in kindergarten in the Netherlands. For a hands-on lesson his teacher took the class out to a garden where instead of planting seeds, they planted fish bones leftover from supper. After school the teacher alone went back and planted complete fish with heads protruding above the ground. The next morning it seemed to the children that the "bone seed" had grown overnight to become a crop of fish. As the story was retold, it was never clear to me whether the point of the lesson was just a fun practical joke or a critical thinking exercise where the children were supposed to consider whether fish bones and plant seeds are really of the same category.

For our purposes, the lesson is about memory. Several factors that cause long term accurate recollection were present in my grandfather's memory of this event: personal involvement, unexpected and unique experiences, emotions (humor), vivid imagery, frequent mental rehearsal, frequent retelling of the story to others over the years. Eighty years later Grandpa Herwich could still laugh at the teaching methods in his Dutch kindergarten.

Acknowledging debt to Bauckham's research on long term memory, his list of unforgettable experiences (with my modifications in order to condense) is as follows:

• Unique, unusual, unexpected events (like healings, miracles, and exorcisms) are memorable.

• Events that are personally important and relevant tend toward long term memory (like matters of the Messiah's arrival and eternal destiny in heaven or hell).

• Events in which one is emotionally involved are memorable (Mark 9:6, 14:72, as in being a participant in a great cause with struggles and opposition).

• Memories involving vivid imagery are remembered well (Mark 2:4, 4:37-38, 6:39-40, 7:33-34, 9:20, 10:32, 50, 11:14).

• Memories often include irrelevant and odd details (there were "other boats," Mark 4:36).

• Reliable memories rarely include precise dates as on July 15 but do include time of day and relationships to seasons and holidays (as in the Gospel of John).

• The "gist" of a memory (even with details essential to the main point) is more likely to be retained than purely secondary details. (Bauckham's own conclusion is that this explains the variation in the Gospel accounts but unity on the core facts.)[161]

• Frequent retelling of a story shortly after an event tends to sharpen not diminish memory. "Frequent recall is an important factor in both retaining memory and retaining it accurately."[162]

Conclusions from research on human memory discount any notion that the eyewitnesses to Jesus forgot His life and teachings in the period between His life and the written Gospels. The life of Christ included the sort of events and teaching which would not be easily forgotten.

". . . memories for unusual events are least likely to be false memories. Memorable events stick with us; it is with the ordinary and the everyday that our memories may sometimes deceive us."[163]

"The eyewitnesses who remembered the events of the history of Jesus were remembering inherently very memorable events, unusual events that would have impressed themselves on the memory, events of key significance for those who remembered them, landmark or life-changing events for them in many cases, and their memories would have been reinforced and stabilized by frequent rehearsal, beginning soon after the event. They did not need to remember – and the Gospels rarely record – merely peripheral aspects of the scene or the event, the aspects of recollective memory that are least reliable. Such details may often have been subject to performative variation in the eyewitnesses' telling of their stories, but the central features of the memory, those that constituted its meaning for those who witnessed and attested it, are likely to have been preserved reliably. We may conclude that the memories of eyewitnesses of the history of Jesus score highly by the criteria for likely reliability that have been established by the psychological study of recollective memory."[164]

87

Conclusion on the Gospel History of Jesus A.D. 30-60

Information on the life and teaching of Christ was not forgotten but preserved reliably in the short period between the end of the earthly ministry of Jesus (A.D. 30-33) and the composition of the written Gospels (no later than the A.D. 60's, probably no later than the 50's).

Chapter 8

The Life of Jesus in the Epistles

The particulars of the life and teaching of Jesus must be derived from the Gospels. However, the major outlines of His life story are also revealed in the New Testament epistles. There is value in consideration of the historical Jesus as contained in the epistles.

Many, even in conservative schools of thought, would date the composition of the epistles even earlier than the Gospels. By this conclusion, the epistles are even closer to the time of Jesus than the Gospels.

Thus, for those who have doubts about the traditional authorship and early dates for the Gospels, consideration of the life of Christ from the epistles may be even more crucial. Raymond Brown (Union Seminary, New York), Martin Hengel (Tubingen), John Bowker (Cambridge), Timothy Luke Johnson (Emory) and Bruce Metzger (Princeton) hardly represent the Christian right. Yet, they all accept at least seven Pauline epistles as genuine from the pen of the Apostle Paul with specific dates in the A.D. 40's and 50's.[165]

Thus, the life of Jesus in the epistles can be useful to confirm the essential outline of Jesus' life as given in the Gospels. To those who remain doubtful about the Gospels, the epistles may be even easier to prove as authentic and close to Jesus' time. The epistles prove the basic history and claims of Jesus are original to His time.

The Outline of Jesus' Life in the Epistles

Using only Paul's comments on the life and teaching of Jesus, Paul Barnett makes the following outline of Jesus' life:

The Historical Jesus: His Life

1. He descended from Abraham (Galatians 3:16).

2. He was a Son of David (Romans 1:3).

3. He was naturally born but [perhaps?] supernaturally conceived (Galatians 4:4).

4. He was born and lived under the Jewish law (Galatians 4:4).

5. He welcomed people (Romans 15:5, 7).

6. His lifestyle was one of humility and service (Philippians 2:7-8).

7. He was abused and insulted during his life (Romans 15:3).

8. He had a brother named James (Galatians 1:19) and other brothers (1 Corinthians 9:5).

9. His disciple Peter was married (1 Corinthians 9:5; cf. Mark 1:30).

10. He instituted a memorial meal on the night of his betrayal (1 Corinthians 11:23-25).

11. He was betrayed (1 Corinthians 11:23).

12. He gave testimony before Pontius Pilate (1 Timothy 6:13).

13. He was killed by Jews of Judea (1 Thessalonians 2:14-15).

14. He was buried, rose on the third day and was thereafter seen alive on a number of occasions by many witnesses (1 Corinthians 15:4-8).[166]

Barnett comments that 1 Corinthians 8:9 proves Jesus' poverty but also that He gave up riches in heaven to be born poor. Paul refers to the crucifixion in Galatians 2:20 and 3:1, 13; 1 Corinthians 2:2 and many other places. Thus, the basic history of Jesus can be proven to date close to the time of Jesus by the record in the epistles.

Furthermore, the early church remembered the teaching of Jesus. Sometimes the Lord's teaching came to Paul by oral tradition which was never recorded (e.g. 1 Corinthians 7:10 on divorce). Other times tradition ("delivering" and "receiving" as in Jewish oral transmission) does have parallels in the Gospels (e.g. the Lord's Supper in 1 Corinthians 11:23ff. is similar in phraseology to Luke 22:19ff., see also "tradition" in 1 Cor. 11:2). Barnett gives another list of texts in the epistles which repeat still earlier teachings that indeed go back to Jesus' own time:

The Historical Jesus: His Teachings

1. The Lord's Supper 1 Corinthians 11:23-25; cf. Mark 14:22-25

2. Divorce and remarriage 1 Corinthians 7:10-11; cf. Mark 10:1-12

3. The laborer deserves wages 1 Corinthians 9:14; cf. Matthew 10:10; Luke 10:7

4. Eat what is set before you 1 Corinthians 10:27; cf. Luke 10:7

5. Tribute to whom due Romans 13:7; cf. Mark 12:13-17

6. Thief in the night 1 Thessalonians 5:2-5; cf. Luke 12:39,40

In addition to these more direct sayings, Paul makes numerous indirect allusions to the teachings of Jesus. For example:

7. Practical ethics Romans 12:9 - 3:10; cf. Matthew 5 –7

8. The return of Jesus 1 – 2 Thessalonians; cf. Matthew 24[167]

Since these epistles can be proven to be authentic and to date from a time close to Jesus, we could construct the basic history for the life of Jesus even if the Gospels did not exist.

Perhaps the most important text is 1 Corinthians 15:3-8. On historical grounds this can be proven to go back very close to Jesus' days and shows that the history and doctrine of Jesus originated from the earliest of times.

The Creed in 1 Corinthians 15:3-7

In 1 Corinthians 15:1-3 Paul again refers to delivering and receiving earlier tradition. In v.3 Paul had "delivered" the message (the one in vv. 3-7) when he founded the church in Corinth. The letter of 1 Corinthians was written around A.D. 55-57, but Paul's initial ministry in Corinth had occurred around A.D. 51. This date is secure because Paul in Corinth was dragged before the court of Roman Governor Gallio (Seneca's brother). Gallio likely took office in midsummer A.D. 52, and Paul stayed in Corinth for 18 months (Acts 18:11).[168]

Thus, the message Paul delivered in Corinth had already been the "traditional" Christian message by A.D. 51! This brings the date of this creed to around 18 years after Jesus' ascension. Yet, there are clues within 1 Corinthians 15:3ff. that point back even earlier.

First, "Cephas" (v.5) is Peter's Aramaic name, and this gives a clue to an earlier time. Second, ". . . the threefold usage of 'and that' " follows an "Aramaic and Mishnaic Hebrew" means of narration.[169] Third, a number of words in these verses are unlike Paul.[170] It is likely Paul is quoting an earlier creed that is possibly an Aramaic original. Thus, it is likely this creed goes back to ". . . two to eight years after the crucifixion or from about A.D. 32-38."[171]

Contrary to the impression of Bible critics, the basic facts of Jesus' life and teachings about Him can be proven to be **extremely early** on solid historical grounds. They were categorically **NOT** made up long after the time of Jesus by people who had no eyewitness credibility.

From the beginning the message has been salvation by faith in the Lord Jesus Christ. The Gospel is the good news of Jesus' death to pay for our sins. His burial and His resurrection were attested to by many eyewitnesses, including Peter and the other apostles, and also by His skeptical half-brother James and to more than 500 brethren at one time. This historical information and theological claims can be traced via the dating for 1 Corinthians 15 almost to the time of Jesus.

Embedded Hymns and Creeds

The epistles contain pre-formed hymns and creeds (i.e. doctrinal statements) that were quoted by the biblical authors. When an epistle is given a date, the origin of such creeds should be viewed as even earlier. The list of possible creeds within the epistles is quite long.[172]

We must limit ourselves to several examples as illustrative of the 30 or so important Bible texts that are most likely to be embedded hymns or creeds (Romans 1:3-4, 4:25, 8:31-39, 10:9-10, 11:33-36; 1 Corinthians 12:3, 1 Corinthians 15:3-7; Ephesians 1:3-14, 5:14; Philippians 2:6-11; Colossians 1:15-20; 1 Timothy 3:16, 6:13; 2 Timothy 2:8; 1 John 4:2). Romans 10:9-10 may be an earlier baptismal creed giving the historical facts of Jesus' death and resurrection and the doctrinal message He is the risen Lord (i.e., deity). [173]

Almost everyone agrees that Philippians is a genuine letter from Paul and to be dated no later than the early A.D. 60's. Furthermore, nearly all conclude that Philippians 2:6-11 gives an embedded Christological hymn. By singing such hymns, the early Christians would be grounded in doctrine. "Most think that Paul wrote but did not create these lines; they are probably a prePauline hymn that the Philippians knew and that Paul may have taught them at the time of his first visit."[174] Paul's initial visit to Philippi would have been A.D. 49-50.[175] Therefore, the essential doctrines of Christ were already "traditional" before this.

The modern attempt to make the deity of Christ a brand new doctrine invented at the Council of Nicea in A.D. 325 is the real myth. The historical outline of the life of Jesus and the Christological doctrines contained in the epistles can be proven to pre-date the writing of the epistles. In conclusion, the life and claims of Jesus Christ go back to His own time.

Transition to Secular History

With good reason the Gospels have been attributed as genuine to Matthew, Mark, Luke and John and within the living memory of eyewitnesses. The epistles can even more easily be proven to be authentic and from an early time. Furthermore, they contain quotes from creeds and hymns that date even closer to the historical Jesus.

Most who reject the New Testament portrayal of Jesus' life as being inaccurate never study the background of the Gospels extensively. For them matters of authorship and dates are not of interest because they already have closed minds. By some means that often does not involve the hard work of actual study, they have caught the impression that the Bible is non-historical or mythological. They reason "if the authors were ignorant, what makes the difference whether their writings are authentic and can be dated close to the time of Jesus?" The next chapter covers the many evidences that the Gospels do give an accurate history of the time. Some details from 2,000 years ago can no longer be verified. However, when the Gospels do overlap with known secular history they show themselves to be trustworthy. The next three chapters concern facts in the Gospels that also appear in ancient non-Christian sources or archaeology.

Chapter 9

Gospel People Also Mentioned in Non-Christian Sources: Jesus and Followers

The life, teachings, and claims of Jesus Christ are connected to the flow of secular history in His time. Having trusted in Jesus as ones Savior from sin, it is then consistent to accept the Bible as of divine origin without error in its original texts as given by the apostles and prophets.

Yet, in purely historical research one should suspend this conclusion and work towards a more modest goal. Human knowledge of the past is simply too limited to verify every historical claim in the New Testament. However, we can probe the reliability of the Gospels on many key points.

Many regard the Bible as pure myth. This conclusion must arise from attitudes caught from group-think or group acceptance rather than real research. With a reasonable and limited goal of showing the New Testament gives basic reliable history on the points where it can be tested, we will find the statements in the four Gospels are certainly not mythology.

In unpublished research I have tried to keep a list of people in the Bible who are also mentioned in non-Christian sources in ancient history.[176] Of course, it is best to classify these into categories of proven, probable, and merely possible. Archaeological artifacts can often raise disputes over authenticity or dating. Also, sometimes a name was so common a reference is in dispute as to whether it is the person in the Bible or another with the same name.

At the time of this writing we could list approximately 105 persons in the Bible who are also mentioned in non-Christian sources (ancient books or archaeological inscriptions such as coins, monuments, or buildings). Perhaps an additional 10 would be in the "wait-and-see" or "possible" category.

95

The general trend over time has been that more and more names come to the surface. However, the process usually involves a "two steps forward - one step back" path. Over time some archaeological conclusions are challenged, but also over time more and more information arises that confirms the Bible.[177]

As this book concerns Jesus' history we will limit material to people and places in the four Gospels. (Pages 153-156 provide historical confirmation for Acts showing Luke was a careful researcher in Acts and thus also for the Gospel of Luke.) It will also be necessary to give only a survey of this topic. The goal is to show the Gospels are not myth. If the goal were to exhaust historical details, we would need to write an encyclopedia not a brief chapter. Stress will be placed upon literary references to Bible characters as these are often stronger evidence than some archaeological artifacts that remain in dispute.

Finally, consider that the method adopted **excludes Christian sources. We could learn much more about New Testament people if we included the writings of early Christians.** Being a committed Christian I am intrigued by the foundational premise of the common intellectual game. "All Christians are suspect of intelligence or motive. Therefore, nothing they wrote of their own origins may be seen as credible." Granted, the writings of the early church fathers were not infallible. They were not all wrong either! Thus in order to study history fully, they should be included. Yet, in order to establish the reliability of the New Testament it is best to yield for the sake of argument. We will use only non-Christian sources to show the Gospels are not myth.

Chapter 11 will consider places in the Gospels, especially the accurate topography in the Gospel of John. Bible characters who are also mentioned outside of the Bible and early Christian authors may be broken into three categories: Jesus and His followers, Jewish religious officials, and Jewish/Roman political rulers. Chapter 9 concerns Jesus and His followers. Chapter 10 will consider Jewish and Roman people in the Gospel accounts.

Many do not realize that John the Baptist, James (Jesus' half-brother), and Jesus Himself are mentioned outside the Bible in non-

Christian sources. Also, it is likely an inscription on an ossuary ("a bone box") names the man who carried Jesus' cross to the crucifixion site. Other than references to Jesus, the main literary source for most New Testament people comes from Josephus.

Josephus was a Jewish historian who lived from approximately A.D. 37-100. Having been to Rome, he knew the Jewish war against Rome (beginning in A.D. 66) would be a hopeless effort. Josephus was the Jewish commander in the Galilee region but was taken prisoner of war by the Romans. He went to Rome and was shown great favor by emperors Vespasian, Titus, and Domitian. Emperor Titus urged Josephus to write a history of the Jews, and King Agrippa 2 testified to its accuracy. Josephus wrote *The Jewish War* in Aramaic. It was translated into Greek in A.D. 77-78. In A.D. 93-94 Josephus wrote *Jewish Antiquities*.[178] In addition to references to Jesus, Josephus wrote about John the Baptist and Jesus' half-brother, James.

John the Baptist

John the Baptist was known by virtually all in Judea. Josephus attests to his popularity, his virtue, his call to baptism, and his execution by Herod Antipas. In addition, Josephus refers to the scandalous divorce, which gave rise to John getting into trouble.

"Herod himself now quarreled with Aretas, king of Petra, whose daughter he had married. But Herod had since fallen in love with Herodias, wife of his half-brother [also named] Herod, and he promised to marry her and dismiss Aretas' daughter. However, she heard about the agreement, and asked Herod for permission to visit Machaerus. From there she hurried on to her father in Arabia, and told him of Herod's plans. This and a boundary dispute led Aretas to attack Herod, whose whole army was destroyed. Herod wrote about this to Tiberius, who was furious, and ordered Vitellius, governor of Syria, to declare war on Aretas. But to some of the Jews, Herod's disaster seemed to be divine vengeance for his treatment of John, surnamed the Baptist. Although John was a good man and exhorted the Jews to lead righteous lives and practice justice toward their colleagues and piety to God, Herod had put him to death. John taught that baptism must not be employed to obtain pardon for sins committed, but as a consecration of the body, implying that the soul was already purified by proper behavior. When others also joined the crowds around John and were greatly aroused by his preaching, Herod grew alarmed that such eloquence could lead to rebellion. Therefore, he decided that it would be better to strike first and get rid of him, rather than wait for an uprising. Although John was brought in chains to Machaerus and put to death in that stronghold, the Jews decided that the destruction of Herod's army was God's vindication of John." *Antiquities*, 18.106ff.[179]

James: Jesus' Half-Brother

Scholars are debating the authenticity of an ossuary with the inscription "James, son of Joseph, brother of Jesus." Opinion seems to have shifted back in favor of its authenticity. Yet, because of the remaining controversy, material on this artifact has been included in endnote 182. If established as genuine, this would add the name "Joseph" to people confirmed by the writings of Josephus. The historicity of James and certainly Jesus does not at all depend upon this ossuary. James was mentioned long ago in Josephus.

"This elder Ananus, after he himself had been high priest, had five sons, all of whom achieved that office, which was unparalleled. The younger Ananus, however, was rash and followed the Sadducees, who are heartless when they sit in judgment. Ananus thought that with Festus dead and Albinus still on the way, he would have his opportunity. Convening the judges of the Sanhedrin, he brought before them a man named James, the brother of Jesus who was called the Christ, and certain others. He accused them of having transgressed the law, and condemned them to be stoned to death. The people of Jerusalem who were considered the most fair minded and strict in observing the law were offended by this." *Antiquities* 20.197ff.[180]

The elder Annas is the one mentioned in John 18:13. Josephus tells us this man's son Annas took an "opportunity" to kill James in the transition between Roman governors. With Festus dead but before the new governor Albinus could arrive, Annas tried and stoned James. It is interesting that Josephus condemns the Sadducees for this atrocity and the people of Jerusalem were offended by this injustice.

Evidently James, the leader of the Christian church in Jerusalem (see Acts 15:13ff. and Galatians 2:9) had a good reputation even among the people of the city. This text in Josephus is also important in that it refers to "Jesus who was called the Christ." This undisputed reference to Jesus with His adherents claiming Him to be the Messiah leaves readers with the impression that Josephus must have previously referred to Jesus with more detail. There are 21 different Jesuses (Yeshua or Joshua) in Josephus' writings. Thus, Josephus must have already given his reader background information about "Jesus who was called the Christ."[181] This brings us to the important text in Josephus.[182]

Josephus on Jesus

The standard text of Josephus' main reference to Jesus reads this way:

> "About this time lived Jesus, a wise man, if indeed one ought to call him a man. For he was the achiever of extraordinary deeds and was a teacher of those who accept the truth gladly. He won over many Jews and many of the Greeks. He was the Messiah. When he was indicted by the principal men among us and Pilate condemned him to be crucified, those who had come to love him originally did not cease to do so; for he appeared to them on the third day restored to life, as the prophets of the Deity had foretold these and countless other marvelous things about him. And the tribe of Christians, so named after him, has not disappeared to this day." *Antiquities* 18:63-64[183]

This wording exists in all Greek manuscripts and was known before A.D. 300.[184]

Since it is known Josephus was not a Christian, many have argued that this text has been altered.[185] Yet, Josephus *must have said something* about Jesus here because his later reference to "James, the brother of Jesus who was called the Christ" presupposes his readers already know something about this Jesus. Otherwise, Josephus would have identified Him with more detail to distinguish from the numerous people named Jesus at that time.

In previous decades many suggested the original Greek text of Josephus read something like this (note the italics):

"Now there arose about this time *a source of further trouble* in one Jesus, a wise man who performed surprising works, a teacher of men who gladly welcome *strange things*. He led away many Jews, and also many of the Gentiles. He was the *so-called* Christ. When Pilate, acting on information supplied by the chief men among us, condemned him to the cross, those who had attached themselves to him at first did not cease *to cause trouble*, and the tribe of Christians which has taken this name from him, is not extinct even today.[186]

F.F. Bruce's above reconstruction of Josephus' wording into this form takes only four steps and is reasonable. First, there is only one letter difference in Greek between "truth" and "strange."

Secondly, Josephus labels Jesus the "so-called Christ" in the following section involving James the brother of the "so-called Christ" (*Antiquities* 20.197ff.). Therefore, it is reasonable that this was Josephus' original wording and was deleted by Christian copyists.

Suggested changes three and four involve adding the two italicized references to Jesus as a source of trouble. In the greater context around this passage about Jesus, Josephus is giving a list of troubles during Pilate's time. Perhaps Christian copyists deleted Josephus' original reference to Jesus being "trouble."

Bruce's four suggested changes all are reasonable and would turn the text into something written by a non-Christian. It also explains how a Christian scribe might drop out the description "so-called" before Christ and references to Jesus being a source of trouble. If one changed "strange" to "truth", then we may be close to explaining how Josephus' original words were easily altered to the existing phrase in all extant Greek manuscripts.[187]

In 1971 Professor Schlomo Pines (Hebrew University in Jerusalem) revealed a manuscript tradition that comes down from an Arabic, as opposed to a Greek, translation of Josephus. This Arabic manuscript comes from the 10th century historian, Agapius, but according to Charlesworth (Princeton) preserves the wording from the 4th century.[188]

In his modern translation of Josephus into English, Paul Maier follows this Arabic textual line at this key point. He says this "corresponds so precisely to previous scholarly projections of what Josephus originally wrote that it is substituted (for the traditional Greek revision of Josephus) in the text above."[189]

"At this time there was a wise man called Jesus, and his conduct was good, and he was known to be virtuous. Many among the Jews and the other nations became his disciples. Pilate condemned him to be crucified and to die. But those who had become his disciples did not abandon his discipleship. They reported that he had appeared to them three days after his crucifixion and that he was alive. Accordingly, he was perhaps the Messiah, concerning whom the prophets have reported wonders. And the tribe of the Christians, so named after him, has not disappeared to this day."[190]

Josephus must have said *something* about Jesus at this point in his book because the references about James the brother of Jesus seems to presuppose a previous explanation. One could follow F.F. Bruce's proposed reconstruction to easily explain how an original by a non-Christian could morph into the existing Greek text. Perhaps it is safer to use the form of the Josephus text coming down from Arabic. The historical results end about the same.

While the results give only sparse information about Jesus, the important historical truths remain. Jesus lived in Judea at the time of Pilate. He was known to be wise and holy. Pilate condemned him to crucifixion. Jesus' followers believed Him to be alive again. The Christian movement attracted Jewish and gentile disciples and continued to expand.[191]

The Talmud on Jesus

Jewish oral traditions were finalized in writings (The Talmud) about three centuries after Jesus.[192] The earliest period called the Tannaitic period dates from A.D. 70-200 and seems to include some reliable but sparse references to Jesus. The most likely text is *Sanhedrin* 43a.

> "Jesus was hanged on Passover Eve. Forty days previously the herald had cried, 'He is being led out for stoning, because he has practiced sorcery and led Israel astray and enticed them into apostasy. Whosoever has anything to say in his defense, let him come and declare it.' As nothing was brought forward in his defense, he was hanged on Passover Eve."[193]

This early Jewish perspective is definitely hostile, but it gives a few historical points. Jesus did exist and lived in Judea. He aroused the hatred of the Jewish establishment. (No mention here of the Romans.) By this assessment, he was guilty. In fact, He had no defense. He was executed on Passover Eve (as in John 19:14). As Jews typically stoned for execution "hanging" may refer to Roman authority. Crucifixion can be compared to hanging as in Galatians 3:13 and Luke 23:39. Jesus was regarded as a magician, but His power arose from black magic not God.

Another Talmudic reference seems to mention Jesus in connection with a trial for heresy. Rabbi Eliezer is challenged for his orthodoxy because years earlier he had conversed with a follower of Jesus named Jacob.[194]

Joseph Klausner, a Jewish scholar, concluded that Rabbi Eliezer was born about A.D. 30 or 40. "Klausner accepts the conclusion that the arrest of R. Eliezer took place in A.D. 95 and that Eliezer was recalling his encounter with Jacob of Kefar Sekanya about A.D. 60. Jacob would have been around 50 or 60 years old by then if he heard Jesus teach some 30 years previous to the meeting with Eliezar.[195] Klasner thought it was possible that the "Jacob" in question was James, the brother of Jesus and presiding elder of the church in Jerusalem.

F.F. Bruce described Talmudic ridicule of the "gospel" in texts that alter the word "evangelism" into similar words meaning "falsehood or perversion of the scroll." The Talmudic text involves the grandson of the great Gamaliel mentioned in Acts 5:34 and the tradition is best dated to shortly after A.D. 70.[196]   Since the text quotes the proverb about letting your light shine and not adding to the Law, there may be references to the dispute over the authority of the new Christian books (see Matthew 5:16-17). F.F. Bruce suggests: "The *Euangelin* in question was most probably an Aramaic form of the Gospel according to Matthew, the favorite Gospel of the Jewish Christians in Palestine and the adjoining territory."[197]

A final reference to Christians and the "Nazarenes" may occur in a synagogue prayer cursing Christians as heretics. Barnett dates this prayer (Benediction Twelves) to the A.D. 80's.

"For the renegades let there be no hope, and may the arrogant kingdom soon be rooted out in our days, and the Nazarenes and the minim perish as in a moment and be blotted out from the book of life and with the righteous may they not be inscribed. Blessed art thou, O, Lord, who humblest the arrogant."[198]

Josephus, an historian, and the rabbinic traditions do refer to Jesus and the rise of Christianity. These writings may not give details, but they do parallel the bare outlines of Jesus' life in the Gospels. They place Him in Judea at the time of Pilate. They show Jesus was the basis for great controversy and was killed. Both Josephus and the Talmud hint Jesus did wonders (or was a magician).

Next we turn attention to gentiles who write of Christ and the early Christians.

Early Roman Sources For Jesus

Three main Roman authors refer to Christ and the early Christians. Their writings occurred about the same time. All were around A.D. 110.

■ Tacitus and Christ

Cornelius Tacitus (about A.D. 55-120) wrote an estimated 30 history books including *The Annals of Imperial Rome* and *The Histories*. He was son-in-law to Julius Agricola, the Roman governor of Britain, A.D. 80-84. Tacitus himself was the governor of the Roman province of Asia which is now in Western Turkey. In A.D. 109 Tacitus wrote about Jesus in *The Annals of Imperial Rome:*

"But neither human resources, nor imperial munificence, nor appeasement of the gods, eliminated sinister suspicions that the fire had been instigated. To suppress this rumor, Nero fabricated scapegoats – and punished with every refinement the notoriously depraved Christians (as they were popularly called). Their originator, Christ, had been executed in Tiberius' reign by the governor of Judaea, Pontius Pilatus. But in spite of this temporary setback the deadly superstition had broken out afresh, not only in Judaea (where the mischief had started) but even in Rome. All degraded and shameful practices collect and flourish in the capital. First, Nero had self-acknowledged Christians arrested. Then, on their information, large numbers of others were condemned - not so much for incendiarism as for their anti-social tendencies. Their deaths were made farcical. Dressed in wild animals' skins, they were torn to pieces by dogs, or crucified, or made into torches to be ignited after dark as substitutes for daylight. Nero provided his Gardens for the spectacle, and exhibited displays in the Circus, at which he mingled with the crowd – or stood in a chariot, dressed as a charioteer. Despite their guilt as Christians, and the ruthless punishment it deserved, the victims were pitied. For it was felt that they were being sacrificed to one man's brutality rather than to the national interest." *Annals* 15.44[199]

Tacitus refers back to the burning of Rome in A.D. 64. Many believed Nero himself had ordered the arson in order to make room for his grand building projects. In order to quell rumors of his own involvement, Nero cast blame upon Christians for burning the city. Tacitus had no use for Christians. Descriptions include:

"notoriously depraved, deadly superstition, degraded, shameful, anti-social, guilty, deserving of ruthless punishment."

Yet, Nero's arrest of a "large number" and their resulting "comic" tortures (including being torn to pieces by dogs, crucifixion, and being ignited as torches at parties) aroused sympathy for Christians and further disrespect for Nero.

Regarding historical information on Christ, Tacitus mentioned the place: Judea, the general time: the reign of Tiberius, Christ's execution by Pontius Pilate as a criminal, the continued growth of Christianity past the time of Christ's death, and Christianity's spread from Judea to Rome in large numbers. Pliny the Younger, another Roman author, also mentioned early Christianity.

■ Pliny the Younger and the Christians

Gaius Plinius Secundus lived from A.D. 61-113. He is called Pliny the Younger to distinguish him from his more famous uncle Pliny the Elder. Pliny the Elder researched and wrote on natural history. He died studying nature too closely in A.D. 79 at the eruption of Mt. Vesuvius as it destroyed the city of Pompeii.

Pliny the Younger was the Roman governor of the province of Bithynia (A.D. 111-113), a region now in Turkey along its north coast of the Black Sea. He was constantly writing letters back to the Roman Emperor Trajan, hoping to maintain his favor. In *Epistles* X.96 Pliny wrote the Emperor. Trajan replied with general approval and advice in *Epistles* X.97.

"My Lord: It is my custom to consult you whenever I am in doubt about any matter; who is better able to direct my hesitation or instruct my ignorance? I have never been present at Christian trials; consequently I do not know the precedents regarding the question of punishment or the nature of the inquisition. I have been in no little doubt whether some discrimination is made with regard to age, or whether the young are treated no differently from the older; whether renunciation wins indulgence, or it is of no avail to have abandoned Christianity if one has once been a Christian; whether the very profession of the name is to be punished, or only the disgraceful practices which go along with the name. So far this has been my procedure when people were charged before me with being Christians. I have asked the accused themselves if they were Christians; if they said 'Yes,' I asked them a second and third time, warning of the penalty; if they persisted I ordered them to be led off to execution. For I had no doubt that, whatever kind of thing it was that they pleaded guilty to, their stubbornness and unyielding obstinacy at any rate deserved to be punished. There were others afflicted with the like madness whom I marked down to be referred to Rome, because they were Roman citizens. Later, as usually happens, the trouble spread by the very fact that it was being dealt with, and further varieties came to my notice. An anonymous document was laid before me containing many people's names. Some of these denied that they were Christians or had ever been so; at my dictation they invoked the gods and did reverence with incense and wine to your image, which I had ordered to be brought for this purpose along with the statues of the gods; they also cursed Christ; and as I am informed that people who are really Christians cannot possibly be made to do any of those things, I considered that the people who did them should be discharged. Others against whom I received information said they were Christians and then denied it; they meant (they said) that they had once been Christians but had given it up: some three years previously, some a longer time, one or two as many as twenty years before. All these likewise did reverence to your image and the statues of the gods and cursed Christ. But they maintained that their fault or error amounted to nothing more than this: they were in the habit of meeting on a certain fixed day before sunrise and reciting an antiphonal hymn to Christ as God, and binding themselves with an oath – not to commit any crime, but to abstain from all acts of theft, robbery and adultery, from breaches of faith, from repudiating a trust when called upon to honour it. After this, they went on, it was their custom to separate, and then meet again to partake of food, but food of an ordinary and innocent kind. And even this, they said, they had given up doing since the publication of my edict in which, according to your instructions, I had placed a ban on private associations. So I thought it the more necessary to inquire into the real truth of the matter by subjecting to torture two female slaves, who were called 'deacons'; but I found nothing more than a perverse superstition which went beyond all bounds.

Therefore I deferred further inquiry in order to apply to you for a ruling. The case seemed to me to be a proper one for consultation, particularly because of the number of those who were accused. For many of every age, every class, and of both sexes are being accused and will continue to be accused. Nor has this contagious superstition spread through the cities only, but also through the villages and the countryside. But I think it can be checked and put right. At any rate the temples, which had been well nigh abandoned, are beginning to be frequented again; and the customary services, which had been neglected for a long time, are beginning to be resumed; fodder for the sacrificial animals, too, is beginning to find a sale again, for hitherto it was difficult to find anyone to buy it. From all this it is easy to judge what a multitude of people can be reclaimed, if an opportunity is granted them to renounce Christianity." *Epistles* X.96[200]

Pliny stated that some he judged had been Christians for 20 years. This places the origin of Christianity in this region at least to the A.D. 80's. In fact, Pliny says by his tenure as governor Christians came from all social categories: all ages, all ranks, cities, villages, and rural. Tactitus also reported large numbers of Christians in Rome. Pliny hoped by legal pressure "a *multitude* of people could be reclaimed."

Both Tacitus and Pliny give alarm to the number of Christians. While they may exaggerate for propaganda purposes, they are similar to worries expressed within the book of Acts. In Acts 17:6 the missionaries have "upset the world." In Acts 19:24ff. the commercial side of the idolatry racket was being affected by the popularity of early Christianity. In Acts 28:22 the Roman Jews said that they knew about Christianity and that "it is spoken against everywhere." Tertullian, a century later than Pliny, made the same point about the growth of Christianity.

"We are but of yesterday, and we have filled everything you have – cities, tenements, forts, towns . . . even the camps, tribes, palace, senate, forum. All we have left you are the temples." *Apology* 37.4[201]

As does Acts 19, Pliny's letter written from the same area, Roman "Asia," indicates that pagan temples had been close to being abandoned, idol services had been neglected, and it had been difficult to sell fodder for sacrificial animals. From Pliny we have information about the early Christians. Real Christians would not worship idols or the emperor. They would not curse Christ (1 Corinthians 12:3). They had formal meetings on a certain day of the week. They sang hymns to worship "Christ as God." (The deity of Christ was definitely **not** a doctrine that started at the Council of Nicea in A.D. 325!). They made vows about holy living. They had a group meal of an innocent kind. In other words, rumors about drinking blood and eating flesh were symbolic of communion not literal. There were also ranks of authority in the early church such as deaconesses. Pliny was a close friend of our next Roman author, Suetonius.

■ Suetonius and Christ

Gaius Suetonius Tranquillas lived from A.D. 69 to about 140. He was the chief secretary to Emperor Hadrian and thereby had access to imperial records and the best of libraries. Writing in about A.D. 110, two references in *The Twelve Caesars* overlap with Christianity. In *Life of Claudius* 25.4 Suetonius wrote, "Because the Jews at Rome caused continuous disturbances at the instigation of Chrestus, he expelled them from the city."[202] "Most scholars believe Suetonius (or his source) simply got the vowels confused" so that "Chestus" refers to "Christus."[203]

The Jews in Rome evidently had debates and friction over the claims of Christ as early as A.D. 49. Some translate "disturbances" as "riots."[204] Suetonius' reference to Jewish expulsion from Rome confirms Acts 18:2. "And he [Paul] found a Jew named Aquilla, a native of Pontus, having recently come from Italy with his wife Pricilla, because Claudius had commanded all the Jews to leave Rome."

A second reference to Christians occurs in Suetonius' *Life of Nero* 16.2. As with Tacitus, here is a reference to crazy Nero persecuting Christians. "Punishments were also afflicted on the Christians, a sect professing a new and mischievous religious belief." [205]

In addition to Tacitus, Pliny, and Suetonius other possible references to Christ or early Christianity exist within ancient literature. [206]

Christ and Pompeii Inscriptions

Several puzzles have been found in the ruins of Pompeii A.D. 79:

```
R  O  T  A  S
O  P  E  R  A
T  E  N  E  T
A  R  E  P  O
S  A  T  O  R
```

We will depend upon Paul Barnett for an explanation.

"The reconstruction that is accepted by many indicates that the inscription is Christian. The letters in the square can be redistributed, with none spare, to make two A's, two O's and the word *PATERNOSTER* (Latin: 'Our Father') in both arms of a cross.

```
            A
            P
            A
            T
            E
            R
A P A T E R N O S T E R O
            O
            S
            T
            E
            R
            O
```

A and *O* stand for the Greek letters alpha and omega, symbols for God in Revelation 1:8, 21:6 and 22:13. If this is a correct understanding it means that there were Christians in Pompeii by the seventies. This should cause no surprise, given the large Christian community in nearby Rome in the sixties, as attested by Tacitus."[207]

Non-Christian references to Jesus or to Christ may not be detailed, but they do show that the outline of Jesus Christ's life and claims in the Gospels are historical. He did exist, have a public ministry, arouse opposition, performed "wondrous things" or "magic," was killed by the Jewish establishment and Pontius Pilate. His followers increased in great numbers and geographical extent. They worshipped Him as God.

Early church writings, of course, mention many more characters from the Gospels, but even a non-Christian source, Josephus, refers to John the Baptist and James, Jesus' half-brother. We should include Simon of Cyrene before moving to the historicity of various Jewish and Roman religious/political leaders mentioned in the Gospels. [208]

Archaeology and Simon the Cyrene

In 1941 an ossuary was discovered in the Kidron Valley in Jerusalem. It reads, "Alexander the Cyrene, Son of Simon." According to Mark 15:21, Simon of Cyrene was forced to carry Jesus' cross, and he had sons named Alexander and Rufus. As odd as it sounds, this ossuary is likely a reference to the man compelled to carry Jesus' cross and his son. Barnett calls the identification "most likely." Evans calls the identification "very suggestive."[209-210]

Chapter 10

Gospel People Also Mentioned in Non-Christian Sources: Jewish and Roman Leaders

High Priest Annas

The Gospel of Luke dates the ministry of John the Baptist during the time when Annas and Caiaphas were high priests. John 18:12-17 says that after they arrested Jesus they "led Him to Annas first" (see also Acts 4:6).

Josephus also made several references to Annas, i.e. Ananus. In *Antiquities* 18.26 (Maier, 262) "Quirinius, appointed Ananus, the son of Seth, as high priest."[211] In the section concerning the younger Ananus (the one in Acts 23:2) Josephus makes reference to the Ananus of Jesus' time. "This elder Ananus, after he himself had been high priest, had five sons, all of whom achieved that office, which was unparalleled (*Antiquities* 20.197)."[212]

Annas was high priest from A.D. 6 to A.D. 15. Although deposed, people still called him "high priest" much as former presidents still retain their title after their time in office.[213] As long as he lived, Annas had great influence over his five sons, one grandson, and son-in-law, Caiaphas, who all became high priests.

High Priest Joseph Caiaphas

The New Testament mentions Caiaphas nine times (Matthew 26:3, 57; Luke 3:2; John 11:49ff., 18:13, 14, 24, 28 and Acts 4:6). Caiaphas initiated the plan to kill Jesus because He was gaining popularity by His "many miracles" (KJV, John 11:47ff.). Caiaphas presided over the formal Jewish trial of Jesus (Matthew 26, John 18).

Caiaphas' tenure as high priest was unusually long. He held this office from A.D. 18-36. This means Caiaphas was high priest during Jesus' entire ministry, and he must have been a "good" politician in order to please the Romans so long. Josephus mentioned Caiaphas by name when Roman governor, Valerius Gratus, installed

111

him in office (*Antiquities* 18.26).[214] From Josephus we learn his first name was Joseph. Josephus mentioned Caiaphas again in a section concerning Pilate's recall to Rome to answer charges. While the office of governor of Judea was vacant, Vitellius, the governor of Syria, visited Jerusalem and "removed Joseph Caiaphas from office" (*Antiquities* 18.85).[215]

The *Biblical Archaeology Review* Sept./Oct. 1992 issue gives the story of an ossuary that probably held the bones of high priest Caiaphas.[216]

"The ossuary marked 'Joseph Son of Caiaphas' contained the bones of a 60-year-old man. Thus we may not only have the ossuary of the man who according to the Gospels, presided at the trial of Jesus, we may even have his bones."[217]

The Caiaphas ossuary ("bone-box") is white with ornate geometric deigns. It is among the most elaborate of the more than 800 ossuaries found in Jerusalem.

Herod the Great (73 – 4 B.C.)

Herod the Great overlaps with the life of Jesus at the time of His birth. Matthew 2 presents Herod's paranoid reaction to the Magi inquiring about the promised King of the Jews. When they did not return to tell Herod the whereabouts of Jesus, Herod ordered all the boys in Bethlehem age two and under to be massacred. Critics sometimes believe this to be myth as there is no record outside the Gospel of Matthew.[218] Yet, Herod was famous for both his paranoia and cruelty. Murdering children and/or striking out at anyone with credentials to be king would have been normal procedure for Herod. The Gospel claim of such is quite believable.

So much information exists about Herod the Great we are forced to abbreviate greatly.[219] Herod remodeled the Temple in Jerusalem, built a monument that still exists over the traditional burial site to the Patriarchs in Hebron (Machpelah), built the Caesarea Harbor, Masada, Herodium, and palaces at Jericho. Richardson lists 83 of Herod's building projects.[220]

Many ancient authors outside the Bible mention Herod. In addition to Josephus, Harold Hoehner's articles in *The Zondervan Pictorial Encyclopedia of the Bible* and *Dictionary of Jesus and the Gospels* cite two additional Talmudic writings (*Baba Bathra* and *Kiddushim*) and six gentile authors (Plutarch, Dio Cassius, Appian, Strabo, Tacitus, and Pausanius). Two merit attention. Regarding the beauty of the Temple, the Talmud says:

> "He who has not seen the Temple in its full construction has never seen a glorious building in his life. Which Temple? – Abaye, or it might be said, R. Hisda, replied, The reference is to the building of Herod. Of what did he build it? – Rabbah replied, of yellow and white marble . . . . He intended at first to overlay it with gold, but the Rabbis told him, leave it alone for it is more beautiful as it is, since it has the appearance of the waves of the sea." (*Gemara, Sukkah* 51b; cf. also b. *Baba Bathra* 3b).[221]

Herod's cruelty was legendary. Later we will list some of his atrocities. Because Herod killed three of his own sons, Emperor Augustus is quoted as making a pun of the close relationship between the words for "son" and "pig" in Greek. Augustus said, "I would rather be Herod's pig than his son" (Macrobius, *Saturnalia* 2.4.1).[222] Because Jews would not eat pork, pigs would not be slaughtered, unlike Herod's own family members. Coins and numerous inscriptions mention Herod. The author owns several coins with anchors on them that commemorate the building of Caesarea Harbor. Another has a bird (eagle) on it. This would be offensive to Jews as a graven image. All other coins have objects such as anchors, ceremonial bowls, helmets, palm branches, and cornucopias. "The eagle is said to represent the golden bird Herod placed above the Temple entrance."[223] Josephus wrote that Herod had erected a golden eagle (the symbol of Rome) over the gates of the Temple. When offended Jewish men (most likely students), tore down this eagle, Herod had these leaders burnt alive.[224] Herod's eagle coin is probably related to this event.

Richardson devotes an appendix to 22 inscriptions mentioning Herod.[225] They involve places in Israel but also far away: Masada, Jerusalem, Ashdod, Delos, Athens, Rhodes and Rome. Herod endowed the Olympic games, which had "fallen on hard times."[226] There were references to Herod in the Agora in Athens and on the Acropolis. Herod had sided with Anthony and Cleopatra against Augustus. When Augustus won the battle at Actium, Herod went in person to Rome and switched sides. This no doubt explains the fact that Herod built the majority of buildings in the town founded by Augustus to commemorate his victory, Nicopolis in Greece meaning ("city of victory").[227]

Herod had relationships with the major players of his day. Though he sided with Anthony and Cleopatra, Cleopatra also tried to seduce Herod. He was the only man known to resist her wiles.[228] Cleopatra at other times coveted oases at Jericho and Ein Gedi because of dates, palm wines, balsam (used for headaches and as an eye salve), and the cosmetics of the region. Anthony gave these areas to Cleopatra and forced Herod to pay rent on them.

Herod's family tree is quite complicated. At various times there were at least 10 wives and 15 known sons.[229] Court intrigue among these wives and sons plus a lifetime of threats and danger from shifting Roman politics, and guilt twisted Herod into deep depression, paranoia, and psychosis. He murdered his brother-in-law (drowned in a pool), his uncle, his wife's grandfather, and his "favorite" wife (Mariamne). He kept calling out in pain to his "favorite" wife and preserved her body in honey for frequent visits. To continue the list, Herod killed his mother-in-law (she tried to escape Jerusalem to Cleopatra by hiding in a coffin). He killed three of his "close friends," including another brother-in-law.

Fearing no one would mourn his death, Herod ordered all the leading men in the nation to gather in the hippodrome in Jerusalem. Upon news of Herod's death, the army was supposed to kill all these men and was also supposed to kill one person from every family in Israel so that there would be no rejoicing on the day of his death. His sister Salome cancelled this order when Herod died. In all, he killed three of his own sons, but Antipater was executed only five days before Herod's death because the son in prison rejoiced prematurely at reported news of his father's death.

With elaborate pomp (and relief by the people) Herod was buried in the place he constructed for that purpose, the Herodium. Even today the massive Herodium can not be overlooked, but Herod's crypt had been unknown until recently. The announcement of the discovery of Herod's burial chamber finally came on May 9, 2007.[230]

Josephus reported Herod died around the time of a lunar eclipse (perhaps March 13, 4 B.C.) at about age 70. "He had a terrible craving to scratch himself, his bowels were ulcerated, and his privates gangrenous and wormy."[231] He tried to recover at the hot springs in Callirrhoe, and then returned to Jericho. Herod tried to stab himself, but his cousin stopped him. His bier was of gold with gems.

> "There was a solid gold bier, adorned with precious stones and draped with the richest purple. On it lay the body wrapped in crimson, with a diadem resting on the head and above that a golden crown and the scepter by the right hand. The bier was escorted by Herod's sons and the whole body of his kinsmen, followed by his Spearmen and the Thracian company, Germans and Gauls, all in full battle order; headed by their commanders and all the officers, and followed by five hundred of the house slaves and freedmen carrying spices. The body was borne twenty-four miles to Herodium where by the late king's command it was buried. So ends the story of Herod. *Antiquities*, 17.193;17.8.3

Herod was "great" in terms of building projects, and he was a great politician in the sense of being able to retain his client status power despite sometimes first choosing to side with a loser. However, Herod was also insane and cruel.

Historical knowledge of Herod outside the Bible fits the characteristics described in Matthew. He was paranoid. He had no trouble murdering the innocent.

After Herod's death, his kingdom was divided into three parts ruled by three sons: Archelaus, Herod Philip, and Herod Antipas. All three are also mentioned in both the Gospels and secular history.

Archelaus (c. 23 B.C. – A.D. 16)

After Herod the Great's death, his son Archelaus ruled in the province of Judea from 4 B.C. to A.D. 6. In Matthew 2:13ff., the Bible says Mary and Joseph left Bethlehem for safety from King Herod in Egypt. After Herod's death, they returned to Israel. When Joseph "heard that Archelaus was reigning over Judea in place of his father Herod he was afraid to go there" (Matthew 2:22). Therefore, instead of returning to Bethlehem in Judea, the family returned to Nazareth in Galilee.

Herod had designated Archelaus as king and two other sons, Philip and Antipas as "tetrarchs." Those who resented Herod for putting up his golden eagle in the Temple and for burning the leaders who cut it down caused a riot. To restore order Archelaus ordered his army to attack the mob at Passover season with the result of 3,000 deaths.

As Antipas contested the will (Herod was insane and had written six wills), the two brothers traveled to Rome to have a settlement. During Archelaus' absence, further riots led to Romans being trapped in the city. The Romans then burned the Temple porches and plundered the treasury. There were between 1½ and 2½ months of chaos. The Syrian governor arrived with three legions to assert order.

After a few more years of shaky rule a delegation of Jews and Samaritans, who seldom agreed on much, petitioned Rome to depose Archelaus. The last straw was Archelaus divorcing his wife Mariamne to marry Glaphyra who in turn had been previously married to Archelaus' brother. The citizens had all they could tolerate when Archelaus married his brother's wife.

Rome banished Archelaus to Gaul in A.D. 6 (to Vienna which is south of Lyon, France). Glaphyra chose to share his exile. This explains why from that time Judea was ruled by Roman governors, while Herod Antipas ruled Galilee.

Most of the information about Archelaus comes from Josephus. He is also mentioned in Dio Cassius, *Roman History*.[232] Though Herod had willed Archelaus be king, Archelaus had refused the crown and title pending Roman settlement of the will. During his time, he was made "ethnarach" not king. This is the title that appears on Archelaus' coins.

Philip the Tetrarch (c. 20 B.C. – A.D. 33/34)

Another of Herod's sons, Philip, is mentioned in Luke 3:1 as being "tetrarch" of regions that are today on the northeast side of the Sea of Galilee. They include the Golan Heights and places now in Lebanon and Syria. Josephus wrote, ". . . Philip improved Panias at the source of the Jordan and called it Caesarea [Philippi]. He also raised Bethsaida on Lake Gennesaritis [Sea of Galillee] to city status by adding townspeople."[233] Caesarea Philippi is the place of Peter's confession of Jesus in Matthew 16. The Roman temple Philip built at Caesarea – Philippi appears on his coins as does the graven image of Augustus and Livia. Philip's coins say "tetrarch." Near Bethsaida Jesus fed the 5,000 (Luke 9:10). Philip called it Bethsaida-Julius in honor of Augustus' daughter Julia.[234]

Unlike Archelaus, the population was happy with Philip's rule. He married Salome, Herodias' daughter, who had danced and asked for John the Baptist's head on a platter. He was also her uncle on her father's side and her great uncle on her mother's side. They never had children.[235] After Philip's death, his area was given to Herod Agrippa I, the brother of Herodias.[236/237]

Herodias/Herod Antipas (c. 21 B.C. – after exile in A.D. 39)

Herodias was the granddaughter of Herod the Great. She was married in succession to two uncles. Both Josephus and the New Testament mention and criticize her marriage to Herod Antipas. Not only did it break up two homes, but it involved prohibited incestuous relationships. A niece married her two uncles in succession and in the process left one living husband for his brother.

Josephus called the first husband simply "Herod" while the New Testament calls him "Philip."[238] It is preferable to follow Hoehner. The man's full name was probably "Herod-Philip" and all sources are correct. Thus, Herod-Philip, Herodias' first husband is to be distinguished from Philip the Tetrarch.[239] Hoehner also comments that the origin of this scandal was a trip in which Herod Antipas lodged with his brother Herod-Philip and Herodias:

"When Antipas traveled to Rome around A.D. 29, he visited his brother Herod (Philip), who apparently lived in one of the coastal cities of Palestine. While there he fell in love with his niece as well as his brother's wife, Herodias. She agreed to marry Antipas when he returned from Rome, provided that he divorce his first wife (Josephus, *Antiquities* 18.5.1/109-110). Antipas's first wife learned of the plan and fled to her father, Aretas IV, who considered the matter a personal insult and later retaliated against Antipas.[240]

Though Josephus does not mention John the Baptist's criticism of this elite and wicked couple, he does refer to this scandal in separate comments on both Herodias and Herod Antipas.

Regarding Herodias, Josephus wrote:

". . . Herodias took upon her to confound the laws of our country, and divorce herself from her husband while he was still alive, and was married to Herod [Antipas] her husband's brother by the father's side, he was tetrarch of Galilee . . ."[241]

Immediately following this material on Herodias' bad behavior, Josephus refers to her daughter. The New Testament does not give her name. Josephus does, and also adds she was married to Philip the tetrarch. ". . . her [Herodias] daughter Salome was married to Philip, the son of Herod, the tetrarch of Trachonitis . . ." Josephus adds that they had no children.[242]

Josephus also refers to the immoral marriage between Herod Antipas and Herodias' in a previous section. Though he does not mention John the Baptist's preaching against this marriage or the dance at the birthday party, Josephus' comments about John the Baptist (see pp. 97-98) being righteous and popular are **immediately preceded** by references to the scandalous Antipas-Herodias affair.

Josephus' purpose is to recount how Antipas' first wife's father was enraged at the divorce. He was King Aretas also mentioned once in the Bible in 2 Corinthians 11:32.

"About this time, Aretas (the king of Arabia, Petrea) and Herod had a quarrel, on the account following: Herod the tetrarch had married the daughter of Aretas, and had lived with her a great while; but when he was once at Rome, he lodged with Herod, who was his brother indeed, but not by same mother; for this Herod was the son of the high priest Simon's daughter. However, he fell in love with Herodias this last Herod's wife, who was the daughter of Aristobulus their brother, and the sister of Agrippa the Great. This man ventured to talk to her about a marriage between them; which address when she admitted, an agreement was made for her to change her habitation, and come to him as soon as he should return from Rome: one article of this marriage also was this, that he should divorce Aretas's daughter. So Antipas, when he had made this agreement, sailed to Rome; but when he had done there the business he went about, and was returned again, his wife having discovered the agreement he had made with Herodias, and having learned it before he had notice of her knowledge of the whole design, she desired him to send her to Marcherus, which is a place on the borders of the dominions of Aretas and Herod, without informing him of any of her intentions. Accordingly Herod sent her thither, as thinking his wife had not perceived anything; now she had sent a good while before to Macherus, which was subject to her father, and so all things necessary for her journey were made ready for her by the general of Aretas's army, and by that means she soon came to Arabia, under the conduct of the several generals, who carried her from one to another successively; and she soon came to her father, and told him of Herod's intentions. So Aretas made this the first occasion of his enmity between him and Herod . . . ."[243]

Following this, Josephus recounts Aretas' attack upon Herod Antipas because Antipas had divorced his daughter. The people credited Antipas' military setback to his execution of the righteous and popular John who had an extensive preaching and baptizing ministry.

119

From Josephus we learn the Baptist's execution took place at Macherus. Given the context, it is reasonable to infer that the topic of the scandalous marriage led Josephus to think next about John's preaching on virtue, his approval by the masses, and his execution by Herod Antipas.

When Herod the Great died, Antipas had gone to Rome to contest Archelaus over their father's will. A previous will had named Antipas heir. Antipas ended up ruling Galilee and Perea (the land of the east bank of the Jordan).[244] Antipas built Sepphoris. Being only four miles from Nazareth, many believed that Joseph and Jesus would have worked on building projects (carpentry or masonry) in Sepphoris.[245] Antipas also built Tiberias as a capital city in honor of Emperor Tiberius.[246] Antipas' coins bear the title "tetrarch" and *The Dictionary of Biblical Archaeology* mentions two inscriptions with his name.[247]

Luke 23:6-12 says that Pilate and Antipas had been enemies. When Pilate learned that Jesus was from Galilee and that Antipas was in the city for Passover, Pilate sent Jesus to Antipas for an examination. Herod wanted to see Jesus do some entertaining magic tricks and had wanted to see Jesus for a long time. Jesus would not even speak to Antipas. After Antipas dressed Jesus in a "gorgeous robe", he sent him back to Pilate. "Now Herod and Pilate became friends with one another that very day, for before they had been enemies with each other" (Luke 23:12).

Gospel sources for intimate details of Jesus' trial before Antipas, the Lord's silence, and the resulting attitude change between Pilate and Antipas probably came from the Christians within Herod's staff. The New Testament mentions two: Luke 8:3 "Joanna the wife of Chuza, Herod's steward" and Acts 13:1 "Manaen, who had been brought up with Herod the tetrarch." The Chuza family name appears on various Nabatean inscriptions including one at Petra.[248] Chuza was probably Antipas' finance minister. Manaen was perhaps a childhood friend and/or raised together with Antipas in school or in child-care.

Non-Christian sources such as Josephus and Tacitus mention Jesus being tried by Pilate. There is no mention of an examination by

Antipas. However, the cause of enmity between the two leaders may be a subject in Philo's writing. No doubt Pilate and Antipas were at odds over the "Galileans whose blood Pilate had mixed with their sacrifices" (Luke 13:1). Philo (a Jewish writer from Alexandria, Egypt at the time of Jesus) writes that Pilate had some golden shields bearing the name (but not the image) of Tiberius erected in the former palace of Herod the Great. In *Legatio ad Gaium* 299-305 Philo wrote that four of Herod's sons protested Pilate's actions to Emperor Tiberius. The Emperor rebuked Pilate and ordered him to take these shields from Herod's old palace in Jerusalem to the Temple of Augustus in Caesarea. Antipas was certainly one of the main spokesmen who accused Pilate. This explains the hatred between the two.

Secular history may also explain Pilate's decision to change directions and use the trial of Jesus to repair relations with to Antipas. Several scholars believe Pilate's benefactor in Rome was Sejanus, an anti-Semite. However, Sejanus was executed as a traitor to Tiberius on October 18, A.D. 31. This perhaps left Pilate vulnerable, as the authorities would now be tracking Sejanus' friends who also had a strong anti-Semitic policy. Therefore, secular history does not specifically mention Jesus' trial before Antipas but may explain and indirectly verify Pilate's attempt to reconcile and to make Jewish friends. Also, this change in political conditions fits Pilate caving in to the Jewish religious establishment at Jesus' trial. The tipping point seems to be John 19:12 when "the Jews" (probably a term for religious authorities) threaten Pilate with charges he is "no friend of Caesar" and that he "opposes Caesar."[249] Even if the tie between Sejanus and Pilate is not conclusive, this was hardly a time for Pilate to appear anti-Semitic.[250]

After the trial of Jesus, Antipas fades from the Gospels. However, Josephus mentions the demise of Antipas and Herodias. When Gaius (Caligula) became emperor he elevated his childhood friend Agrippa (see endnote 237) and gave him the title king. This prodded Herodias to urge Antipas to go to Rome and also ask for more favors including the title of king. This move backfired badly as Josephus remarks:

"Antonia, Tiberius' sister-in-law, took a special interest in Agrippa and tried to make him as comfortable as possible during the six months he spent in prison. Then Tiberius died, having appointed Gaius as his successor. One of Gaius' early acts was to put a diadem on Agrippa's head and appoint him king over the tetrarchy of Philip. He also gave him a golden chain equal in weight to the iron one that had bound him, and Agrippa returned home in triumph. Extremely jealous over the success of her brother, Herodias prodded her husband Herod to embark for Rome and petition for the kingship also. He resisted as best he could, but finally gave in, and they sailed to Italy, where they met the emperor at Baiae. During their interview, Gaius was reading letters from Agrippa, in which he indicted Herod for conspiring with Sejanus, a Roman prefect, against Tiberius and for being in alliance now with Artabanus of Parthia against Gaius. As proof, Agrippa cited 70,000 pieces of armor stored in Herod's armories. Gaius asked whether the arms were there, and when he received an affirmative, he took away Herod's tetrarchy and added it to Agrippa's kingdom banishing Herod to Lyons in Gaul. He would have permitted Herodias to return and enjoy her property, but she chose exile with her husband.[251]

Antipas and Herodias ended their days in exile and obscurity.[252] Contemptible though she was, Herodias chose to follow her husband into exile when Caligula would have permitted her to remain with her possessions in Judea because she was Agrippa's sister. Her "noble" choice may have also involved total distrust and hatred of her brother Agrippa who would now rule in her husband's place.

This would be a logical point to move to Pontius Pilate who was contemporary with Antipas during Jesus' ministry. Antipas ruled Galilee, and Pilate Judea. However, before any Pilate study we have to include several minor non-Herodians mentioned in the Gospels.

Quirinius

Christians are familiar with Quirinius if for no other reason than listening to recitations of the Christmas story each year. "Now in those days a decree went out from Caesar Augustus, that a census be taken of all the inhabited earth. This was the first census taken while Quirinius was governor of Syria" (Luke 2:1-2).

Publius Sulpicius Quirinius was most definitely an historical figure. He was born in Lanuvium. His first wife was Appia Claudia. His second wife was Aemillia Lepida a descendent of Sulla and Pompey.[253] He died in A.D. 21. Classical references to him include: Tacitus, *Annals* 2.30, 3:22, 23, 48; Suetonius, *Tiberius* 49; Strabo, *Geography* 12.6.5., and Florus, *Roman History*, 2:31. Also, several references in Josephus mention this Quirinius (*Antiquities*, 18.1.1-2, 26;20:102).[254]

After Archelaus was deposed in A.D. 6, the Romans ordered a census of Judea. According to Josephus, this was carried out by Quirinius, the governor of Syria.

"Quirinius, a Roman Senator of consular rank, was also sent by Caesar to be governor of Syria assessor of property there and in Judea, where he was to sell Archelaus' estate. While the Jews reluctantly agreed to register their property, a certain Judas of Gamala claimed that this was tantamount to slavery . . . and [he] called for a revolution." *Antiquities*, 18.1.1-2 [255]

Quirinius himself is historical, and he was governor of Syria at the time of this additional census in A.D. 6 mentioned by Josephus. Luke was aware of Quirinius' census and the tax revolt by Judas as shown by Acts 5:37.

How does Quirinius' census as governor in Syria (A.D. 6-9) relate back to the taxation which compelled Joseph to go to Bethlehem a decade earlier? There are options that solve this question. However, choosing the correct option is difficult.

Regarding Roman censuses in general, no all-inclusive world-wide decree was mentioned in secular history. Augustus did order regional censuses in Gaul (France), Cyrene (Libya) and Egypt.[256] Ben Witherington III (Asbury Seminary, Methodist) offers this explanation about a world-wide census:

". . . it is not certain that Luke in 2:1 means that Augustus took one enormous census of the whole empire. The language is general and may mean no more than that the various parts of the empire were subject to various censuses during the time of Augustus. What the Greek in fact says is that Caesar decreed that 'all of the Roman world be enrolled' (Thorley). Both the present tense of *apographo* ('to enroll') and the use of *pas* ('all') suggest that Luke means that Caesar decreed that the enrollment, which had previously been going on in some parts of the empire, should now be extended to all parts, including client states. The Roman historian A. N. Sherwin-White states, "A census or taxation-assessment of the whole provincial empire . . . was certainly accomplished for the first time in history under Augustus."[257]

Perhaps Augustus' cumulative program over time reached an empire wide registration which would be regarded as the entire "civilized world." Evidence regarding Roman census habits points to a fourteen year cycle. "The sequence of known dates for the censuses clearly demonstrates that one was taken every fourteen years."[258]

While secular history does not mention any orders in Judea to return to ancestral homesteads, two relevant documents come from Egypt. One refers to orders by the governor to return to homesteads for tax purposes. The second papyri contain an oath that seems to distinguish those permanently living at a residence as opposed to others on an "extended stay", who nevertheless count another locality as "home" for tax purposes.[259]

While these come from Egypt, traditions of loyalty to a family home would likely be even stronger in Israel. Under the Law of Moses land remained in families. Even if sold, the prices in Israel were supposed to be proportioned to the number of years until the Jubilee year when land returned to the original family (see Leviticus 25:10 "each of you shall return to his own property" and 25:23 "The land, moreover shall not be sold permanently . . .").

Augustus' taxation scheme involved all the empire whether by instantaneous decree or eventual realization of a long-term goal.

Having Jews returning to their family homestead also makes sense. Next we return to Quirinius. It is known he was governor of Syria (A.D. 6-9) and ordered a census after Archelaus was removed in A.D. 6 to prepare for Judea being ruled directly by Roman governors. How does this relate to Mary and Joseph going to Bethlehem previously when Herod the Great ruled? There are four main possibilities:

1. Quirinius served two terms as governor of Syria. He ruled from A.D. 6-9 but also previously at the time of Jesus birth. Charles Ryrie accepts this view in his *Ryrie Study Bible* note on Luke 2:2. British scholar Sir William Ramsey maintained this view based upon an inscription called *Lapis Tiburtinus*. The inscription refers to an honorable Roman officer who entered the office of imperial legate for a second time. However, the name on the inscription is mutilated. This could refer to a previous term for Quirinius being the governor of Syria, but it is not definitive. Further discovery could turn up another name.[260]

2. There were two governors named Quirinius. "Some recent archaeological evidence has shed new light on an old and vexing problem relating to Christ's birth . . . . Jerry Vardaman has discovered the name Quirinius on a coin in micrographic letters, placing him as proconsul of Syria and Cilicia from 11 B.C. until after the death of Herod. The evidence contributed by Vardaman supports the view there were two Quiriniuses . . . ."[261]

3. Luke 2:2 should be translated, "This census was *before* that [census] when Quirinius was governor of Syria," or "This census took place *before* Quirinius was governor of Syria."[262] Harold Hoehner favors this view. The Greek word *"protos"* is rendered "before." Luke was writing decades after Jesus' birth. Perhaps he believed his readers, Jewish and especially Roman (e.g. Luke 1:3 Theophilus"), would recall the more famous tax revolution during the days of Quirinius' term as governor of Syria in A.D. 6. In order to avoid this misunderstanding that could easily arise, Luke intended to make clear that the census bringing Mary and Joseph to Bethlehem was before the more disruptive one later involving Quirinius.

4. Quirinius may have ordered the census at the time of Jesus' birth in his role as imperial consul of the East before he took the office of governor. Thus, Luke refers to "governing" or "administering" this census, or Luke uses the title "governor" of Quirinius because he later held that office also.

Most Bible students would have no reason to study the entire life of Quirinius. He was consul in Rome 12 B.C., proconsul of the province of Asia, advisor to future emperor Gaius Caesar during the future emperors' battle with Armenia, and only then governor of Syria.[263]

Perhaps it was in Quirinius' role as "consul" that he "governed" a census even outside his normal jurisdiction. There are examples of Romans asserting tax authority even over distant areas of client kings such as Herod the Great. Herod was both crazy and terminally ill at this time. Perhaps a higher official from outside the area would supervise the census.[264]

Any of these views could explain how Quirinius could relate to a census at the time of Jesus' birth. Regardless of which one may be preferred, Quirinius was a historical figure and eventually governed Syria.

Lysanias: Tetrarch of Abilene

Along with Tiberius, Pilate, Herod the tetrarch, Philip the tetrarch, and high priests Annas and Caiaphas, Luke 3:1 says "Lysanias was tetrarch of Abilene" when John the Baptist began preaching in the wilderness.

There was an earlier Lysanias mentioned in *Dio* Cassius and Josephus, *Antiquities* 14.13.3/14.330; 15.4.1/15.92. He was executed by Mark Anthony in 36 B.C.[265]

An inscription refers to "Lysanias the tetrarch." D. Edmund Hiebert concludes this inscription dates from A.D. 14-29.[266] The *Dictionary of Biblical Archaeology* mentions a second inscription reading "Lysanias the tetrarch."[267] McRay comments, ". . . an inscription has been found from the time of Tiberius (A.D. 14-37) that names Lysanias as tetrarch in Abilene near Damascus."[268]

Some references in Josephus also refer to this later Lysanias. "It seems a necessary assumption that Josephus referred to two different men named Lysanias."[269] Bock suggests *Antiquities* 19.5.1/ 19:275; 20.7.1/20.138 as the strongest.[270]

"Claudius now confirmed Agrippa as king and added to his domain Judea and Samaria as well - all the lands formerly ruled by his grandfather Herod [The Great] but also Abilene, which had been governed by Lysanias."[271]

There seems to have been a dynasty with the Lysanias family name in this region. Some references in Josephus concern the time of Agrippa 1 (A.D. 40-44) and, therefore, are best taken to be the recent Lysanias not the one who died in 36 B.C. Josephus, taken with at least two inscriptions mentioning Lysanias, confirms that Luke was careful in his historical data.

Pontius Pilatus

Hundreds of millions of people recite Pilate's name in the Apostle's Creed. "I believe in God the Father Almighty, maker of heaven and earth; and in Jesus Christ His only Son, our Lord who was conceived by the Holy Spirit, born of the Virgin Mary, suffered under Pontius Pilate . . . ."

This is historical truth. In non-Christian sources Pilate was mentioned by Josephus, Tacitus, and Philo. In 1961 Italian archaeologist Antonio Frova discovered a 2' by 3' stone in an ancient theater in Caesarea, Israel. The full inscription was easily reconstructed to read "Pontius Pilatus Prefect of Judea has presented the Tiberium to the Caesereans."

Many archaeology and history books, as well as, the internet will supply pictures.[272] Though Pilate had already been referenced outside the Bible by three other authors, this was the first archaeological inscription giving his name. In addition, it shows that the Gospels were correct to call Pilate "prefect" not "procurator." By contrast, Tacitus and Josephus use a later title that changed under Claudius in A.D. 41-54. Yet, in Pilate's time A.D. 26-36/37 his title would have been "Prefect" not the later "Procurator" used by Tacitus and Josephus. (See p. 155 for more examples of Luke being careful with professional titles.) A procurator was more a financial officer whereas a prefect like Pilate was more a military commander.[273]

Coins produced during Pilate's tenure show images of a wand and a libation bowl with a ladle. Both seem designed to be provocative to Jews. The wand is an augur's staff used by pagan priests (like a sorcerer's staff). The ladle and bowl remind one of meat broth being poured out over pagan sacrifices cooking in the fire. This must not have gone over very well with the Jews (Jewish author Philo especially returned the insults). Pilate stopped issuing these coins in A.D. 31 (after the fall of anti-Semitic Sejanus, see pp. 131-133).[274]

According to Paul Maier, Pontius, the family name belonged to the hill country tribe of the Samnites, known for being "a scrappy breed." He translates *Pilatus* as "armed with a javelin."[275] This would be a good name for a military governor. Pilate's 10-year rule (A.D. 26-36) was the second longest of any Roman governor. Despite his insults, we can assume he had much skill in keeping the divisive province together most of the time.

Tacitus, *Annals* 3:33-34, wrote about a debate in the Roman Senate in A.D. 21 concerning wives traveling with husbands on foreign assignments. The Romans approved this. Therefore, we read of Pilate's wife in the New Testament (Matthew 27:19). By the way, a wife's dreams would have spooked a Roman. "Everyone knew about Calpurnia's dream of Caesar's torn and bloodied toga on the eve of the Ides of March."[276] Her traditional name was Procula. Normally, Pilate would live in Caesarea (hence the inscription slab found there) as it was the Roman Capital of Judea. When visiting Jerusalem for work or Jewish holidays, they no doubt stayed in Herod's old palace near Herod's three towers. Does it not make more sense that the Governor and Mrs. Pilate stayed in Herod's palace, not the soldiers' barracks in the Fortress Antonia? Thus, the location for Jesus' trial would be in

Herod's old palace and the real Via Dolorosa ran from Herod's palace to Calvary not Fortress Antonia to Calvary.[277]

Roman author Tacitus mentions Pilate in connection with Christ. More has been said above, but the actual quote is brief if we delete references to Christians being martyred. "Their originator, Christ, had been executed in Tiberius' reign by the governor of Judea, Pontius Pilate" (Tacitus, *Annals*, 15.44.4).

Philo, the Jewish author from Alexandria, was a contemporary of Jesus and Pilate. We will save additional information from Philo about Pilate's golden shield debacle for now. Yet, we must quote Philo's insults in *De Legatio ad Gaium* 38. Philo in this portion is quoting Herod Agrippa I.

"The Jews 'exasperated Pilate to the greatest possible degree, as he feared lest they might go on an embassy to the Emperor and might impeach him with respect to other particulars of his government – his corruptions, his acts of insolence, his rapine, his habit of insulting people, his cruelty, and his continual murders of people untried and uncondemned, and his never-ending gratuitous and most grievous inhumanity.' "[278]

Josephus also gave many examples of the rocky relationship between the Jews and Pilate. In *Antiquities* 18:55 he relates how Pilate was the first governor to bring shields with images of Caesar into Jerusalem.

"Pilate, having been sent by Tiberius as procurator of Judea, moved his troops from Caesarea to winter quarters in Jerusalem. But by night he brought into the city busts of the emperor that were attached to the military standards, when our law forbids the making of images. For this reason, the previous procurators used standards that had no such ornaments. The next morning, the Jews were indignant and hurried to Pilate in Caesarea, imploring him to remove the images. When he refused, deeming it an insult to the emperor, they prostrated themselves around the palace for five days and nights. On the sixth, Pilate took his seat on the tribunal in the stadium, and when the Jews again pleaded, he gave a signal. The people were suddenly surrounded with a ring of troops three deep, their swords drawn, and Pilate threatened death if they did not stop the tumult. But they bared their necks, declaring that they would rather die than transgress the laws. Astounded at such religious zeal, Pilate immediately transferred the images from Jerusalem to Caesarea." [279]

Next Josephus continues in *Antiquities* 18:60 with tension between Pilate and the Jews over Pilate constructing a water aqueduct. Pilate used money dedicated to God in the Temple (*corban*) to construct a municipal water supply. The water ducts brought water 25 miles to Jerusalem from the south. The uproar over Pilate's use of Temple funds may overlap with the Passover disturbance of Luke 13:1-2 when Pilate killed some Galileans (Herod Antipas' subjects) visiting Jerusalem and mixed their blood in with animal sacrifices. [280]

"Later, he spent money from the sacred treasury to construct an aqueduct to bring water into Jerusalem. But the people were angry at this enterprise and surrounded Pilate's tribunal when he visited Jerusalem. Anticipating the riot, Pilate had ordered many of his troops to mingle with the crowd, disguised as civilians, and on his signal, they clubbed the abusive Jews. Although Pilate had ordered them not to use swords, a large number were killed, some from the blows, others in the stampede which followed." [281]

It seems likely there had been an agreement between Pilate and the Temple authorities on the use of this money. If so, the religious authorities abandoned Pilate when the population grew angry about the project. At the trial of Jesus, we see a mixture of Pilate continuing to provoke these leaders yet at the same time caving in to keep them happy. He puts up an inscription above Jesus, "The King of the Jews" and refuses to take it down. He is exasperated with these people but submits to their demands.

Given Pilate's obnoxious coins, and the Jewish leaders returning insults (as in Philo), they disliked each other very much. Yet, Pilate tries to befriend Herod Antipas by sending Jesus to him (Luke 23:6-12), and he relents when the Jews threaten to accuse him of opposing Caesar (John 19:12ff.). Why?

The incident of the golden shields and probably the fall of anti-Semitic Sejanus may explain Pilate's actions at Jesus' trial. Some explanation has been included in the previous section about Herod Antipas. We will review slightly but now use additional quotes from contemporary scholars.[282]

Hoehner writes, "According to Philo it seems that Pilate obtained his position via his mentor Sejanus, the commander of the Praetorian Guard" (Philo, *Leg. Gai.* 159).[283] F.F. Bruce supports this connection between Pilate and Sejanus. ". . . Pilate may well have been his nominee."[284]

In A.D. 31 Sejanus was executed for treason against Emperor Tiberius. The head of the Praetorian Guard (personal bodyguards to Caesar) and virtual co-ruler of the empire, he was executed October 18, A.D. 31. (*Dio Cassius*, Book 58:9-15 especially 10-11 relates Sejanus' downfall.)

If Sejanus had been Pilate's patron, this would help explain Pilate's unwilling but accommodating spirit at Jesus' trial. All of Sejanus' friends would be in deep trouble. However, even without any close tie between Sejanus and Pilate, all those who had followed Sejanus' anti-Semitic policies would now avoid mistreatment of Jews in order not to draw any dangerous attention or display similarities to the now dead powerful leader.

Philo says Pilate brought golden shields to Herod the Great's former palace in Jerusalem that would have been Pilate's own residence when visiting the city. This time the gold gilded shields would have not had the emperor's image as had the military standards in the previous conflict soon after Pilate entered office. These golden shields only had the emperor's name. Thus, Pilate may have not expected any objection.

Philo's account in *Leg.* 299-305 says Pilate would not remove these shields despite local appeals. Therefore, four of Herod's sons appealed in a letter to Tiberius. Hoehner says, Antipas and Philip the tetrarch were "certainly" among the four and that Antipas "may have been the spokesman for the group."[285]

Maier agrees that Antipas was a principal leader in the charge to embarrass Pilate in the removal of these golden shields bearing Caesar's name. It worked. The Emperor was very angry and ordered Pilate to remove the shields back to the Temple of Augustus in Caesarea.[286]

The golden shield incident helps explain why Pilate and Antipas "had been enemies with each other" (Luke 23:12). The fall of the anti-Semitic Sejanus in A.D. 31 may explain why Pilate saw a need to make peace with Antipas by sending Jesus the Galilean for trial (Luke 23:12) and also why Pilate gave in so quickly to the religious leaders who wanted Jesus dead when Pilate would have let him go (see Acts 3:13 and John 19:12ff.). Caesar's choice of Antipas over Pilate in the matter of the golden shields, and the anti-Semitic Sejanus' fall meant Pilate had better yield. This would be true whatever Pilate's past with Sejanus, but a matter of physical (not just political) life and death if Sejanus were Pilate's main contact back in the capital.

"Philo who extols Tiberius's liberal policy toward the Jews, records the episode when Pilate had set up gilded votive shields bearing the name, though not the image, of the emperor in the former palace of Herod in Jerusalem (an incident to be distinguished from his earlier placement in Jerusalem of standards bearing the embossed figure of the emperor). Prominent Jews, including the four sons of Herod, appealed to Pilate to remove the shields. But when he refused to hear their request, they wrote to the Emperor Tiberius. Upon receiving the letter, Tiberius was enraged and immediately replied, ordering Pilate to remove the shields from Jerusalem and place them in the temple of Augustus at Caesarea (*Leg. Gai.* 299-305*).* Unlike the previous incident of the standards, prominent Jews and Herod's sons were able now to write directly to Tiberius, an event made possible by Sejanus's execution by Tiberius on October 18, A.D. 31. Tiberius was now trying to reverse Sejanus's anti-Semitic policies and hence gave a quick response to the Jew's request.

But why would Pilate have done such a thing when he had already been defeated in the incident of the standards? It seems that with the removal of his mentor Sejanus, whose anti-Semitic policies he had followed, Pilate wanted to dissociate himself from Sejanus and ingratiate himself with Tiberius. Consequently, he brought into Jerusalem shields that had no image but bore the name of the emperor. But the plan backfired and Tiberius was sorely displeased. The most likely time for this incident to have occurred is at a Jewish festival when the sons of Herod would have been in Jerusalem, possibly the Feast of Tabernacles in A.D. 32."[287]

Josephus wrote of the military standard riot. Pilate backed down. He wrote of the Temple money for the aqueduct. Pilate was again vilified. Then Sejanus was executed. Next we learn from Philo that Tiberius ordered Pilate to remove golden shields with only a name not images on them. Pilate then tried to make friends with Antipas and the Jewish religious leaders at the trial of Jesus, perhaps to save his job or even his life. Pilate chose personal safety over the ideal of a Roman Judge, *fiat justitia ruat caelum,* ("Let justice be done, though the heavens fall").[288]

Ironically, it was perhaps during Pilate's rule that full control over death penalty cases was taken from the Sanhedrin and given to the Roman governor. The Babylonian Talmud in *Shabbath 15a* says, "Forty years before the destruction of the Temple, the Sanhedrin . . . did not adjudicate capital cases." Also, the Palestinian Talmud in *Sanhedrin* 18a and 24b says, "Capital punishment was abolished forty years before the destruction of the Temple." Maier concludes ". . . a literal reading of the sources would indeed point to 30 A.D."[289] Thus, it could be that Pilate himself had something to do with the requirement that he get involved in his own personal dilemma involving the most important capital punishment case in human history.

As did Tacitus, Josephus refers to Pilate in connection with the trial of Jesus. Previous material covered the details (see pp. 99-101). Whether we use the standard Greek text of Josephus or adopt the Arabic tradition, both refer to "Jesus" and both say "Pilate condemned him to be crucified," *Antiquities* 18.63.

Pilate must have felt he had conciliated Herod Antipas enough to be safe ("friends with one another now that very day," Luke 23:12). Still he did not enjoy the situation.

There were limits to how far he would go to make Jews happy. He quit minting offensive coins, but he would not take down his *titulus* over Jesus cross (John 19:19, 22, "The king of the Jews" and "what I have written I have written"). Pilate may have wondered "what next?" The answer was a crazy Samaritan false prophet that ended Pilate's career.

Josephus gives details of Pilate's recall in his *Antiquities* 18.85.

"The Samaritans too were not exempt from troubles. A demagogue persuaded them to go with him to Mount Gerizim, where he would show them the sacred vessels which Moses had supposedly buried there. A great multitude arrived at the mountain armed, but Pilate blocked their route of ascent with infantry and cavalry. In the clash that followed, some were killed and the rest scattered or taken prisoner. Pilate then executed the ring-leaders.

After the uprising was quelled, the Samaritan council went to Vitellius, the governor of Syria, and accused Pilate of massacre. Vitellius sent Marcellus, one of his friends, to take charge of Judea, ordering Pilate to return to Rome and defend himself before the emperor against the Samaritan charges. And so Pilate, having spent ten years in Judea, hurried to Rome in obedience to Vitellius' orders. But before he reached Rome, Tiberius had already died."[290]

Moses did not bury anything in Mt. Gerizim. He only looked into the Promised Land from Mt. Nebo (Deuteronomy 34). In addition to this Biblical mistake, the Samaritans made the mistake of being armed as they followed their fanatic to Mt. Gerizim. Pilate ruthlessly blocked the way up the mountain. Vitellius listened to the Samaritan grievances and ordered Pilate to vacate office and travel to Rome for trial before Tiberius. Given Tiberius' earlier anger against Pilate in the matter of the golden shields, Pilate must have been very nervous on this trip. However, Tiberius died on March 16, A. D. 37 before Pilate reached the city. This is the last historical reference to Pilate. Perhaps the next emperor continued with the trial, but Gaius Caligula dropped "most of the cases carried over from Tiberius' administration."[291]

Eusebius in *Church History* 2.7 quotes a Greek report that Pilate committed suicide. Yet, no other sources confirm this.[292] By contrast Origen does not mention Pilate's suicide. In *Contra Celsum* 2.34 Origen responded to pagan critic Celsus' comments that no divine punishment happened to Pilate, e.g. Pilate did not have "madness." Origen countered "And yet he does not know that it was not so much Pilate that condemned Him . . . as the Jewish nation . . ." The text continues with references to Pilate's wife's dream. If Pilate had committed suicide or suffered serious tragedy, Origen would not have conceded Celsus' point that Pilate suffered no judgment.[293]

Perhaps Caligula would not have cared about Tiberius' squabbles with Pilate over the golden shields years before or have worried about the Samaritans who, after all, had been armed and irrational. Maier concludes, "nothing grossly negative, it seems, ever befell Pilate."[294]

Pontius Pilate was certainly not a make-believe person. We actually know much about him from sources beyond the Bible in early ancient writings.[295]

Conclusion on People in the Gospels

The broad outline of Jesus' life is contained in Jewish and Roman sources outside of the Bible. Other Bible characters such as John the Baptist and James have parallels in ancient literature.

Jewish religious leaders (Annas and Caiaphas), Jewish political leaders (Herod the Great, Archelaus, Herod Philip, Herodias, Antipas) and Roman political leaders (Quirinius, Lysanias, and especially Pilate) mentioned in the Gospels are also mentioned by ancient non-Christian writings and artifacts. The Gospels are rooted in history not mythology. In the case of Luke's Gospel, many additional names, places, and customs also have parallels between the book of Acts and non-

Christian sources. Since our subject is the four Gospels and Jesus' history, this information has been included on pages 153-156. Material from Acts also shows that the author of the Gospel of Luke was a careful historian.

The people in the Gospels are not mythological but historical. This brings the study of people mentioned in the Gospels to a close. Now we must further consider places mentioned in the Gospels.

Chapter 11

Places in the Gospels

Many places in the Gospels can be shown to be real not fictional. In order to confirm that the Gospels are not mythological, there is value in showing that references to places are no more fictional than are references to people. Both are historical.

Numerous places could be included, but we will be forced to select only sites most significant to the life of Christ and detailed references from the Gospel of John which prove that the book was written by one with an accurate knowledge of the geography of that time period.

Significant Places in the Life of Christ

The Church of the Nativity in Bethlehem, Capernaum, the Upper Room, and the Church of the Holy Sepulcher are probably authentic sites from the birth, ministry, and death/resurrection of Jesus. Additional places can be researched by consulting books on New Testament archaeology, Bible encyclopedias, or the many "coffee table" type books on the Holy Land.[296]

■ Church of the Nativity – Bethlehem

The Church of the Nativity in Bethlehem is the oldest church in continuous use in the world. Most early churches were destroyed by the Persians (A.D. 614) or Moslems (A.D. 638), but when the Persians saw a painting of the Magi in Persian dress they left this church alone. Constantine's mother, Helena, had the church erected sometime before A.D. 333. The mosaic floor beneath the present floor probably is original, and the red limestone columns still exist from the original church.[297]

The entire building dates from Byzantine Emperor Justinian A.D. 527-565. The door has been lowered so that Moslems could not ride horses into the sanctuary. High above the existing entrance one can still see the lintel from the original massive door.

137

The Church of the Nativity has been long regarded by scholars as the correct site for Jesus' birth. Roman Emperor Hadrian A.D. 117-138 desecrated a site that had already been regarded as the place of Jesus' birth back into the first century. By planting a grove of trees there in honor of the Roman God Adonis, Hadrian's plan backfired, as he actually preserved knowledge of the location. Writing in A.D. 150, Justin Martyr said, "But when the child was born in Bethlehem, since Joseph could not find lodging in the village, he took up his quarters in a certain cave near the village, and while they were there Mary brought forth the Christ and placed him in a manger, and here the Magi who came from Arabia found him."[298] *The Protoevangelium of James* (second century, 18.1;19.2) and Origen in *Contra Celsus* 1.51 (c. A.D. 248) both indicate Jesus was born in a cave.[299] That a cave would be used for a stable would not be without logic. Today the cave walls have been enlarged to accommodate visitors and are covered with tapestry. It may not look like a place for a manger, but this probably is the correct place.

Paul Maier says, "Though final proof is necessarily lacking, the surprising answer lurks closer to probably than possibly."[300] McRay concludes, "The place where Jesus was born has never been seriously disputed . . . . There appears little reason to doubt its essential trustworthiness."[301]

■ Capernaum – Synagogue

Jesus moved to Capernaum (the village of Nahum) after His rejection by His boyhood town Nazareth. Many events in the life of Jesus took place in Capernaum.

At Capernaum Jesus taught in the synagogue and encountered demons (Mark 1:21-28). There He healed Peter's mother-in-law (Mark 1:29ff.), and the whole city gathered at the door. In Capernaum Jesus healed the paralytic who had been lowered through a hole in the roof (Mark 2:1ff.). The context in which Jesus called His disciples to be fishers of men mentions Capernaum (Matthew 4:13, 19). There Jesus healed the centurion's servant after the Jewish elder testified the centurion had built them a synagogue (Matthew 8:5ff; Luke 7:1-10). The nobleman's son was healed in Capernaum (John 4:46) though

Jesus was in distant Cana. Near the shore Jesus had His disciples cast a hook. Inside the first fish was a coin with which to pay taxes and silence critics (Matthew 17:24). In the synagogue in Capernaum, Jesus claimed to be the bread of life (John 6:17, 24, 59).

Beautiful white colored slabs and columns of the synagogue in Capernaum are now a main tourist attraction (see cover). These date from the A.D. 300's according to McRay or A.D. 200's according to Finegan.[302] However, in 1975 black basalt foundation stones were discovered below the existing whitish limestone structure. This proves this location was the place of the Capernaum synagogue in Jesus' time. "Certainly the remains of the synagogue in which Jesus preached."[303]

■ Peter's House

Perhaps an even more impressive find than the Capernaum synagogue is a building a few steps south (closer to the Sea of Galilee). Here the Catholic Church has built a shrine over an octagonal church dating from the A.D. 400's. Beneath this old Byzantine church there is a house. A large room in this house was a place of special veneration. While the house was built about 60 B.C., "Sometime about the middle of the first century A.D. the function of the building changed."[304] It had roughly 158 inscriptions in Greek, Syrian, Aramaic and Latin with paintings of flowers, fruit, crosses, and a boat with oars.[305] These inscriptions can be translated:

"Christ have mercy," "Lord Jesus help," "fish," and possibly "Peter."[306]

While definitive proof is lacking, most scholars believe these are actually the ruins of Peter's house in Capernaum: Maier (Western Michigan) "quite probably Peter's house"; Charlesworth (Princeton) "Peter's house in which Jesus lived . . . . has probably been discovered;" Charlesworth in *Jesus and Archaeology* also writes, ". . . it seems to be Peter's house" and ". . . I fully agree with . . . ." (then he quotes J. Murphy-O'Connor who is a main advocate that this is Peter's house); von Wahlde (Loyola), "Almost all scholars now espouse this view;" Finegan (Pacific School of Religion, Berkley), "It is well possible, therefore, that it was the relatives of Peter who had remained in Capernaum and had transformed Peter's house in this way . . . ;"

Shanks (editor, *Biblical Archaeology Review*) and Strange (University of South Florida) do not believe the name Peter can be read with confidence but still conclude, "a considerable body of circumstantial evidence does point to its identification as St. Peter's house."[307]

The places of Jesus' birth and home during His ministry have probably been identified. This is also true for the sites of the Passion Week.

■ The Upper Room

The Upper Room was the place for the Last Supper (Luke 22:11-13) and the place for the coming of the Holy Spirit upon the church (Acts 1:12-14). The room was large enough to accommodate 120. The building shown as the Upper Room by tour guides was built in 1099 with the portion now existing remodeled in 1342. It is called the "cenacle" after the Latin for a "dining room" on the upper floor.

Since this church was built long after Jesus, it cannot possibly be the structure of the Upper Room. However, the location of it or the next building, the Dormition Church, probably does mark the spot of the original Upper Room. Underneath both buildings are the ruins of the Holy Zion Church that was first mentioned in literature by A.D. 530. This was the largest church in Jerusalem at the time of its construction, even larger than the Church of the Holy Sepulcher. It was 200' by 130'. It encompassed both today's cenacle and the Dormition church. The Persians destroyed this church building in 614. However, this church was built upon the spot of two even earlier churches.

The earliest remains were from the 1st century. Plaster has graffiti on it reading, "Conquer", "O Savior", "Mercy" or "O Jesus that I may live."[308] When Emperor Hadrian visited Jerusalem in A.D. 130, he found a church here which Christians said was the Upper Room (Finegan)[309]. *The Dictionary of Jesus and the Gospels* claims materials from this early church, dated A.D. 73-135, still remain.[310] McRay dates the ruins in the A.D. 80's. Following Bargil Pitner, he supports the view that Jewish Christians built the first church in the decade after their return from Pella to Jerusalem in A. D. 73. Some Herodian stones from the recently destroyed Temple were used in building on this site.[311] Therefore, the present structure is not the actual Upper Room, but the general location seems correct.

■ Golgotha and the Tomb

The place of Jesus' death was called Golgotha in Aramaic ("place of a skull," Mark 15:22) or Calvary in Latin (Jerome's Latin translation). Jesus' tomb was very close. "Now in the place where He was crucified there was a garden and in the garden a new tomb . . . the tomb was **nearby** . . ." (John 19:41-42).

The place called the "Garden Tomb" has no basis to be regarded as authentic. This tomb, discovered in 1885 by British General Gordon, never had better credentials than the traditional Church of the Holy Sepulcher. Modern archaeological clues should remove any doubt as to the latter's authenticity.

In A.D. 135 Roman Emperor Hadrian had the then traditional site for Jesus' cross and tomb covered. He "built a huge rectangular platform of earth over this quarry for a temple dedicated to Venus."[312] In thinking to desecrate the location, Hadrian put a huge statue of Aphrodite (Venus) over the place where the cross had stood. Over the burial tomb he placed a statue of Jupiter. In trying to erase the location, he ensured the memory of location that is authentic to a high degree of probability.

Gentile Christians had remained in the city even after the Romans expelled the Jews in A.D. 70. Therefore, an unbroken line of Christian leaders from apostolic times to the legalization of Christianity under Constantine would have remembered the location of the crucifixion and resurrection of the Lord Jesus.

When Queen Helena, Constantine's Mother, visited Jerusalem, she was shown the place of Jesus' cross and tomb. Constantine ordered the rock of Golgotha (Calvary) uncovered (the top 16' are uncovered). The original Church of the Holy Sepulcher was dedicated in A.D. 335. The Persians looted and damaged the church in A.D. 614 and Caliph el-Hakim destroyed much of it in 1009. Much of the present church dates from 1149, but remains from Constantine's original church are within the present building.[313] Of course, more important is that the place of the cross and the tomb are probably within this building.

The biggest objection to the authenticity of the Church of the Holy Sepulcher had been that it is presently within the city walls. Jesus was crucified not in but "near the city" (John 19:20) and "outside the gate" (Hebrews 13:12).

Beginning in the 1960's excavations beneath the church gave three details supporting its authenticity. (Final reports were published in 1980-87.) The church location was outside the city wall at the time of Jesus but only until A.D. 41-44, when Herod Agrippa built a wall enclosing this area. This helps confirm that traditions supporting the Church of the Sepulcher are correct and that the New Testament gives accurate information (for beginning only 10-15 years after Jesus this location was within the city walls!).

The fact that the location of the Church of the Holy Sepulcher was within the city walls in Helena's time is another support for its authenticity. If the locals were just guessing at a site, they would have found one outside not inside the walls. The compelling reason to show Helena a place now inside the walls was that it is authentic.

Secondly, it was discovered that there are tombs nearby. This not only conforms to John 19:42, but further supports the fact that this location had been outside the walls.[314] By tradition no graves could be within the walls. Evidently, Joseph of Arimethea had wanted to be buried near a busy road just outside the city (even if a place of execution was also nearby).

Thirdly, it has been shown this location had been a rock quarry. "The excavations disclosed that beneath the church is a rather extensive stone quarry . . ."[315] This fits within descriptions that Nicodemus' tomb had been "hewn out in the rock" (Matthew 27:60) and "cut into the rock" (Luke 23:53).[316] It is possible that New Testament authors had a double meaning when they quoted Psalm 118:22 (see Mark 12:10; Acts 4:11; 1 Peter 2:7). Jesus Himself is the rejected stone who became the cornerstone for God's plan. A parallel may also be that Golgotha was a hill only because it was rejected as good building material for Jerusalem. Stone all around it was selected, which only caused Golgotha to become even higher than its natural state. This rejected location, like the rejected Savior, would be a central place in world history (John 12:32 as an illustration). Incidentally, the rock inside the Church of the Holy Sepulcher has a split in it, possibly from an earthquake (Matthew 27:51, 54).

Jewish Scholar Dan Bahat of Bar-Ilan University in Israel can be expected to be objective on the location of Golgotha and Jesus' tomb. His conclusion is, ". . . we now know that its location perfectly fits first-century conditions . . . . we really have no reason to reject the authenticity of the site."[317]

Major places in the life of Jesus are definitely not mythological. With high probability the Church of the Nativity is the place of His birth, the synagogue and Peter's house in Capernaum (where Jesus lived during his ministry) have been identified, the Upper Room, and Golgotha with the nearby location of Jesus' tomb are probably at the site for The Church of the Holy Sepulcher in Jerusalem.

Next, we will continue to study places but concentrate on places in the Gospel of John to show that the author of John knew his facts.

Geography and John's Gospel

This sub-section is best appreciated by remembering that Bible critics often view the Gospels as pure hype, creative fiction, and mythology. Also, the location of many Bible places had been totally lost until comparatively modern times. As an introductory example Bethsaida, the hometown of Andrew, Peter, and Philip (John 1:44) was only discovered by ground-penetrating radar in 1987 and only identified as Bethsaida in the 1990's.

Against the background of former ignorance and wild charges of skepticism, seemingly small things like the location of cities at least establishes that the life of Christ in the Gospels is not mythological regarding both places and people.

Professor Urban C. von Wahlde, Professor of Theology at Loyola University in Chicago, is an example of a critical scholar. He is not in the inerrancy theological camp. Yet, he reacts to the critical extreme of those who have concluded the Gospel of John is just creative myth. While books on archaeology or the standard Bible encyclopedias would often also have this information, we will condense von Wahlde's study, *"Archaeology and John's Gospel."*[318]

■ An Overview of Places in John's Gospel

The goal of von Wahlde's research is to update significant new discoveries about places in John's Gospel: ". . . our understanding of these sites is growing almost daily."[319] The truth is that, new facts are discovered so quickly that book publishers literally can not keep up. "Our primary focus is on the question of the historical reliability of this topographical information."[320]

Thirteen references to places in John's Gospel do not appear anywhere else in the New Testament. With seven more places that are mentioned in the synoptics, the Gospel of John gives additional details never found in the synoptics. These twenty cases have allowed scholars in the past to question the accuracy of John, especially when John stands alone. This is no longer an option. We must delete and condense, but for arrangement we follow a breakdown of von Wahlde's list by the three main geographic areas in New Testament Israel.

■ John and Places in Galilee

Bethsaida was the hometown of Andrew, Peter, and Philip. Jesus criticized the place for lacking faith (Matthew 11:21-24). It is the site for the multiplication of the loaves, and near where Jesus walked on water (Luke 9:10-17). Josephus mentioned the city (*Ant.* 18.2.1/28). Philip the tetrarch raised it to a city status and renamed it "Bethsaida-Julia" in honor of Augustus' wife Livia who had been adopted into the Julian clan. As mentioned above, this location was only finally confirmed in the summer of 1999 (but the park had opened to the public in March 1998).[321]

Cana of Galilee is only mentioned in John's Gospel within the Bible (four times, 2:1, 11, 4:46-54, 21:2). In this place Jesus attended a wedding, turned the water into wine, healed the "royal" official's son. Nathaniel who went fishing with Jesus after the resurrection was from "Cana of Galilee" (21:2).

Josephus mentions Cana of Galilee in his own biography *Life* 16/86. The town's existence has never been in doubt, but its location had been uncertain. Von Wahlde concludes that the combination of archaeology and reports of pilgrim trips to the Holy Land in earlier times allows identification of Khirbet Qana with the Biblical Cana of Galilee. A definitive study on Cana was only finished in 1999.[322]

Previous sections cover the identification of Capernaum (the village of Nahum) which was the place of Jesus' residence after Nazareth's rejection of Him. We need not repeat studies on the Capernaum Synagogue or the identification of St. Peter's house (see pp. 138-140).

Additional information about Capernaum comes from recent archaeology. Low lake levels in the 1990's revealed piers, a breakwater, and remarkably fish pools near the harbor indicating a substantial fishing trade in the town. There is also evidence of a Roman camp in Capernaum. Luke says a Roman Centurion paid for the synagogue (Luke 7:5). Because Capernaum was a provincial border town between Antipas' jurisdiction in Galilee and the tetrarchy of Philip, it makes sense there was also a tax office there (Matthew 9:9).

Tiberius was another Galilean city not mentioned in the synoptic gospels. John refers to Tiberias in 6:1, 23, and 21:1. Information on Tiberias outside the Bible comes from Josephus.[323] It was founded on a cemetery and, therefore, Jews who lived there were rendered unclean. It was also a place of hot springs and beauty by the Sea of Galilee. Herod Antipas moved the capital of Galilee from Sepphoris to Tiberias in A.D. 24.[324]

The Gospel of John lists real, not fictitious, places from Galilee. This is also true of Samaria.

■ Samaria - Jacob's Well

In John 4:4-6 Jesus passes through Samaria and rests near Jacob's well in a Samaritan city called Sychar. "In verse 6 of the Johannine text this well is identified as a *pege* (a running spring), whereas in verses 11, 12 it is called *phrear* (a dug-out well). The well near Shechem is just such a combination of dug-out well and running water."[325]

John 4:11 says "the well is deep." In A.D. 670 it was estimated to be 240 feet. Measurements in 1838 and 1875 were 105'and 75' respectively. Across the centuries, debris seems to have filled in at the bottom. The original depth must have been "very deep" indeed. The nearby village of "Askar" is probably the Sychar of John 4:5, and remains of the alternative Samaritan Temple on Mt. Gerizim mentioned in John 4:20 are also nearby.[326] It is possible for tourists to drink of the same well that Jesus did.

Next we will consider locations in Judea but outside of Jerusalem.

■ Rural Judean Places in John's Gospel

John 11:54 refers to a place near Jerusalem called Ephraim. Jesus could retire there with the disciples to get away from His enemies who were planning to kill Him. Yet, this "wilderness" or "desert" place was close enough to Jerusalem to return easily. No archaeological evidence has been found on this Ephraim, but it is mentioned in the Old Testament, Josephus, the Mishnah, and the Talmud. Only John among the Gospels mentions Ephriam.[327]

Bethany near Jerusalem was the hometown of Mary, Martha, and Lazarus. All four Gospels mention this town, but only John 11:18 gives the distance from Jerusalem (15 *stadia* or 1.75 – 2 miles). Bethany has long been consistently identified with modern el-Azariyeh. The Gospel of John gives the correct distance.

Closer to Jerusalem, John 18:1 mentions the Kidron Valley. This place is well known, but one unfamiliar with the area might make a mistake. Technically, the Kidron Valley can flow with water in the winter months. Thus, John 18:1 is correct to say Jesus and His disciples crossed over the "ravine" (NASB) or the "brook" (KJV).

■ John's Gospel and Places in Jerusalem

John 2:13ff. contains the story of Jesus' anger over the money-changers and livestock vendors in the Temple vicinity. Several archaeological and cultural facts explain this event.

The exact location could be in the outer courts of the Temple (the court of the gentiles) or the royal porch on the south side of the Temple. It is also known there were many vendors on the street level in the southwest corner of the Temple near what is now called "Robinson's Arch." Shanks calls this area "the Times Square of Herodian Jerusalem."[328] A stone vessel was found that had an engraving of two small birds with the Hebrew word (*corban*, "dedication" or "gift", see Mark 7:11).[329] This stone was for sale in the shops near the Temple. It was probably a souvenir of offering two doves or pigeons in gratitude to God for the birth of a child (Luke 2:21-24). Perhaps the livestock so close or within the outer courts of the Temple is what angered Jesus. "The discovery of 'double and triple Hulda Gates' near which there was a massive stairway and passageways leading from the stables into the Temple area makes the driving out of oxen and sheep from the Temple area by Jesus in John 2:15 an entirely realistic scene –not just a concoction."[330]

Another factor in Jesus' anger was the cheating or exorbitant charges to people who had come to worship, and also that this hypocritical dealing was conducted in the Temple. The atmosphere of prayer and worship was turned into a "den of thieves" (see Luke 19:46; Matthew 21:13; Mark 11:17, and Jeremiah 7:11). In addition to the offense of locating livestock and commerce within the Temple itself, the bankers had schemes to guarantee high profits. They charged fees to turn "pagan" coinage with images on it into coins that were acceptable for Temple use. They obviously made money on both ends of the deal. Not only did they charge a fee to exchange the money into approved coinage, the Temple also received all the money back in the end because the customer would put it into the Temple offering boxes.

Beyond having livestock, wheeling and dealing within the Temple precincts, and gouging fees, yet another hypocritical custom could have angered Jesus. While presumably pagan coins could not be used for Temple offering because of graven images, the authorities instead required the use of the Tyrian shekel. This shekel, which was deemed perfectly acceptable, had images of the pagan god Melkart-Hercules on the front and a Tyrian eagle on the back.[331] The Tyrian shekel was known to have a high silver content ("over 90%").[332] It was quite hypocritical to force the public to exchange coins to avoid impure pagan money, and then use coins with pagan idols on them because they had more "pure" silver. Any or all of these reasons could have precipitated Jesus' righteous anger and the cleansing of the Temple.

A second location within Jerusalem that has been illuminated by archaeology is the Pool of Siloam (John 9:1-12). This is the place where Jesus commanded the man born blind to "Go, wash in the Pool of Siloam . . . . So he went away and washed, and came back seeing" (John 9:7).

This pool is mentioned both in the Old Testament (2 Kings 20:20; Isaiah 8:6; Nehemiah 3:15) and Josephus *War* 6.7.2/363. Within the New Testament, only John refers to this pool.

A pool identified with the Pool of Siloam has been known for over 100 years. Yet, in June 2004 archaeologists discovered a second pool close to the first. It has steps leading to it on all sides. There is a paved area for assembly. In short, at the very least the Pool of Siloam was once quite large (50 meters long) and had areas for "lounging." "It is not impossible that at the time of Jesus the 'traditional' pool was the first of two related pools . . . In any event, the accuracy of the Johannine information is clearly established . . . ."[333]

Von Wahlde's study on archaeology in John's Gospel also includes material on places previously studied in this book, such as places involving Pontius Pilate. As in endnote 277 of this book, von Wahlde also concludes that Pilate's residence in Jerusalem (and, thus, the place of Jesus' trial) was not in the Antonia Fortress or the northwest corner of the Temple. Instead, the Roman governor's residence was Herod's old palace near Herod's three towers.

In addition to the location of the praetorium (the place of Jesus' trials), it may be possible that archaeologists are correctly identifying the "pavement" (*Gabbatha* in Hebrew) mentioned in John 19:13.

There is a gateway approach to Herod's old palace which would provide a spot for a high place (*bema*) for judgment that is still outside the residence. This would provide a place for Pilate to judge outside his residence so the Jews would not enter a gentile dwelling and could thereby avoid defilement.[334] This part of the city is the highest location in Jerusalem. It is also on a "surface area consisted of bedrock."[335] McRay also agrees we know the place of Jesus' trial.

"The praetorium (i.e. residence of Roman authority) must have been the Herodian palace. Therefore, the large podium Broshi found must have been that on which Jesus stood before Pilate. In Greek it was called "stone pavement" (*lithostrotos*) and in Hebrew an "elevated place" (*Gabbatha*, John 19:13).[336]

Von Wahlde closes his study on *Archaeology and John's Gospel* with material concerning the Church of the Holy Sepulcher as the authentic location for the cross and the tomb (see pp. 141-143).

We are not yet ready for a conclusion about places in John's Gospel. The most impressive location establishing the accuracy of John's Gospel has been bypassed until now in order to give it a separate treatment: the pool of Bethesda.

■ John's Gospel and the Pool of Bethesda

In John Chapter five there is reference to a pool in Jerusalem. Jesus finds a man there who had been lame for 38 years. He, along with many others, were waiting for the waters to be "stirred up" (John 5:7) hoping for a cure. Jesus commands him, "pick up your pallet and walk" (John 5:11).

In describing this place, John writes in the present tense seeming to indicate this material was written before the Temple's destruction in A.D. 70. John 5:2 gives a specific location:

"Now there is in Jerusalem by the sheep gate a pool, which is called in Hebrew Bethesda, having five porticoes."

As late as 1968, it was suggested this place was mythological. Since the Gospel of John was viewed as creative fiction, the five covered porches would then stand for the five books of Moses. The lesson would be that the Law of Moses cannot heal anyone.[337] Prior to the Dead Sea Scrolls, there had been no literary evidence outside the Bible to this pool.

However, the *Copper Scroll* from Qumran (3Q15 11.12) contains this line "in *Bet'Eshdatayin*, in the pool at the entrance to its smaller basin."[338] This phrase is a dual form in Aramaic and means "place of twin outpouring" reflecting that the Bethesda pool had two basins.[339]

The Bethesda pool was excavated between 1957 and 1962 with publications following decades later and new work still ongoing. This pool is indeed near the area of the sheep gate. There were two basins in a "trapezoidal form, surrounded on four sides by porticoes . . . ."[340]

The fifth porch occurred along the west to east line bisecting the two large basins. Thus, the pool of Bethesda had two basins with four covered porches around the sides and a fifth in the middle. When water would flow from the northern basin into the southern basin, it would have produced churning. Furthermore, the steps leading to the pool have intermittent landings that would "allow considerable numbers of people to descend into the water."[341]

When the Gospel of John stood alone in the description of the pool of Bethesda, it had still been correct all the time. The pool had five porches and was accessible and popular with people and "stirred" (John 5:7).

"Whatever we may continue to learn about the original purpose of the pools, the discovery of this pool in close proximity to what was known from documents as the Sheep Gate was one of the most significant factors leading to a reappraisal of the topological data of the Gospel. The discovery of the pools proved beyond a doubt that the description of this pool was not the creation of the Evangelist but reflected accurate and detailed knowledge of Jerusalem" [142]

Just as the people in the Gospels are not fictional, the places are not make-believe either. Von Wahlde counted 13 places in John not mentioned at all in the synoptics plus another seven with details about a place only given by John. Out of these twenty, he concludes, ". . . sixteen have been identified with certainty" and "two can be narrowed to within a relatively restricted locale."[343]

The Gospel of John can be shown to be accurate by a study of the places it includes. ". . . the Johannine account contains remarkably accurate knowledge." ". . . the intrinsic historicity and accuracy of the references should be beyond doubt."[344]

Beyond accuracy in place, the Gospel of John gives many references to details that support its claim to be based on eyewitness information.

The Gospel of John and Details

John 1:14, 19:35, and 21:24 claim the book originates from a truthful eyewitness. Numerous details in the book are written from the perspective of one involved in the events. Anderson counts 98 reports in the Gospel of John about "seeing" something, hearing something 30 times, smelling twice, tasting once, and touching four times, with a reference to a cold temperature in John 18:18, 25.[345]

John preserved Aramaic words: John 1:38, 41; 4:25; 5:2; 9:7; 19:13, 17, and 20:16 translating many for Greek readers. He explains Jewish rituals 2:6, 13, 23; 4:9; 5:1, 9, 10, 16, 18; 6:4; 7:2, 22, 23; 9:14, 16; 11:55; 12:1; 13:1; 18:20, 28, 39; 19:31, 40, 42. These include things like jars used for cleansing (2:6), Jews becoming unclean by entrance to a gentile dwelling (18:28), and purity in burial practices (19:31, 42). Aramaic words and Jewish customs show the book as originating in early memories from the land of Israel.

References to specific distances such as 15 *stadia* in 11:18 or 30 *stadia* in 6:17-19 or elevations such as going up or down, show familiarity with the events. There was "much water" near Aenon (3:23). Jacob's well was "deep" (4:11). Philip, Andrew, and Peter were from Bethsaida (1:44, 12:20-21).[346] Thomas was a twin ("Didymus" in John 11:16; 20:24). The servant whose ear was cut was named Malchus (18:10). It was his right ear. One around the courtyard who confronted Peter was a relative of Malchus (18:26).

Regarding time notations in John's Gospel, Jesus came to Nicodemus at night (3:2). Jesus called his disciples at the tenth hour (1:39). He met the woman at the well at the sixth hour (4:6). He healed the official's son at the seventh hour (4:52-53). Jesus was crucified at the sixth hour (19:14). Sometimes events occur on the same day (5:9; 20:19). Yet, the wedding in Cana was on the third day of Jesus' trip (2:1). After meeting the woman at the well, Jesus stayed in Samaria two days (4:40-43). Lazarus had been dead four days when Jesus arrived on the scene (11:17).

Other indirect claims of precise knowledge include: the lame man had been ill for 38 years (5:5), there was "much grass" at the multiplication of the loaves (6:10), the loaves were barley (6:9-13), Jesus and the disciples caught 153 fish (21:11).

In numerous ways the Gospel of John indirectly claims familiarity with the events. Modern skepticism about the book being creative fiction do not explain these details, because such trivia occurs in offhand remarks. They best fit personal familiarity with the events. From an even greater survey of such details than in this present condensed review, Anderson gives these conclusions:

" . . . The Gospel of John is far closer to the historical Jesus than most scholars have claimed or thought for almost a century."

"... a verdict of radical and pervasive ahistoricity is overreaching and wrong . . . . Much of John's tradition appears to be authentic
. . . ."[347]

In addition to defending the Gospel people and places, one could study customs of the time. One important archaeological find overlaps with crucifixion procedures.

Archaeology and the Crucifixion

The practice of crucifixion was well known from ancient literary references.[348] However, prior to 1968 remains of a crucifixion victim had never been found. Bible critics doubted that nails were used to affix people to crosses. The victims must have been tied. Also, they doubted that those who died on crosses were given proper burials. The expectation was that the remains would just be discarded in a pit.

In 1968 the ossuary of a man named *Yehohanan* was discovered near Jerusalem. He had been crucified a few years before Jesus. "*Yehohanan* had been impaled by iron spikes through his hands to a crossbeam and through his ankles to a vertical stake."[349] Those on crosses would be forced to push up on their nailed feet in order to breathe. After their legs were broken, they would die of suffocation (John 19:31). *Yehohanan's* right leg (the only one available for study) had been "brutally fractured . . . . by a single strong blow."[350] The fact that *Yehohanan* was given a proper burial shows that it is false to think executed criminals were just thrown into a pit. They were both nailed and buried as reported in the Gospels.[351]

With this point we will end presentation of evidence that the Gospels are reliable. However, something must be included about Luke as the author of Acts.

Luke as an Historian

While beyond the scope of studies on the Gospels or history of Jesus, accuracy in the book of Acts reflects back upon the Gospel of Luke. As the author of the book of Acts, Luke can be shown to be a careful and trustworthy author. In order to be brief we will use lists. The reader can research each person, place, or custom by consulting Bible encyclopedias or good commentaries on the book of Acts.[352]

The following people in Acts are historical persons mentioned in non-Christian sources:

153

Gamaliel (5:34; 22:3); Judas the rebel (5:37); King Herod Agrippa I (12:1-4, 20-23); Sergius Paulus, Roman Governor of Cyprus (13:6-12); James, the Lord's brother (15:13); Gallio, Roman Governor of Achaia (18:12-17); Erastus (19:22); Demetrius (19:24ff.); the Egyptian rebel (21:38); Ananias (23:1-5); Felix (cp. 24); Drusilla (24:24); King Agrippa II (25:13, 26:32); Festus (25-26) and Bernice (25:13).

Numerous places within Acts are real places. While the major places are so familiar as to no longer cause amazement, it helps to remember these were often lost until modern times. The theater in Caesarea (in Acts 12:19 -23 where Agrippa I made his blasphemous speech and was struck down) was only discovered in the 1960's. The Temple of Diana (Artemis, Acts 19:29) seated around 24,000 but was only discovered on the last day of 1869.

Specific places or artifacts related to places in Acts show Luke knew his facts. An inscription exists from the ruins of the "Synagogue of the Freedman" (Acts 6:9). Straight Street in Damascus where Paul stayed after his vision (9:11) can be identified. Athens did have altars to "unknown gods" (17:23). Signs designating the "middle wall of partition" (Ephesians 2:14; Acts 21:27-30) were found in 1871 and again in 1935. They are in museums in Istanbul and Jerusalem. These warned of the death penalty for gentiles who trespassed beyond the court of the gentiles further into the Temple.

Various other customs recorded in Acts ring true, and several events are confirmed outside the Bible. In Acts 14:8ff. Paul and Barnabas heal a lame man in Lystra. The people identify them as the gods Zeus and Hermes and begin to sacrifice oxen to them. The Roman poet Ovid records a legend of gods visiting this location in the past. All turned them away except one old couple named Philemon and Baucis.[353] Evidently, the citizens in Lystra believed Paul and Barnabas were a second round of visits by the pagan gods.

Historical events in Acts that are mentioned outside the Bible include: a famine in the days of Claudius (11:28-29), Agrippa's death after his speech in Caesarea (12:20-23) and Claudius' eviction of the Jews from Rome (18:2). All are mentioned in other ancient writings. [354]

By the reference to a regional border, Luke again proves himself knowledgeable. In Acts 14:6 Luke implies that when Paul and Barnabas left Iconium and moved to Lystra and Derbe, they were crossing a regional border into Lycaonia. Since Roman records had included all three cities within Lycaonia, critics had often charged Luke made an error in putting a border between them. It is now known that the border existed only between A.D. 37 and A.D. 72 and at no other time.[355] This period, of course, is the exact time for Paul's travels.

Finally, Luke's accuracy is most impressive in the matter of giving precise titles for office holders. One may use the United States as a comparison. Pennsylvania is a "Commonwealth" not a state, Louisiana has "parishes" not counties. Brooklyn is a "Borough." The polyglot and patched-together Roman Empire had diverse titles for office holders. Confusion on such minute details would be extremely easy.

In many cases a title may have only been known from the book of Acts. However, even when Luke stood alone, he has always proven to be correct.

In Acts 13:7 the governor of Cyprus is called a "proconsul." This referred to an area under the Roman senate's authority not one under the emperor's control. Critics had charged Luke with a mistake. It is now known the switch happened in 22 B.C. Luke was correct.

In Acts 16:19, 35 Luke called the city officials in Philippi *"praetors."* Other Roman colonies called their leaders *"duumvirs."* However, Cicero said Philippi was an exception. There they were called "praetors."[356]

No other ancient literature ever called officials *"politarchs"* except Acts 17:6. In 1876 the main arch of the *Via Egnatia* into Thessalonica was located. The arch called the city leaders *"politarchs."* At least 17 other references are now known.

Luke also used the correct title for Gallio in Achaia, "proconsul" (Acts 18:12); for the city leaders in Ephesus, "Asiarchs" (Acts 19:31); and for the leader at Malta, simply "chief" (Acts 28:7).

The historical competence of Luke should be regarded as established. The knowledge and care with which he wrote Acts indicates he would have been just as careful with the history and teaching of the Lord Jesus Christ when he wrote the Gospel of Luke.

Conclusions on People and Places in the Gospels

Even if we withhold information about the New Testament from writings of the early church, non-Christian data alone is sufficient to show the four Gospels **are definitely not mythology**. Many people, places, customs, and events can be shown to be true. Since the Gospels can be shown to be reliable in areas that can be tested, one should trust the author's integrity and competence on other historical matters. No doubt the real reason many people criticize the Gospels is that they record the miraculous.

Chapter 12

Jesus, History and Miracles

My philosophy professor with absolute certainty told us that there are no absolutes. He said we could not be certain that the desk he was sitting on was real or that he himself was real. I raised my hand to state I absolutely believed that a scrambled egg would not win the gold medal in the next Olympic pole vault competition. Furthermore, I was absolutely certain that everyone in the room possessed an attached head.

One should be skeptical about any claims to miracles. Only a fool believes everything. However, only a fool believes nothing. No amount of evidence can make faith in the Lord Jesus Christ unnecessary, but enough evidence exists to make faith reasonable.

While being skeptical about miracle claims is wise, it is not wise to rule out the miraculous simply based upon a closed worldview before checking out any evidence as to what happened. A final determination should be based on history not philosophy alone.

Bible critics have long placed faith in Jesus in a "no-win situation." They *a priori* deny the miraculous regardless of changing philosophical trends over time. Worldviews morph over the generations but denial of the possibility of miracles remains constant.

The Newtonian view of the Universe was that it is regulated by natural laws. Though Newton himself was a Christian, many took natural law to shut out the miraculous. Nothing contrary to normal rules of the Universe could ever happen.

However, in the modern world of Einstein's relativity, critics of Christianity now rule out the miraculous because everything is relative.[357] Why? Assuming natural laws, one should posit a Lawgiver. Assuming relativity, then anything, including miracles could happen. If for the sake of argument, we concede there are no absolutes, this actually opens the door to the possibility of the miraculous. Lutheran theologian and historian John Warwick Montgomery made the connection between relativity and the possibility of miracles:

"But can the modern man accept a 'miracle' such as the resurrection? The answer is a surprising one: The Resurrection has to be accepted by us just because we are modern men – men living in the Einsteinian-relativistic age. For us, unlike people of the Newtonian epoch, the universe is no longer a tight, safe, predictable playing field in which we know all the rules. Since Einstein, no modern has had the right to rule out the possibility of events because of prior knowledge of 'natural law.' The only way we can know whether an event *can* occur is to see whether in fact it *has* occurred. The problem of 'miracles,' then, must be solved in the realm of historical investigation, not in the realm of philosophical speculation. And note that a historian, in facing an alleged 'miracle,' is really facing nothing new. All historical events are unique, and the test of their facticity can only be the accepted documentary approach that we have followed here. No historian has a right to a closed system of natural causation, for as the Cornell logician Max Black has shown in a recent essay, the very concept of cause is 'a peculiar, unsystematic, and erratic notion,' and therefore 'any attempt to state a universal law of causation' must prove futile.' "[358]

An open mind involves not ruling out miracles before examining the historical evidence for them. Jesus of Nazareth is a unique person. While faith is necessary, in the end many conclude it is unreasonable and contrary to the evidence to deny Jesus' claims whereas it is reasonable to trust Him as Savior.

Hostile Witnesses to Jesus' Miracles

A college student was moping in the library after a class with the above mentioned philosophy professor. She said his lecture had just destroyed her faith in Jesus' miracles. My response was to say that it is odd a teacher 2,000 years later can assert Jesus had no power. His enemies at the time admitted He did. They just claimed Jesus' power came from Satan not God.

We cannot now review the previous arguments for authorship, early date, and general historical reliability of the Gospels. It has already been established that the Gospels are authentic as to authorship. They were written within the lifetime of the eyewitnesses of Jesus. They are not mythology but trustworthy in general historical matters where they can be checked.

Given the early dates for the composition of the Gospels, fascinating questions arise about miracle claims. If untrue, how did the Gospel authors ever get away with asserting Jesus' **enemies** believed He could do miracles? It would have been one thing for the Gospels to invent stories that Jesus' followers claimed He had powers. It is a different matter to assert confidently **those who hated Him agreed He had such supernatural powers**. If untrue, this would have been easily discredited a lie. If true, what does this say about Jesus?

Time after time the New Testament lists Jesus' enemies as hostile witnesses that He could perform miracles. High Priest Caiaphas advised the council of chief priests and Pharisees that Jesus be killed due to His popularity as a miracle worker. "What are we doing? For this man is performing many signs" (John 11:47, see also 11:47-53). Herod Antipas seems to have worried the miracle-working Jesus might be John the Baptist returned to haunt or punish him. "And King Herod heard of it [i.e. the miracles, see 6:13], for His name had become well known . . . that is why these miraculous powers are at work in Him" (Mark 6:14, see also Luke 23:8). Nicodemus prior to his conversion said, ". . .Rabbi, we know that You have come from God as a teacher; for no one can do these signs that You do unless God is with him" (John 3:2). The apostolic preaching assumes Jesus' opponents concede His miracles (Acts 2:22, 4:16, 10:37-38, 26:26).

Those who hated Jesus still believed He could do miracles. After an exorcism in which a blind and mute man was healed, the crowds concluded Jesus must be "the Son of David," that is the coming Messiah. The opposition does not even try to argue that this miracle is a fraud. Instead, they challenge the power source by which the miracle was done. According to them, Jesus' power comes from "Beelzebul, the ruler of demons" (Matthew 12:22-24, see also Mark 3:22).[359]

Other passages give the same pattern. There is a split over Jesus' source of power, but everyone agrees that He had the ability to work miracles:

> "After the demon was cast out, the mute man spoke; and the crowds were amazed, and were saying, 'Nothing like this has ever been seen in Israel.' But the Pharisees were saying, 'He casts out the demons by the ruler of the demons' " (Matthew 9:33-34).

> "The crowd answered, 'You have a demon! Who seeks to kill You?' " (John 7:20).

> "The Jews answered and said to Him, 'Do we not say rightly that You are a Samaritan and have a demon?' Jesus answered, 'I do not have a demon but I honor My Father, and you dishonor Me' " (John 8:48-49).

> "A division occurred again among the Jews because of these words. Many of them were saying, 'He has a demon and is insane. Why do you listen to Him?' Others were saying, 'These are not the sayings of one demon-possessed. A demon cannot open the eyes of the blind, can he? ' " (John 10:19-21).

It is astounding that hostile witnesses concede Jesus' powers. Such evidence as exists outside the Bible points in the same direction. The enemies of Christianity in earlier times agreed He could do miracles. They just put Him in the category of a "magician" or "sorcerer." In order not to disrupt the flow of argument here, possible sources outside the Bible placing Jesus in the magician category will be relegated to the footnotes for those with interest.[360]

The opposition provides strong proof Jesus could do miracles, but Jesus' followers were witnesses with great proven integrity.

The Character of Christ's Disciples

The early Christians would make credible witnesses in any court. They were raised with Jewish convictions against bearing "false

160

witness" (Exodus 20:16). Many of them died brutally still asserting Jesus is the Son of God (confirmed by miracles) and that He rose from the dead. More studies about the disciples as credible witnesses will come in the following material on the greatest miracle of all, the Resurrection. (See also pp. 77-81 for discussion of John the Baptist's doubts and Jesus' claim to miracles as being authentic judged by the principle of embarrassing statements being true statements.)

Jesus' Miracles: Public and Involving Proven Cases of Need

Other miracle claims often involve only private encounters. Allah gave private revelations to Mohammed. The angel revealed golden plates to Joseph Smith. In many instances, one can challenge whether the recipient of the miracle was even really sick. He or she could be a fake planted in the crowd to give the appearance of a miracle, or both "sickness" and "recovery" are entirely psychological.

Many of the miracle stories in the Gospels do not allow these challenges. They are entirely public. Mass numbers of people, friends and foes, could easily tell whether the miracle did or did not take place. The miracle accounts of Jesus also involve people who were demonstrably infirm. There are numerous examples of public miracles for those with proven needs:

1. Mark 1:21-28; Luke 4:31-37:
In a public synagogue meeting, Jesus cast out a demon. "Immediately the news about Him spread everywhere into all the surrounding district of Galilee" (Mark 1:28).

2. Matthew 8:1-4; Mark 1:40-45; Luke 5:12-16:
With "large crowds" observing, Jesus touched a leper (a startling thing to do when the man had an obvious problem). The result of the healing was that large crowds gathered and Jesus "could no longer publicly enter a city . . . they were coming to Him from everywhere" (Mark 1:45).

3. Matthew 9:2-8; Mark 2:1-12; Luke 5:17-26:
Because the crowds were blocking the entrance, friends of a paralyzed man lowered him through a hole in the roof.

4. John 5:1-9:

At a public pool with a multitude around it, Jesus healed a lame man "who had been thirty-eight years in his sickness" (John 5:5). The man had not been a disciple. He did not even know Jesus (John 5:13). He certainly had not pretended to be handicapped for 38 years just to get some attention.

5. Matthew 12:9-14; Mark 3:1-6; Luke 6:6-11:

During a synagogue service, Jesus healed a man with a "withered hand." This was another public occasion involving a man with an undeniable problem.

6. Matthew 8:5-13; Luke 7:1-10:

Jewish elders request that Jesus heal a centurion's servant because the officer had donated to build the synagogue in Capernaum. He was obviously a well-known person.

7. Luke 7:11-17:

Jesus encountered a funeral procession with a "sizeable crowd from the city." He raised the widow's son from the coffin. "This report concerning Him went out all over Judea and in all the surrounding districts" (Luke 7:17).

8. Matthew 8:28-34; Mark 5:1-20; Luke 8:26-39:

The demon-possessed man who lived in a cemetery was undeniably sick. The people of the region had tried to restrict him with chains. His change of character and the loss of 2,000 swine would have been noticed by a large number of people in the area.

9. Matthew 9:18-26; Mark 5:21-43; Luke 8:40-56:

While the raising of Jairus' daughter from the dead was witnessed by a limited group, everyone outside the house knew this girl was dead. "This news spread throughout all that land" (Matthew 9:26).

10. Matthew 9:27-35:

Two blind men are healed and "spread the news about Him throughout all that land" (Matthew 9:31, see also 9:33-35).

11. Matthew 14:13-21; Mark 6:30-44; Luke 9:10-17; John 6:1-15:

The crowd of 5,000 men plus women and children believed Jesus multiplied the loaves and fish. They were convinced enough "to come and take Him by force to make Him king . . ." (John 6:15).

12. Mark 7:31-37:

The crowd brings a deaf man to Jesus. Though he tells the group not to tell anyone "they continued to proclaim it . . . saying 'He has done all things well; He makes even the deaf to hear and the mute to speak' " (Mark 7:36-37).

13. Regarding public miracles Matthew 15:29-31 says: "Departing from there, Jesus went along by the Sea of Galilee, and having gone up on the mountain, He was sitting there. And large crowds came to Him, bringing with them those who were lame, crippled, blind, mute, and many others, and they laid them down at His feet; and He healed them. So the crowd marveled as they saw the mute speaking, the crippled restored, and the lame walking, and the blind seeing; and they glorified the God of Israel."

14. Matthew 15:32-38; Mark 8:1-9:

Another group of 4,000 men plus women and children witnessed the multiplication of loaves and fish.

15. Matthew 17:14-21; Mark 9:14-29; Luke 9:37-43:

Crowds observed the failure of the disciples to help a boy brought by his father, "but Jesus rebuked the unclean spirit, and healed the boy and gave him back to his father" (Luke 9:42).

16. John 9:

Jesus heals a man born blind who is identified by his parents. Neither the man nor his parents had been followers of Jesus. He had not faked blindness since birth.

17. Luke 11:14:

Jesus heals a mute person, "and the crowds were amazed."

18. Luke 13:10-17:
In a public synagogue service, Jesus healed a woman who had been bent over double for 18 years. It is unlikely she faked it for 18 years.

19. Luke 14:1-6:
At a Pharisee's house Jesus heals a man with "dropsy." This refers to body swelling by retention of liquid, another obvious need that was clearly not a fraud.

20. Matthew 20:29-34; Mark 10:46-52; Luke 18:35-43:
With a large crowd observing, Jesus healed some blind men including Bartimaeus.

This list is by no means complete. John 20:30-31 and 21:25 assert many miracles were not recorded in the Gospels. Many were public and involved people who could not have feigned illness in order to gain attention. Perhaps the most astounding miracle, outside of Jesus' own resurrection, is the raising of Lazarus.

In John 11 Lazarus died and had a public funeral. With witnesses Jesus requested that the tomb be opened, and He called Lazarus forth. This resulted in some of the witnesses accepting Jesus as Savior. However, others ran to the opposition to report the miracle. They did not believe in Jesus, but they did believe He had raised Lazarus. This is the context for the admission by the chief priests, Pharisees and possibly even Caiaphas himself that Jesus could do miracles (John 11:46-50).

These things are astounding, but perhaps the most telling point in the narrative comes in John 12:9-11, and 17-19:

"The large crowd of the Jews then learned that He was there; and they came, not for Jesus' sake only, but that they might also see Lazarus, whom He raised from the dead. But the chief priests planned to put Lazarus to death also; because on account of him many of the Jews were going away and were believing in Jesus" (John 12:9-11).

"So the people who were with Him when He called Lazarus out of the tomb and raised him from the dead, continued to testify about Him. For this reason also the people went and met Him, because they heard that He has performed this sign. So the Pharisees said to one another, 'You see that you are not doing any good: look, the world has gone after him' " (John 12:17-19).

The Gospel of John not only claims that Lazarus died and had a public funeral, but that Lazarus later showed up in Jerusalem to testify about Jesus. If untrue, this assertion could easily be refuted. In addition, verse 17 says that people who witnessed the raising of Lazarus were testifying to Jesus' ability to do miracles during the "Palm Sunday" parade. If untrue, this also could easily be discredited.

If Lazarus never appeared alive and healthy in the city or, if no one in the procession ever testified to Lazarus' restoration to life, then the rest of the story also collapses.

If the Gospel witnesses were just making up stories, why take the risk of including features like this if they never happened? Yet, if they did happen, what does it say about Jesus that Lazarus appeared in the city after his own funeral or that witnesses to Lazarus' exit from the tomb were testifying and pointing to Jesus along the parade route!

Evidently, the opposition gave up on trying to counter the evidence. Instead of refuting Lazarus or the witnesses, they conceded Jesus' ability to work miracles and decided both Jesus and Lazarus would have to die so they could preserve their religious authority. Yet, not far from the Palm Sunday account, John 12:42 says, "many even of the rulers believed in Him."

Many of Jesus' miracles were public. They involved people who had proven infirmities with little or no possibility they could be frauds. The apostles could run around preaching that the opposition had witnessed the miracles just as much as believers did.

"But many of the crowd believed in Him; and they were saying, 'When the Christ comes, He will not perform more signs than those which this man has, will He?' " (John 7:31).

"But though He had performed so many signs before them, yet they were not believing in Him" (John 12:37).

"Men of Israel, listen to these words: Jesus the Nazarene, a man attested to you by God with miracles and wonders and signs which God performed through Him in your midst, just as you yourselves know - " (Acts 2:22).

". . . saying, 'What shall we do with these men? For the fact that a noteworthy miracle has taken place through them is apparent to all who live in Jerusalem, and we cannot deny it' " (Acts 4:16).

"*You know of* Jesus of Nazareth, how God anointed Him with the Holy Spirit and with power, and how He went about doing good and healing all who were oppressed by the devil, for God was with Him" (Acts 10:38).

"For the king knows about these matters, and I speak to him also with confidence, since I am persuaded that none of these things escape his notice; for this has not been done in a corner" (Acts 26:26).

Jesus was a great teacher. Yet, the cause for His popularity must be found by another explanation. The masses followed Him because they believed He demonstrated His claims. The historical rise of Christianity against all odds is best explained by His ability to confirm His teachings by His powers.

Conclusion on Jesus' Miracles

Certain facts should be admitted by all people, Christian or non-Christian. The New Testament comes from the first century and has not been altered to any significant degree. It contains the witness of people who were ethical and sincere. It would be contrary to human nature for them to suffer death for something they knew to be a hoax, especially when there could be no hope for earthly gain. The New Testament also contains the astounding claim that many of Christ's **enemies** believed He could do miracles. It would be the ultimate in stupidity to make such claims if they were false. Everyone in 1st century Israel would have known whether such public miracles took place or not, and the authorities could have easily discredited Christian writings if the opposition did not in fact concede that Jesus could do miracles.

However, it is also an historical fact that thousands of people became Christians even though it meant persecution and horrible death. They were in a position to know if these miracles took place, and yet, they decided to believe Jesus was sent from God.

Persecution which attempts to change people's long cherished beliefs is often met with resistance. However, persecution that attempts to keep people in an entrenched belief that they have adhered to all their lives is hardly ever necessary. Such would be expected to be totally effective. If a dedicated Moslem, for example, were in a situation where he would face death to become a Jewish rabbi, one would expect very few devoted Moslems to ever suddenly convert to Judaism. Likewise, the Jewish people of the 1st century would have been expected to remain committed Jews even without any persecution whatsoever. Persecution when applied with such severity as faced the early Christians would have been expected to be virtually 100% successful in keeping people in the heritage into which they were born and raised. This is particularly true if they could tell the claims about Christ's public miracles were totally fraudulent (Remember the nature of the claims is such that they would have been able to know with ease if they were false.)

Yet, it is a fact that Christianity arose against brutality and martyrdom. People gave up their ancestral and cherished beliefs to become Christians and faced great political and social pressures, even the likelihood of death. The only explanation for their unwavering faith is that the miracles of Christ were so convincing they gladly forsook Judaism to follow Him. All history is based upon probability. The same facts, which should be acknowledged by all, make it reasonable to conclude that Christ's miracles actually happened, and make it unreasonable to conclude they did not. The literary integrity of the Gospels, the ethical and psychological character of the disciples, the claims of public miracles witnessed by friends and foe alike, and the mass exodus of people into Christianity despite the horrors of persecution are best explained by the historicity of Christ's miracles. In fact, the only satisfactory way to explain these things is to believe Christ was a miracle worker.

Of course, the resurrection of Jesus Himself is the greatest miracle of all. If Jesus rose from the dead, then we must all pay close attention to what He teaches. The historical evidence is compelling that He did in fact defeat death.

The Resurrection

The tomb of Jesus was empty on the first Easter morning. If not, His opponents could and would have turned the sepulcher into an exhibit or loaded His body on a wagon to display it for all of Jerusalem to see. Either would have effectively eliminated the rise of Christianity. The question facing us is no different than 2,000 years ago. Jesus' tomb was empty. How did this happen? Incredibly, none of the natural explanations make sense. Factual circumstances box one into the resurrection being the best explanation of the undeniably empty tomb.[361]

■ Public Events

The Gospels record certain public events that had to be true in order for the preaching and writings of the early Christians to be credible. The trials of Jesus involving the Sanhedrin, Caiaphas, Herod Antipas and Pilate must have occurred. References in Josephus and Tacitus (see Chapter 9) grant Jesus' trial and crucifixion as historical. The procession of the cross through the streets, Jesus' public execution by a busy road, Joseph of Arimethea's visit with Pilate to request Jesus' body for burial, and the posting of guards at the tomb, all must have been credible. If not, the gospel accounts would have been easy to dismiss.

Matthew 27:45, 51-54, 28:1-6 give specific and startling details (darkness for three hours [noon – 3:00pm], an earthquake, the veil in the Temple being torn in two). If creating fiction, it would not be safe to include such public details unless all would agree they happened. Many would know if they were true or fraudulent, but if true, what does this say for the rest of the account in the Gospels? Those in that day would have every social incentive not to become Christians. Yet, shortly the apostles would preach Christ's trial, death, and the empty tomb as undeniable facts to those in Jerusalem (e.g., Acts 3:13-15). Such evidence as does exist outside the Gospels confirms these public events, even darkness in the middle of a spring day.[362]

Public events surrounding the "Passion Week" must have been true in order for Christianity to get started. If there had been no trial, crucifixion, request for Jesus' body, guards, darkness, earthquake, or torn veil, why would anyone believe the rest of the story? Most important, the empty tomb should be included in any list of known facts (for reasons explained below). The only question is how did Jesus' body exit this tomb?

■ The Swoon Theory

Was the tomb empty because Jesus never died on the cross? Perhaps He merely fainted. Later He was able to recover and leave the tomb.

The soldiers, whose task was execution, knew a corpse when they saw one. After Joseph of Arimathea (a Sanhedrin member) asked Pilate for Jesus' body, "Pilate wondered if He was dead by this time, and summoning the centurion, he questioned him as to whether He was already dead" (Mark 15:44). The centurion affirmed Jesus' death. John 19:34 adds that the on-site execution detail "saw that He was already dead," but to be certain "one of the soldiers pierced His side with a spear."

John, who solemnly affirms to his readers that he was an eyewitness, affirms as an incidental comment that he observed blood and water flow from Jesus' wounded side. *The Journal of the American Medical Association* published a detailed study *On the Physical Death of Jesus* co-authored by a pathologist, a medical graphics artist (both from Mayo Clinic) and a pastor. Water flowing from Jesus' side was probably "pericardial fluid . . . . in the setting of . . . impending acute heart failure . . ."[363]

The swoon theory can not overcome the historical and medical facts that Jesus died on the cross.

"Clearly, the weight of the historical and medical evidence indicates Jesus was dead before the wound to his side was inflicted and supports the traditional view that the spear, thrust between his right ribs, probably perforated not only the right lung but also the pericardium and heart and thereby ensured his death. Accordingly, interpretations based on the assumption that Jesus did not die on the cross appear to be at odds with modern medical knowledge."[364]

■ The Wrong Tomb Theory

If the women and then the disciples went to the wrong tomb, they may have discovered it empty and in hysteria started the resurrection rumor.

Based upon the "principle of embarrassment" statements likely to produce embarrassment would not be creative fiction but true. If merely composing stories, the Gospel authors would not have begun the Easter narrative with *women* discovering anything, nor would they portray the disciple's initial reaction of disbelief.

The wrong tomb theory miserably fails to explain the known facts. If the disciples had gone to the wrong tomb, then the Jewish and Roman authorities were still guarding the right tomb and would have had access to Jesus' body. They could have stopped the spread of Christianity by turning the real tomb into an exhibit or by parading Jesus' body on a wagon through Jerusalem. The authorities could not demonstrate that the disciples were deluded because they knew well that the genuine Jesus' tomb was indeed empty. This same logic destroys the objection that the disciples were having hallucinations. If they were merely seeing things, then the enemies still had Jesus' body in the tomb.

■ The Hallucination Theory

The hallucination view encounters the same objection that the wrong tomb explanation faces. If the disciples were hallucinating, then the authorities could have utterly discredited the apostolic preaching of the resurrection. All they would need to have done is to direct the public to the tomb and body of Jesus.

Furthermore, a corporate hallucination of over 500 people at one time is ridiculous. Over 500 people claimed to see the risen Lord on one occasion (1 Corinthians 15:6).

Also, something beyond hallucinations by followers is needed to explain the turnaround of those who had not believed in Jesus during His earthly ministry. These would not have been impressed or persuaded by the mere hallucinations of people they did not at all respect at the time. Most notably James, the Lord's half-brother thought Jesus was out of His mind (Mark 3:21; John 7:5) until after he had seen Jesus back from the grave (1 Corinthians 15:7). The same logic applies to Saul's conversion to a belief he had formerly hated. James and Saul believed they had actually seen the risen Jesus for themselves. Hallucinations by others could never explain their change.

The disciples were so confident that they had seen the risen Lord that they died for their faith. None of them had doubts or second thoughts about the resurrection. It can scarcely be denied that they sincerely believed they had seen Jesus.

■ The Stolen Body Theory/Before Burial

The official story to explain the empty tomb was that the disciples stole Jesus' body while the guards slept. The choice of this explanation is itself evidence that everyone at the time believed Jesus' body had been buried in the tomb.[365]

Some in modern times have maintained that Joseph of Arimathea and Nicodemus took the body of Jesus from the cross but never placed it in the grave. By contrast, Jewish authorities were convinced that the body was buried in the tomb. If they had believed that Joseph and Nicodemus did not bury Jesus, they would not have requested Pilate for a detachment of guards to protect a particular gravesite. The fact that they knew the location of the tomb implies that they had directly or indirectly observed the burial. They were suspicious that the disciples would steal the body. They would not have taken the disciples word alone as truth. Therefore, it may be safely concluded that the Jewish authorities had independent confirmation and had good reason to believe the body was buried in a specific tomb when they asked Pilate for a guard and when the guard was posted. The disciples also knew the body was in the grave. The women were going to a known location to complete burial customs on Sunday morning. Finally, the Roman soldiers guarded the area believing the body was within the tomb. Their story subsequent to the resurrection was that the body had been stolen as they were guarding it. Thus, no one ever questioned or denied the body was in the tomb when the soldiers arrived and secured it with a seal.

■ The Stolen Body Theory – After Burial

The chief priests and elders bribed the soldiers who had guarded the tomb (Matthew 28:11-15). They obviously believed they had been guarding Jesus' real tomb and that Jesus' body was inside. The religious elite told the soldiers "You are to say, 'His disciples came by night and stole Him away while we were asleep.' And if this should come to the governor's ears, we will win him over and keep you out of trouble" (Matthew 28:13-14). (The very choice of this tactic helps rule out modern explanations about Jesus' empty tomb: the swoon theory, the wrong-tomb theory, the hallucination theory, or any body theft before entombment.)

It is highly unlikely that Pilate never eventually heard about the early Christian claim to the resurrection of Jesus. Both apostolic preaching and the rapid numerical growth of Christianity (Acts 2:41, 3,000 in one day; Acts 4:4, 5,000 men; Acts 6:1,7) would likely have drawn Pilate's attention. The Nazareth decree may have been the Roman response to the empty tomb.[366]

An important undeniable fact regarding the charge that the disciples stole Jesus' body from the tomb is that no court ever prosecuted or tried the disciples for doing so. If Pilate heard this accusation (and he probably did), he never believed there was any basis for a case regarding this serious charge. At the least, the Jewish authorities who crucified Jesus for being a deceiver never even tried to convict the disciples of robbing the grave and then preaching the ultimate apostasy and deception. No such trials (or even continuing charges of grave-robbery) are recorded in the book of Acts. The most serious charge of stealing Jesus' body is quickly dropped. Why? There was no prosecution for grave robbing because there was no case against the disciples. This was true for a number of obvious reasons.

First, guards did not sleep. It was possibly a death penalty offense to fail on a night watch. "If it was not apparent which soldier had failed in duty, then lots were drawn to see who would be punished with death for the guard unit's failure."[367] One possible punishment would be to be stripped naked and burned (including burned to death). [368]

Sleeping on guard duty would have been highly unlikely. Even more improbable would be the entire squad dosing off on such an important assignment. The involvement of both the chief priests and the governor, as well as, the official seal over the tomb show the importance of their military assignment. In addition, had they slept, no one could have possibly slept through all the racket required to steal the body of Jesus.

The stone over the entrance to the tomb may have weighed as much as 3,000-4,000 pounds.[369] Think of a thick stone about 5' or 6' in diameter. This was likely rolled down a slope and blocked with a wedge to seal Jesus' tomb. Then a seal was affixed over both the stone and the sepulcher wall to prevent and warn against any tampering.

Any "sleeping" guards would have been stone deaf not to awaken during the efforts it would have taken to open the sepulcher in the darkness. Some combination of lamps, ropes, animals, and team of men with tools would have roused any sleeping guards.

Furthermore, according to John 20:7, the linen wrappings were left behind as was the face-cloth "rolled up in a place by itself." Just from the arrangement of these cloths, John believed in the resurrection. Evidently, to accept the grave-robbing theory one must not only accept that the guards slept through the commotion but that the disciples took the time to unwind the wrappings, perhaps fold them, and in general tidy up the place before making off with a body under the threat of attack!

Guards on such an important duty facing severe penalties for dereliction would not sleep. They could not possibly have slept during any grave robbing.

Finally, sleeping people do not make reliable witnesses to anything. Those who claim to identify criminals that they saw while they were asleep would not help any prosecutor's case. No arrests were made because there was no evidence whatsoever of guilt.

■ The Disciples as Criminals

The disciples do not fit the profile of criminals. It would have been psychologically and ethically improbable, and physically impossible for them to have robbed the grave (either by overpowering the guards or doing so without waking them).

Regarding psychology, something transformed the disciples from wimps to champions of a Jesus who returned from the grave. It is obvious the disciples sincerely believed Jesus arose from the dead. They willingly died horrible deaths for their faith without the slightest hope of earthly reward or recognition. If they had stolen the body, then they knew their message was a lie. People have died for lies, but it is against human nature to die for a known lie unless there is the possibility of great gain by taking the risk. If the disciples knew their claim of the resurrection was false, it becomes very difficult to find a motivation that explains their willingness to suffer torture and death. If they stole the body, then they knew they were lying; but their dramatic turnabout from cowardice to bold courage demonstrates at least that they sincerely believed they had seen Jesus alive. If anything, it would have taken even greater proof that Jesus was alive to change those who formerly disbelieved Him (such as half-brothers James and Jude or Saul of Tarsus).

Next we must consider ethics and culture. The disciples taught the world its highest system of ethics. Were they all liars? Would they have told lies which they knew would lead innocent people to martyrdom without standing to gain any earthly advantage? Could they have held this conspiracy together without anyone caving in to reveal the "real" truth of grave-robbing? Yet, despite all obstacles they gave a unified front that their witness to a risen Christ was the truth. They were highly ethical and credible witnesses.[370]

Something convincing must have also changed them to alter their inherited culture. They changed the day of worship from Saturday to Sunday to commemorate the resurrection. They believed Jesus was God in the flesh and worshipped Him believing this was not a violation of the commandment "You shall fear **only** the Lord your God, and you shall worship Him . . ." (Deuteronomy 6:13).

It was physically impossible for a timid band of disciples to overpower the guards (let alone remove the body without alarm). Any attempt by these men to challenge the guards would have likely resulted in casualties.

Psychology, ethics, and culture, all cause one to reject the disciples as lying criminals. On the contrary, these factors show it would have taken strong proof for the disciples to first believe in the resurrection and then later to sacrifice all in order to preach the resurrected Jesus as God's Son and Savior.

Jesus Rose from the Dead!

Jesus' tomb was undeniably empty on the first Easter morning. Natural explanations are all dead-ends which fail to satisfy various concrete facts of the situation.

If His body had remained in the tomb, the authorities would have drawn public attention to the remains, and thus expose the early Christians as liars. If they could have done so, they most certainly would have produced Jesus' corpse.

The tomb was empty but the swoon theory will not work. Jesus definitely died. The wrong-tomb theory and hallucination theories likewise fail because then the body would have remained in the real tomb, and the guards would never have made up any grave-robbing explanation for the empty tomb. Obviously, their story itself concedes the point the tomb was empty.

Finally, the grave robbing charge fails to explain the undeniably empty tomb. These guards would not have slept fearing penalties and failure for an assignment given by the top rulers in the province. Had they slept, then no one could have plundered the grave without disturbing them. Also, had they slept they could not have identified anyone as a criminal. This was a ridiculous story that never resulted in any prosecution for Christians. Meanwhile, they kept running around making fools of the authorities by preaching the risen Jesus. Even 2,000 years later, on strictly historical and logical grounds, the far best explanation for the undeniably empty tomb is that the Lord Jesus Christ rose from the dead! [371]

Chapter 13

Review and Conclusions

One of the purposes for this study has been to direct others to the many fine New Testament scholars for additional research. Only the main conclusions from the preceding text and accompanying footnotes will now be condensed and reviewed.

Jesus and History opened with a chapter showing the Gospels must be dated within the first century. First, early church authors such as Clement, Polycarp, Ignatius, and the writer of the *Didache* include allusions or quotations from either the Gospels or the traditions incorporated into them. Second, manuscripts such as p^{52} and the Egertion 2 papyrus show that the 19th century view of Gospel composition past the life span of the eyewitnesses of Jesus is not tenable. If portions of the Gospel of John (p^{52}) were being circulated in Egypt around A.D. 100-125, then the composition of the book must be earlier. Third, scholars such as Hengel (Tubingen), Reicke (Basel) and Wallace (Dallas Seminary) argue that titles were attributed to each of the four Gospels when they first circulated (A.D. 100-125). No alternative authors have ever been given either by the early church fathers or by the titles that were attached to the manuscripts at an early date. The books have always been attributed to Matthew, Mark, Luke, and John. Three of these four are relatively obscure (Matthew a formerly hated tax collector and two non-apostles Mark and Luke). Had they not been the actual authors, these choices would be inexplicable, as well as, the universal attribution to them. No hints or suggestions as to other authors were ever given. Thus, even critical scholars such as Hengel (Tubingen), Brown (Union Seminary, New York), Metzger (Princeton), and Bowker (Cambridge) date the Gosepls within the first century. Having drawn this conclusion, this study then considers each Gospel.

Chapter two examines the Gospel of Matthew. Papias (c. A.D. 95-110) credits Matthew with writing about Jesus in the Hebrew (i.e. Aramaic) language. Additional church fathers follow this view. They were all aware of our canonical Gospel of Matthew in Greek. They assume a connection between the Aramaic writing by Matthew and the

Gospel of Matthew. Scholars disagree as to the connection between Matthew's work in Aramaic and the canonical Matthew. Options include:

▶ Papias' Aramaic writing by Matthew became the major source for our Greek Gospel of Matthew.

▶ Papias made a mistake. Matthew wrote the Gospel of Matthew only in Greek.

▶ Papias refers to Hebrew style not language. Thus, Matthew wrote his Gospel in Greek.

▶ Our Gospel is a direct translation of Matthew's Aramaic original by either Matthew himself or a disciple.

By one of these means Matthew may be regarded as the author of the Gospel of Matthew.

Internal clues support the early church tradition of Matthew being the author. Mark 2:14 and Luke 5:27-28 record the call of Levi. Yet, Matthew 9:9 uses another name, Matthew; and only in Matthew 10:3 do we learn he was a tax collector.

The Gospel of Matthew should be dated prior to the Temple's destruction in A.D. 70. The book refers to Temple sacrifices still in operation (5:23-24) and the Temple tax (17:24-27). Arguments against the Sadducees and a warning to "flee to the mountains" when Jerusalem would be besieged indicate a date no later than the A.D. 60's. Irenaeus dates Matthew to the time "Peter and Paul were preaching in Rome . . ." (*AH* 3.1.1.) which also favors a date no later than the 60's.

Because of its Jewish slant, the Gospel of Matthew probably has its origin in Israel, but there also seems to be an interest in Syria as indicated in Matthew 4:24 (and the earliest quotes or allusions of the book from Ignatius, Bishop of Antioch).

Chapter three concerns the Gospel of Mark. Early church authors such as Papias and Irenaeus claim Mark as the author and that he was Peter's assistant. As with the other Gospels, no other name is given as an author either in writings of the early church or the title "according to Mark" that was attached to the book at an early date. The selection of Mark as the author shows that the early Christians did not make up attributions of authorship. If so, they would have claimed Peter as the author. The selection of non-apostolic and otherwise secondary Mark was based in truth.

Literary analysis of the book indicates Peter's presence as an authoritative source. Peter is mentioned at the beginning (1:16) and end of the Gospel (16:7). Mark 1:36 emphasizes Simon and then refers to his mere "companions." About 21 times the author seems to change an original "we" into a 3rd person "they." This also is a clue Mark (a non-eyewitness) is depending upon Peter for material.

Like Matthew, Mark should be dated pre-A.D. 70. Jesus predicted the Temple's destruction in Mark 13. Because His words were given as a warning of a yet hypothetical future calamity (including at the Second Coming), He Himself made no mistakes. Yet, a later writer would not have referred back upon the Temple's destruction in A.D. 70 with the words found in Mark 13. Mark 13:14 says, "flee to the mountains," but the early Christians fled to Pella (i.e. across the plains). Mark 13:18 advises prayer that the siege not be in winter. The Romans destroyed Jerusalem in August. The text of Mark supports a composition prior to A.D. 70. The church fathers also support a date no later than the A.D. 60's.

Several lines of evidence show the material in Mark's Gospel dates to an even earlier time with origins in Israel. The high priest in Mark 14 is unnamed. Also, people who may have been in potential trouble with authorities are also unnamed. John 18:10 says, Peter cut off Malchus' ear. By contrast, Mark 14:47 only mentions "one who stood by" struck the slave of the high priest. Other examples are in the text of Chapter three. They indicate a probable date for the initial research of Mark's Gospel prior to the end of Caiaphas' tenure (about A.D. 37) when it was still unsafe to identify people involved in such events.

Aramaic words, vivid descriptions of events, and names of those healed or helped by Jesus (Bartimaeus, Jairus, Alexander, Rufus) also favor very early dates for the material in Mark.

While the above data supports an ultimate origin in Israel, the Gospel of Mark contains Latinisms, and early tradition ties the book to Rome. It may be that the book originates in Israel (including Peter's work in Caesarea) but was either finished or first distributed widely in Rome.

Chapter four concerns the Gospel of Luke. As with Matthew and Mark, titles were attached to the early copies of the third Gospel. Whenever a name is attached to a copy or a church father identified the author, it is always Luke.

The author of Acts is also the author of Luke. Therefore, portions of Acts in which the author is traveling with Paul can be isolated by following references to the first person (the "we" sections) in Acts. By the process of elimination, internal clues parallel church tradition identifying Luke as the author. As with Matthew and Mark, it is best to date the composition of Luke prior to the Temple's destruction in A.D. 70. Since Acts 28 ends with Paul in a Roman prison (c. A.D. 61-62) and since the book never mentions the deaths of Peter and Paul or even James (in A.D. 62), it is best to date Acts at A.D. 61-62. This means the Gospel of Luke is even earlier.

Regardless of whether Paul wrote the prison epistles (Ephesians, Colossians, and Philemon) from Caesarea or Rome, it is likely Luke researched (see Luke 1:1-4) his Gospel while Paul was in prison in Caesarea (A.D. 58-60).

Further delineation of the dates for Matthew, Mark and Luke depends upon conclusions of the synoptic problem and whether Mark and Luke began to research or write in Israel.

The synoptic "problem" is not primarily a problem involving the authority of the Bible. The "problem" in view is an explanation of the order of composition of the synoptic Gospels and whether the Gospels written earlier were used by following authors. Matthew, Mark and Luke show considerable overlap in order and verbal similarities. How shall this be explained?

A final answer may not be possible. Ancient habits of oral tradition (Chapter seven) may explain overall similarities but also slight differences between over-lapping materials in Matthew, Mark, and Luke.

A common order is more difficult to explain without some sort of interdependence. It is possible the "pillars" of the church (Galatians 2:9) consulted on the basic outline and order of the proposed written Gospels or that the synoptics follow the general outline of Jesus' life given in Peter's sermon in Acts 10:34ff.

If Mark and Luke gathered material in Israel, then it is possible all three synoptic authors shared their plans or preliminary drafts. There could be an overlap with Peter and Mark and Paul and Luke in Caesarea. This would be even more certain if Colossians and Philemon were written from Paul's Caesarean imprisonment (Colossians 4:10, 14; Philemon 24.) Then Matthew, Mark, and Luke would be in close proximity with all involved in a writing ministry.

While alternatives are feasible and the data might be able to be explained without literary dependence, several observations make a literary dependence more likely. When John the Baptist's death is reported, it is a flashback from the time Herod began to worry that Jesus was John the Baptist's ghost. Also, an Old Testament quote might be modified from the Hebrew but be similar in all three synoptics. Isaiah 40:3, ". . . make straight in the wilderness a highway *for our God"* becomes ". . . make *His* paths straight" in Matthew 3:3; Mark 1:3, and Luke 3:4. Observations like this make a literary dependence more likely. If so, it is best to view Mark as written first with Matthew and Luke adding the Lord's Prayer and the Sermon on the Mount (as opposed to the less likely occurrence of Mark deleting those important sections).

The church fathers believed Matthew, (Aramaic Matthew) was written first. Yet, literary observations can lead to the conclusion of Marcan priority. One reasonable way to incorporate these ideas is as follows: an Aramaic source for Matthew was written in the early A.D.

50's with Mark following in the mid-A.D. 50's. Luke and the Greek Gospel of Matthew follow (their order is in debate) with Luke being in about A.D. 58-60. Finally, comes the Gospel of John.

Chapter five concerns the Gospel of John. The book presents the author as an eyewitness (1:14, 19:35, 21:24).

Papias, reflecting at a time of approximately A.D. 80, refers to the Apostle John and the Elder John in a quote recorded by Eusebius (*HE* 3.39.4). It is probable that the Apostle John and the Elder John are the same person. Even if there were two Johns in view, the Papias' quote itself says nothing about authorship of the Gospel.

Irenaeus identifies the author of the Gospel as an "apostle" in *AH* 1.9.2-3. Internal clues within the text itself support the view that the author is the Apostle John. He is often paired with Peter. The author is the "beloved disciple," a term that probably indicates one of the inner circle of "Peter, James, and John." Yet, Peter is contrasted with the author, and James was beheaded early (Acts 12:2). The Gospel of John never calls the other John, "John the Baptist" nor does it refer to the Apostle John by name. The author felt safe that his readers could understand John "the Baptist" by the simple name "John." There would be no confusion because the readers would identify the author with the Apostle John. In addition, the author was beside Jesus at the Last Supper (John 13:23). The synoptic Gospels emphasize the apostles as the participants at the Last Supper (Matthew 26:20; Mark 14:17; Luke 22:14). Therefore, both external church history and internal clues within the book identify the author as the Apostle John (not another John).

The church fathers saw Ephesus as the place of composition for John's Gospel and hint that John was elderly. Thus, the Gospel of John is often dated to the A.D. 90's.

While final editing may have been in Ephesus in the A.D. 90's, one can also build a case for initial composition in Israel in the A.D. 60's. John 5:2 says, ". . . there is in Jerusalem . . . a pool ... called ... Bethesda." The present tense favors a date prior to A.D. 70 as this pool was destroyed then. Therefore, John may have begun his Gospel earlier, then he moved to Ephesus before the Romans destroyed Jerusalem. There he finished and/or distributed the fourth Gospel.

Chapter six pauses to give conclusions about the four Gospels. The traditional associations with Matthew, Mark, Luke, and John are correct. The synoptics should be dated no later than the A.D. 60's with the Gospel of John having a date no later than the A.D. 90's. While more precise dates can not be given with certainty, it is probable that Matthew, Mark, and perhaps even Luke date to the 50's as explained above and in the relevant chapters.

Chapter seven covers the transmission of information about Jesus from the A.D. 30's to the composition of the Gospels in the A.D. 60's or more likely the A.D. 50's.

Oral traditions among Jewish people would have been much more strictly controlled than modern people may realize. Perhaps materials were memorized in fine detail. An alternative model would allow some variation in stylistic matters and order of reporting an account, but still require facts to be passed on accurately. It is most likely the apostles, church elders, and other eyewitnesses to Jesus supervised the re-telling of the stories about Jesus. Thus, information about Him was reliably transmitted from the end of His earthly ministry (A.D. 30 or 33) to the time the Gospels were composed (A.D. 50's or 60's).

Furthermore, the claims of Jesus can be shown to originate with Jesus Himself. They are not creations of following generations who read them back into the lips of Jesus. Jesus favorite title of Himself is "The Son of Man." This arises from Daniel 7:13-14 and means Jesus claimed to be the coming ruler of God's universal and never-ending kingdom. The early church never used this title (only Acts 7:56). Jesus used the title to claim the authority of God in Mark 2:7, 10, 28 and as an equivalent to "Son of God' at His trial (Matthew 26:63-64; Mark 14:61-62; Luke 22:70).

Other clues in the Gospels show Jesus' claims originate with Himself not the early church. He called the Father "Abba" or "daddy" in Mark 14:36. In the parable of the tenants, Jesus claimed to be the "beloved Son." There is every reason to conclude that the life of Christ as written in the Gospels was reliably preserved in the short time between the life of Christ and the composition of the Gospels a few decades later. Psychological research given in Chapter seven shows events in the life of Christ produce the types of memories that are accurately remembered.

Because most date the Pauline Epistles even before the Gospels, Chapter eight examines the life and teaching of Jesus as recorded in Paul's epistles. Most critical scholars accept the authenticity of at least seven Pauline epistles and date them to the A.D. 40's or 50's. Within these letters we find the same historical outline for the life of Christ that we have in the Gospels. Also, embedded within the epistles are hymns or creeds that were already traditional when Paul wrote these letters. As an example, 1 Corinthians 15:3-7 gives an example of an early doctrinal statement. Paul visited Corinth in about A.D. 51. By that time the historical facts and doctrinal conclusions in this creed were already "traditional."

Chapters nine and ten consider people in the Gospels who are also mentioned in non-Christian sources outside the Bible. Chapter nine shows what Josephus wrote about John the Baptist and James, Jesus' half-brother. Endnote 182 also gives information about the "James Ossuary."

References to Jesus occur in Josephus, the Talmud, Tacitus, Pliny, Suetonius, and others. Clearly the main outline of Jesus' life is not mythological. Chapter ten gives information about religious and political leaders in the Gospels that comes from non-Christian sources. Jewish high priests, Annas and Caiaphas; Jewish political rulers, Herod the Great, Archelaus, Herod Philip, Herod Antipas, and Herodias; and Roman officials such as Quirinius, Lysanias, and Pontius Pilate show that the Gospels overlap with history.

In addition to people, the places in the Gospels are not mythological. Chapter eleven argues we probably know the site of the birth of Jesus in Bethlehem, the synagogue in Capernaum where Jesus taught, Peter's House in Capernaum, the site of the Upper Room,

Golgotha where Jesus died and the place of Jesus' tomb. Also, the accuracy of the Gospels can be demonstrated by the topography given in the Gospel of John. Thirteen places in John's Gospel are not mentioned in Matthew, Mark, or Luke. In seven more instances John adds an additional detail about a place not included in synoptic references to that place. At this time, 16 of the 20 have been certainly confirmed with two more locations that are probably known. The most impressive is the Pool of Bethesda which is mentioned outside the Bible on the Copper Scroll from Qumran. Archaeological work has confirmed John's accuracy in that the pool had five porches and water moving from an upper basin to a lower basin would cause a stirring of the water as mentioned in John 5:7.

Chapter eleven also lists people, places, events and customs in the book of Acts that have been confirmed by sources outside the Bible. While the book of Acts is not one of the Gospels, this accuracy reflects upon the competence of the Gospel of Luke. Chapters nine, ten and eleven establish that the Gospels are historical not mythological. Where they can be tested they show themselves to be reliable. The real reason people reject the Gospel is that they record miracles.

Chapter twelve considers evidence for Jesus' miracles and His resurrection. Most opponents of Christianity adopt a world-view of relativism. Yet, a world-view that claims no absolutes cannot rule out miracles might happen as this would be self-contradictory.

With Jesus one amazing fact is that His enemies conceded He could do miracles e.g. John 11:47ff. (see text on Chapter twelve and endnote 360). They grant the signs and wonders but attribute His powers to Satan not God (Matthew 12:22-24; Mark 3:22). Many of Jesus' miracles were public and helped people with proven needs who could not possibly have been fakes. The disciples had great honesty. It is an historical fact that many in His day believed Jesus could do miracles even though acceptance of His claim to be the Son of God would mean great opposition. The raising of Lazarus is perhaps the greatest miracle outside of Jesus own resurrection from the dead. John 12:9-11, and 17-19 make the astounding claim that Lazarus himself visited Jerusalem after being raised and that those who witnessed his exit from the tomb were attesting to Jesus along the parade route on

Palm Sunday. How could a book make such a statement unless it would ring true to early readers?

Public events such as Jesus' trial and crucifixion would have had to occur (as admitted by writers outside the Bible). Furthermore, public phenomena in Jerusalem such as the darkness and the earthquake must have been known by all to make the rest of the Gospel account credible. (See endnote 206.)

Jesus' tomb had to have been empty on the first Easter morning. If not, His adversaries would have turned it into an exhibit to show that the early Christians were crazy liars. It was empty. Yet, all natural explanations lead to dead ends. A "swoon" theory in which Jesus never died is at strong odds with the evidence. If the disciples went to the wrong tomb or were having hallucinations, then the body would still have been in the real tomb available to disprove the preaching about Jesus' resurrection. The charge that the disciples stole Jesus' body never led to any prosecution because it was too weak to be taken seriously. Guards did not sleep because of the severe penalty. No one could have slept through an effort to roll back the stone. Sleeping people can not testify to having seen any crime. The disciples ran all over Jerusalem in the book of Acts claiming Jesus rose from the dead. No one ever was legally charged with grave-robbing. The tomb was empty, and the most reasonable conclusion is that Jesus rose from the dead. Even Saul (later Paul) and James, the Lord's half-brother changed their minds about Jesus.

Historical evidence does not make faith unnecessary, but it does make it reasonable. Jesus of Nazareth claimed to pay for our sins by His death on the Cross. Then He rose from the dead. He invites and commands us to "believe in Him" so that we can have the gift of eternal life. Jesus is God the Son who died for our sins and rose again. By placing trust in Him and His work on the cross, we share in His life.

Endnotes

Chapter 1 -The Historical Reliability of the Gospels

1. Ellis dates Clement's epistles to the Corinthians at A.D. 69-70. Others conclude this literature's date as 95-96 (Ellis 280 fn. 236). Ellis dates *Didache* to A.D. 50-70 (p. 55). Ellis was research professor at Southwestern Baptist in Ft. Worth, TX. He is my favorite author on these topics at a scholarly and advanced level. See also *The Zondervan Pictorial Encyclopedia of the Bible* 2:125 which dates *Didache* at A.D. 70-110.

2. Regarding Clement: Metzger (*The Canon*) sees possible parallels with Matthew and Luke (p. 41); Barnett lists Matthew, Mark, and Luke (p. 40). Regarding Ignatius: Metzger sees "probable" Matthew and John (p. 45-49), Roberts says "seems" to quote Matthew (p. 56), Barnett lists all four Gospels (p. 40). Regarding Polycarp: Metzger sees "phrases that we find in" Matthew and Luke (p. 62) and Barnett all four (p. 40). Regarding the *Didache*, Roberts "shows" possible knowledge of Matthew (p. 56). Also, Geisler and Nix list Matthew and Luke in their fine chart (p. 294) that should be consulted when a simplified and brief overview of this complex issue is needed. Carson and Moo see "resemblances" to Luke in Clement, Ignatius, and Polycarp with a more likely quote of Luke in *Didache* (p. 216). More early church authors and books could be added. (Metzger was New Testament professor at Princeton Seminary, Barnett the former Anglican Bishop of Sydney, Roberts is Presbyterian with a Ph.D. from Harvard. He blogs at www.markdroberts.com.) Geisler founded Southeastern Theological Seminary in Charlotte). Hengel says the longer ending of Mark 16:9-20 quotes all four Gospels about A.D. 110-120, (pp. 102 and 134).

3. The work of Peter Stulmacher, Martin Hengel, and Joseph Ratzinger (Pope Benedict XVI) affirm the essential veracity of the Gospels giving encouragement that not all of German scholarship is radically liberal.

4. Daniel B. Wallace, *"The Gospel of John: Introduction, Argument, Outline,"* (www.bible.org), accessed 2/13/09. Each of his research papers under New Testament Introductions should be consulted for further research at an intermediate level.

5. See Craig Blomberg (Denver Seminary), *The Historical Reliability of the Gospels*, IVP; Urban C. von Wahlde (Loyola in Chicago) *Archaeology and John's Gospel* and Paul N. Anderson (George Fox University) *Historicity in the Gospel of John* both within *Jesus and Archaeology* edited by James H. Charlesworth (Princeton) published by Eerdmans.

6. See Hengel (pp. 48-54) and Reicke (pp. 150ff. in *The Roots*). Bock (Dallas Theological Seminary), *Jesus According to Scripture*, (pp. 29, 33), and Price, *Original Bible*, (p. 175) seem to agree.

7. See Komoszewski, Sawyer, and Wallace (pp. 139-140).

8. Hengel p. 208; Brown pp. 127, 172, 226, 334; Bowker pp. 307, 309, 311, 313; Metzger (*The New Testament*) pp. 115-117.

Chapter 2 - The Gospel of Matthew

9. Bauckham p. 14. Barnett, *The Birth of Christianity*, p. 159 also gives an early date for Papias, even to the time of Ignatius who died in A.D. 107. Eusebius thought Papias wrote in the time of Ignatius (Eusebius, *HE* 3:36.1-2; 3:39.1)

10. Bock, *Studying the Historical Jesus*, p. 25.

11. Those who enjoy more complete information would not be disappointed in the classic Donald Guthrie (University of London) in *New Testament Introduction*. Hengel believes the longer ending of Mark 16:9-20 quotes all four Gospels about A.D. 110-120 (pp. 102, 134). Wallace lists Irenaeus, Origen, Eusebius, Augustine, and Jerome as supporting Matthean authorship (www.bible.org). Bauckham adds the *Gospel of Thomas*, (p. 236).

12. Daniel B. Wallace, "*Matthew: Introduction, Argument, Outline*," www.bible.org, accessed 02/03/2009. Daniel Wallace (www.bible.org.) writes "only in the first gospel is Matthew called the 'tax-collector' in the list of the apostles . . . . The most logical reason that the writer felt such liberty with his Markan source was because he knew of the identification personally .... Thus, he could either be Matthew himself or an associate who later compiled the work. Against the compiler theory is Matthew 9:9, which records the calling of Matthew, 'it is significant that it is more self-deprecating than Luke's account, which says that Matthew 'left everything' and followed Jesus' while Matthew simply says that he got up and followed Jesus. If the first gospel were not by Matthew, one would be at a loss to explain why the author seemed to deprecate Matthew in such subtle ways. A later compiler who knew and respected Matthew (probably a disciple of his), or worse, a 'school of St. Matthew,' simply does not fit the bill." Carson and Moo suggest Papias understandably erred about Matthew first writing in Aramaic but was still correct that Matthew was the author of the Greek canonical Matthew (p. 146). This is possible, but I prefer with Wallace (see www.bible.org, *Introduction to Matthew*) to give Papias the benefit of the doubt that Matthew wrote *something* about Jesus in Aramaic. "Although Papias could have been wrong

... he is sufficiently early and well connected with apostolic Christianity that he ought to be given the benefit of the doubt." Yet a third option is that when Papias said that Matthew wrote in Hebrew, he referred to a Hebrew style not the Hebrew (Aramaic) language. A fourth view is that despite the comments above, our Greek Gospel of Matthew is a direct translation from an original Hebrew written by Matthew. Bernard Orchard (Catholic, London) following a 1960 article and later book in German by J. Kurzinger (*Papias von Hieropolis*, Regensburg: Pustet, 1983) maintains the third option. Papias means Matthew wrote our Greek Matthew but in a Hebrew literary style (Bernard Orchard, *The Order of the Synoptics,* pp. 129ff. and 198-199). The fourth view is represented by Theodor Zahn (Enlangen, Germany) who argues that Matthew wrote his Gospel in Hebrew and that our Greek Matthew is a direct translation of the Apostle's work (Theodor Zahn, *Introduction to the New Testament,* 2:515). A summary of the major interpretation of Papias' statement about Matthew is as follows:

1. Papias refers to Matthew writing the major **source** that later was incorporated into our canonical Greek Matthew.

2. Papias' reference to a Hebrew (Aramaic) Matthew is a **mistake**. Matthew only wrote the present Greek Gospel never any Hebrew one.

3. Papias referred to a Hebrew **literary style**, but Matthew wrote the canonical Gospel in Greek.

4. Paipas means Matthew wrote his Gospel in Hebrew. Our Greek Gospel is a **direct translation** of Matthew's Hebrew (Aramaic) original.

13. Comments from Robert L. Thomas and F. David Farnell also link the Greek Gospel back to an Aramaic document penned by the Apostle Matthew with Matthew himself as reworking our New Testament book (*The Jesus Crisis*, pp. 42-46). "The anonymity of the Matthean Gospel argues strongly for the validity of tradition that attached Matthew's name to it, for such anonymity is inexplicable apart from its direct association with the apostle Matthew. Matthew was a relatively obscure figure among the Twelve, so no adequate reason exists to explain why the early church would have chosen his name rather than a better-known apostle if he had not indeed written it . . . . Papias referred to an earlier edition of Matthew. This was written entirely in Hebrew (namely, Aramaic) and preceded the Greek version of the gospel. That was perhaps a proto-Matthew, namely, a shorter version that eventually came to be incorporated into (not necessarily translated from but contained within) an expanded Greek version, namely, the canonical gospel of Matthew. Thus, Papias indicated that Matthew wrote first (prior to the other gospels) and that

in so doing, he produced an initial Aramaic edition. The Aramaic edition served as a model and/or source for some of the contents of his Greek edition that he most likely produced as a fresh work soon after he wrote the Aramaic one . . . . Tradition has it that Matthew eventually left the environs of Jerusalem to minister among non-Aramaic speaking peoples. The dominance of Greek in the Hellenistic world would have impelled him to produce another edition. Because he was a former tax collector for the Romans, he would most likely have been conversant in Greek as well as Aramaic, thus facilitating the writing of both versions. Once the Greek Matthew became current in the church, the limited appeal of Aramaic caused that edition to fall into disuse. Papias' statement that 'each interpreted' Matthew's gospel (Aramaic version) 'as best he could' probably hints at the reason why Matthew would have quickly produced a Greek version: to facilitate the understanding of his gospel in the universal language of Greek . . . this view accords with the very early and consistent manuscript ascription of the gospel to Matthew (*KATA MATHTHAION*). The title is not a part of the original text, but no positive evidence exists that the book ever circulated without this title. Moreover, the ascription has a very early date, approximately A.D. 125. As Guthrie notes, 'the title cannot be dismissed too lightly, for it has the support of ancient tradition and this must be the starting point of the discussion regarding authorship'. . . . though patristic witnesses like Papias uniformly spoke about an Aramaic original of the gospel, they accepted the Greek Matthew as unquestionably authoritative and coming from the apostle Matthew himself. They offered no explanation concerning the change in language. Most likely, that indicates their regard for the Greek Matthew as authoritative and substantially representative of the Hebrew *ta logia* . . . . the universal ascription of the Greek Matthew to the apostle Matthew and the failure of tradition to mention any other possible author except Matthew renders unconvincing any suggestion that the early church forgot the true author of the work. Only a brief span of fifty to sixty years passed between its composition and the statements of Papias. A less-prominent apostle such as Matthew would not have been a likely candidate to receive credit for such an important and influential document as the Greek Matthew unless he did indeed write it."

14. The following materials will take up the synoptic problem concerning the time sequence in which Matthew, Mark, and Luke were written and whether a previous Gospel was used as a research source by following authors. Conclusions as to probable dates for Mark and Luke also follow. For the present, we need only explain how these relationships affect the precise dating for the Gospels. Since Acts 28 ends with Paul's first imprisonment in Rome in about A.D. 62, the Gospel of Luke could be dated in the late 50's or 60-61. If one follows church tradition that Matthew was composed first, then Matthew should be dated at least in the 50's. If one follows Marcan priority as the solution to the synoptic problem, then Mark is best dated at least by the 50's.

(See also Daniel Wallace www.bible.org under *The Synoptic Problem*). If a Cesarean provenance for Paul's prison epistles is accepted, then both Luke and Mark could be dated in the 50's (see Chapters three and four).

15. Maier, Eusebius, p. 95. I recommend Paul Maier's fine translations of Josephus and Eusebius both by Kregel. Jesus' words are primarily about the end-times with secondary application to A.D. 70. I have read the Romans were actually camped in the mountains. Flight in that direction would be a bad idea (Matthew 24:16). No one making a fictional account after A.D. 70 would choose these words. Thus, the writing of Matthew is best viewed as pre-A.D. 70.

16. Ellis, p. 290.

17. Irenaeus, *AH* 3.1.1, also Eusebius *HE* 5.8.2.

18. In addition to Irenaeus, *Against Heresies* 3.1.1, other patristic quotes place the composition of Matthew in Judea, the Anti-Marcionite prologue (see Black, *Why Four Gospels?*. p. 39) and Eusebius (*HE* 3.24.6). See Brown 212 fn. 91. Intense debate with Judaism could favor a time close to James' execution in A.D. 62 (See Josephus, *Antiquities* 20:197-203). See also Ellis and J.A.T. Robinson for conclusions that Matthew arises from Jerusalem setting (Ellis p. 291-292, Robinson pp. 75-79). I quote Ellis who essentially agrees with Robinson with a qualification of restraint. This is fascinating when we realize Robinson is a liberal Anglican and Ellis is Southern Baptist.

"J.A.T. Robinson's summary, although perhaps somewhat too sweeping is essentially correct. 'Matthew's gospel shows all the signs of being produced for a community (and by a community) that needed to formulate, over against the main body of Pharisaic and Sadducaic Judaism, its own . . . interpretation of scripture and place of the law, its attitude toward the temple and its sacrifices, the sabbath, fasting, prayer, food laws and purification rites, its rules for admission to the community and the discipline of offenders, for marriage, divorce and celibacy [and] its policy toward Samaritans and Gentiles in a predominantly Jewish milieu . . . .' The canonical Gospel of Matthew was very likely composed in Jerusalem as the Gospel for the Jacobean mission, and that means before A.D. 66 or 67 when the leaders of the mission had departed for Pella and when the Jewish War would have made such work almost impossible."

Riecke also places Matthew in Jerusalem: "With remarkable consistency all pictures developed . . . represent the perspective of the Jerusalem church" (p. 128). Orchard assumes not only a Jerusalem provenance for Matthew but a date before A.D. 44 (pp. 239-244). John

Wenham in *Redating Matthew, Mark and Luke* dates the Synoptics at 40 (Matthew), 45 (Mark), and 54 (Luke).

19. Bock in *Historical Jesus* p. 168. Other scholars give various statistics (Bock 170, fn. 17). See also *Questions about Q* by Bock within *Rethinking the Synoptic Problem* and Daniel Wallace "The Synoptic Problem," www.bible.org. Eta Linneman trained in the German critical school gives alternative statistics in *Is There a Synoptic Problem?* as does my own former teacher Thomas Edgar (Capital Seminary) in *The Jesus Crisis* (cp.3)

20. Endorsements for *The Jesus Crisis* came from Charles Dyer (Moody Bible Institute), Homer Kent (Grace Seminary, Indiana), Norman Geisler (Southern Evangelical Seminary, Charlotte), and Stanley Tousssaint (Dallas Seminary).

21. Bock, *Historical* Jesus, p. 172.

22. Bock, p. 178.

23. Of these perhaps the closest to our theological perspective would be David Alan Black (p. 29 in *Why Four Gospels?*) and John Niemela within (*Three Views on the Gospel Origins*). Niemela's dissertation committee at Dallas Seminary included William Farmer and Harold Hoehner. If Dr. Hoehner advocates this view, it is at least plausible!

24. The previous section contained many names because they seem to be minority views. Often the New Testament experts in the bibliography seem to hold Markan priority (Bauckham, pp. 126, 146 and Hengel, p. 208). Bock and Wallace in our theological camp may have been taught differently in their own work at Dallas Seminary but have changed positions based on research. I. Howard Marshall at the University of Aberdeen no doubt was an influence. I have not included radical liberals in this material or every important New Testament scholar of past history. Information about these may be found in the bibliographic sources. Also, the two source view (Matthew and Luke used Q and Mark) and the four source view (Matthew and Luke used Q, Mark, M & L) may be examined by the books in the bibliography. Research material from additional evangelical scholars who support Markan priority may be found as follows: Blomberg, *Jesus and the Gospels*, pp. 87-90; Bock, *Studying the Historical Jesus*, pp. 167-179; Guthrie, *New Testament Introduction*, pp. 121-236; McKnight, in *New Testament Criticism and Interpretation*, edited by Black and Dockery, pp. 137-172; and McKnight in *Rethinking the Synoptic Problem*, edited by Black and Beck, pp. 65-95; Osborne, in *Three Views on the Origin of the Synoptic Gospels*, edited by Robert Thomas, pp. 19-96; Osborne, *Rethinking the Synoptic Problem*, edited by Black and Beck, pp. 137-151; and Stein, *Studying the Synoptic Gospels*, especially, pp. 94-96, and

Stein in *The Dictionary of Jesus and the Gospels*, edited by Joel B. Green, Scot McKnight, and I. Howard Marshall, pp. 784-792; and Williams, Matthew C., *Two Gospels From One*.

25. Cited by Black, p. 38. Clement's comments concern preaching in Rome but may apply to Mark's transcription of Peter's earlier sermons perhaps in Caesarea, see my comments in the next section on Mark's place of composition. To include the idea that Mark's material may arise from sermon notes need not rule out a later literary revision. Increasingly experts on the Gospel of Mark detect brilliant literary technique (Bauckham, pp. 230ff.). The book begins and ends with references to Jesus as the Son of God (1:1, 15:39). Another *"inclusio"* ("sandwiches") concerns the Apostle Peter who is the primary authority behind the book (1:16, 16:7). Thus, the Gospel of Mark may possibly be traced back to sermon notes, but it has been also reworked into literary form. The point here is that a transcript **could also** explain both deletions and elaborations (not just Marcan priority with Matthew and Luke using Mark).

26. If I read Ellis (333-334) and Reicke correctly, they also do not have dogmatic conclusions on the synoptic order of composition. The synoptics rise at a similar time. Perhaps Matthew, Mark and Luke consulted each other, probably by personal contact in Caesarea in the late A.D. 50's (though Ellis does place Mark before Luke, p. 375). (See also charts on dates of composition in Ellis p. 319, and Reicke p. 166). Bock indirectly mentions the possibility of the order I have concluded above (*Historical Jesus* p. 166 fn. 6). Leading French scholars tend to posit even more sources (L. Vaganay and M.E. Boismard). Bauckham allows for many eyewitness sources (oral and possibly written) and Ellis believes there were many sources used to form the Gospels. Throughout *The Making of the New Testament Documents* Ellis argues for pre-formed traditions being included into New Testament books. (See also Guthrie pp. 138 and 139 for views possibly similar to mine; note French scholars Vaganay and Cerfaux in Guthrie's comments.)

Chapter 3 -The Gospel of Mark

27. See Hengel pp. 48-54 and pages under "superscriptions" in the index, also Reicke, *Roots*, pp. 150ff.

28. Black, *Why Four Gospels?*, pp. 40-41.

29. Ellis, p. 360.

30. Metzger in *The Canon of the New Testament* (Princeton) dates the Muratorian Canon to the bishopric of Pius variously dated A.D. 140-157. See p. 194 and fn. 13.

31. English translation by Ellis, p. 359.

32. See Black's helpful list in *Why?*, pp. 37ff., also Bauckham p. 235.

33. F.F. Bruce, *Canon*, p. 159; Black, p. 39; Bauckham, p. 235 fn.100.

34. Black, p. 38.

35. See Ellis, p. 364 for translations of all three quotes used in the above text.

36. Bauckham, pp. 172-179.

37. See Barnett, p. 78.

38. Barnett, p. 85-86; Bauckham, pp. 156-164.

39. Bauckham, p. 126.

40. 1 Clement 5:2ff., Ellis p. 293.

41. following Ellis, p. 360.

42. Daniel B. Wallace, *"Mark, Introduction, Outline Argument,"* (www.bible.org), accessed 02/03/2009. *See also Zondervan Pictorial Encyclopedia of the Bible* 4:80; *Expositor's Bible Commentary* 8:612; Homer A. Kent, *Studies in Mark*, p. 5; Hengel argues for even more Latinisms p. 259 fn 318.

43. Ellis, p. 360.

44. Ibid., p. 362.

45. Reicke, pp. 168-170; Ellis, pp. 251-254, 266-276. Ellis takes Philippians to originate in the Roman imprisonment but Colossians, Ephesians, and Philemon to come from Caesarea. Thus, Mark and Luke were together in Caesarea. An origin in Caesarea for Mark and Luke is also a possible factor in answering the synoptic problem. Luke knew of Mark's work. Matthew was also in the area. Could Luke, for example, have used both Matthew's Aramaic source and then Mark's Gospel? (whether the Greek Gospel of Matthew was composed before Luke is far less certain, but most believe canonical Matthew

preceded Luke, Bock, p. 43 fn. 2 in *Rethinking the Synoptic Problem.* Yet, Hengel (Tubingen) has strong feelings that our Gospel of Matthew comes after Luke (pp. 169-207, especially, 197ff.). Bowker (Cambridge) also gives the order of Luke then Matthew (pp. 307, 311). Both date Luke and Matthew later than the conclusions in this study. Mark and Luke name "Jairus," Mark 5:22; Luke 8:41. Matthew drops his name in Matthew 9:18-26. Is this a slight support for Luke writing before the canonical Greek Matthew?)

Likely, knowledge of the provenance of the prison epistles would help with the date and place for Mark and Luke, as well as, clear up issues in the synoptic problem. We could view the Aramaic source for Matthew as earliest, Mark at Caesarea about the mid 50's, Luke at late 50's. The Greek Gospel of Matthew could be dated before or after Luke but not later than the 60's.

46. Ellis, p. 375.

47. Black, p. 39.

48. Ibid., p. 40.

49. Ibid., p. 30.

50. See Barnett, pp. 82-89 for additional list of details, emotions, time, and places in Mark. See also Blomberg, *Jesus and the Gospels*, pp. 87-89.

51. Blomberg, p. 89 who follows Stein, pp. 55-57.

52. Bauckham, p. 239.

53. Barnett, pp. 87-88; Bauckham, p.186.

54. Bauckham, pp. 184-197. Bauckham follows Gerd Theissen (University of Heidelberg). J.A.T. Robinson says, "The first draft of St. Mark's Gospel could be as early as 45" (p. 73).

55. Note that Lazarus faced a death threat (John 12:10) and so too would his sister Mary. Therefore, at an early date Mark does not name her.

56. See Hengel, footnote 567 for a list (p. 293).

57. Bauckham, p. 42. See Also Bauckham, pp. 53-54. Eusebius quotes Quadratus who wrote to Emperor Hadrian. Quadratus claimed that some whom Jesus healed had been testifying down to his own time. While

Quadratus wrote about A.D. 117, he refers to an earlier time during his own lifespan. It is likely that some whom Jesus healed, retold their "stories during the whole of their lifetimes" (Bauckham p. 54).

58. We could **tentatively** suggest this order for the completion of the Gospels: Aramaic Matthew source, Mark, Greek Matthew, Luke, and John (or Luke then Greek Matthew and John).

59. Rudolph Pesch in *The Gospel and The Gospels*, edited by Peter Stuhlmacher, p. 109.

60. Bauckham p. 184. Hengel places Mark's provenance in Rome but agrees with Theissen that the author and sources go back to Israel. "The Palestinian 'local coloring,' which Theissen rightly stresses is connected with the fact that the author comes from Jerusalem and the author standing behind him is Galilean" (Hengel p. 259, fn. 318).

61. Gerd Thiessen, *The Historical Jesus,* p. 447 (see also p. 449 regarding Raymond Brown).

Chapter 4 -The Gospel of Luke

62. Reicke says A.D. 100 (p. 150), Hengel (48ff. see 255 fn. 295 on Matthew), Wallace says "The first quarter of the second century." (*Luke: Introduction Argument, and Outline,*" (www.bible.org), accessed 02/03/2009).

63. Bauckham, p. 426. see also Roberts, p. 42, Barnett, p. 89. The date is from Bock's commentary on Luke vol. 1, p. 5.

64. F.F. Bruce, *Canon*, p. 154. Homer Kent dates this prologue to A.D. 150-180 in *Jerusalem to Rome* p. 14. He concluded this is the earliest witness to Luke's authorship. It is likely that the heretic Marcion used a mutilated form of Luke's Gospel (Guthrie pp. 110-111; Hengel 102). Marcion was anti-Semitic and used only Paul's writings. Because Luke was Paul's follower, parts of this gospel were acceptable. Marcion may be dated about A.D. 144.

65. *Against Heresies* 3.1.1. (see also 3.11.8-9 and 3.14.1).

66. In Acts 21:8 the author stays with Philip in Caesarea. In Acts 21:16-17 he comes with disciples from Caesarea to Jerusalem. There he drops away from being with Paul in Jerusalem. The next reference is to Caesarea (Acts 27:1).

67. See material on pages 153-156 that lists examples of the historical accuracy in the book of Acts. This also shows the author of Luke was an excellent historian.

68. Barnett, pp. 92-94.

69. Hegesippus quoted by Eusebius, *Ecclesiastical History* 3:11; 4:22.4 claims Clopas was the brother of Jesus' adoptive father, Joseph. Clopas probably is the Cleopas in Luke 24:18.

70. See Bock's commentary on Luke 1:1-9:50 within *Baker Exegetical Commentary of the New Testament* pp. 5 and 16. He lists 1 Clement 2.1; 5.6-7;13.2;18.1;48.4; and 2 Clement 13:4. Hengel claims Polycarp as quoting Luke (p. 102). He also lists Basilides (A.D. 120/130), Justin (A.D. 150), the secondary ending to Mark (A.D. 110-120), and Marcion (A.D. 144). Wallace in *"Luke: Introduction, Argument, and Outline,"* on www.bible.org also argues that the ancestor to Codex D in Luke-Acts assumes Luke and Acts were a unit before A.D. 150. "One could surmise that patristic writers assumed that Luke and Acts were by one author within two or three decades of their publication."

71. See Ellis, pp. 246, 293, 391 for these dates.

72. See Ellis, pp. 252 and 375.

73. Ellis, pp. 388-389. The Western readings are interesting additions. One can research them in F.F. Bruce's commentary on Acts or Bruce Metzger's *A Textual Commentary on the Greek New Testament.*

74. Elllis, pp. 402-403.

75. See Daniel B. Wallace, *"Introduction to Ephesians"* or *"Introduction to Colossians,"* (www.bible.org), accessed 02/03/2009.

76. Ellis believes Philippians was written during Paul's Roman imprisonment (pp. 275-277), but Ephesians, Colossians and Philemon came from Caesarea, (p. 269ff.).

77. Reicke, p. 165.

78. Reicke, p. 168.

79. Reicke, p. 170. On p. 180 Reicke gives A.D. 60 as Luke's date with Luke's research being A.D. 58-60 with contacts such as: Paul, Mark, and Philip.

80. Above and Ellis, pp. 252, 375, 388-389, 402-403.

81. Ellis, p. 271.

82. Ellis, pp. 271-275.

83. Ellis, p. 245.

84. One last time we revisit the synoptic problem with a more complete background. We can do no more than give probabilities that explain the common order and verbal similarities between the synoptics (Matthew, Mark, and Luke). The final truth may not yet be capable of resolution. A combination of oral recitations of the events and teaching of Christ and/or personal contacts between Matthew, Mark and Luke and/or literary dependence and/or just the timeline of the historical Jesus may all have played a role in the verbal similarities between Matthew, Mark, and Luke. Ones view of the synoptic problem in turn affects issues such as the specific date and place of origin for the Gospels. In general there is sufficient evidence to date the synoptic gospels to the A.D. 60's without resolution to the synoptic problem or concern with details of order or provenance of composition. Then the Gospel deemed to be first may be perhaps dated to the late 50's. Realizing we move into less than certain areas, we now face the issues. How is the similar order and verbal similarities between the synoptics to be explained?

Oral recitation of the events and teaching of Christ may explain much of the verbal similarity (but alone can not explain the close common order). Important scholars on oral tradition incude: Birger Gerhardsson (Lund University, Sweden), J. D. G. Dunn (Durham, UK), Harold Risenfeld (Gerhardsson's teacher) and Kenneth Bailey (N.T. scholar who worked for 30 years in the Middle East, often Lebanon). Bailey's study on oral tradition was given in a 1991 article in the *Asia Journal of Theology*. I have used Bauckham's work to summarize Bailey's observations (Bauckham, pp. 252ff). See also pp. 68-69 in the text.

The older Swedish school of thought believed oral tradition in the early church followed the strict rabbinic model. Students would literally memorize large amounts of information word for word. Given the tie between Judaism and Christianity, this could well have been the model in the early church. Definitely some of the written biblical material originated in oral tradition (e.g., in 1 Corinthians 11:23 "received" and "delivered," and in 1 Cointhians 15:1 "received" and "delivered" (v. 3) are terms for oral truths being passed on as if from a rabbi to a follower). Such oral traditions could explain many of the common wording within the Gospels. Scholars know much about rabbinic oral traditions and memorization. Information about these exact practices, however, dates from a time past the days of Christ and the apostles. While it is logical to assume these habits began a few centuries earlier in Christ's time, one can not be totally certain of this.

Kenneth Bailey instead suggests what he calls "controlled formal tradition." He observed this phenomenon by living in the Middle East. With this system the original eyewitnesses of an event or teaching in the life of Christ would repeat their testimony. Over time the eyewitnesses, apostles, and elders would allow others to retell these events. However, the eyewitnesses and leaders would observe the recitations allowing only limited variation. The names, places, times, and facts were retold with no changes allowed. However, some variations were allowed in minor areas such as introductory formulas and reversal of order. A controlled formal tradition would not allow material changes of substantive fact but would allow a change such as "Then He said" . . . to "Jesus said." Also, the story might allow some variation in the order of phrases. Such a process of oral retelling of the life of Christ could explain the essential agreement but minor variations we see in the synoptic Gospels. It is possible literary dependence between the synoptic Gospels need not have been the factor explaining verbal similarities. Perhaps they arose from oral traditions alone. However, oral tradition alone would not account for the common order of units in the synoptics. Similar ordering of events could just reflect the historical outline of the life of Christ. Yet, the Gospel of John has quite a different inclusion of materials. It is more likely the common synoptic order arose from more than just chance and the historical order of events. See Bock's chart pp. 50-51 in *Rethinking the Synoptic Problem.*

Perhaps personal contacts (such as between Matthew, Mark, and Luke) explain an agreement on the common outline and order of events in the Gospels. An agreement to write books along similar arrangement of material may reflect oral presentations of the life of Christ such as in the sermons in Acts (e.g., Acts 10:34ff.).

While it may be possible that similar wording and order could be explained by oral tradition and personal contacts alone (literary independence view with the authors never seeing each other's actual books), it is more likely there was some sort of **literary** dependence (even if the four "pillars" of the church [Galatians 2:9] verbally agreed on the outline or plan for written work). Ellis sees the four pillars as the authority behind the four Gospels. James and Matthew in Jerusalem for the Gospel of Matthew, Peter and Mark for Mark from Caesarea then Rome, Paul and Luke behind Luke in Caesarea and/or Rome, John writing John with roots in Jerusalem and completion in Ephesus.

Several usages of Old Testament texts give support to literary dependence. Deuteronomy 6:5 says "You shall love the Lord your God with all your heart and with all your soul and with all your **might**" (Massoretic text). However, Matthew 22:37; and Mark 12:30 read, "heart, soul, and **mind**." Isaiah 40:3 says, "Make straight in the wilderness a highway for our **God**." However, Matthew 3:3, Mark 1:3, and Luke 3:4 all apply the quote to Jesus, "make **His** paths straight." (See Stein 45ff.)

The Deuteronomy 6:5 case may be an example of Jesus Himself altering the quote with all three Gospels merely following. However, the example of Isaiah 40 is best traced back not to John the Baptist altering the Old Testament but to a common literary source. By quoting Isaiah, the Gospel author himself is explaining John's message to the readers, not quoting changes John the Baptist had made from Isaiah 40 as he preached. The change more likely comes from the author not John the Baptist. This favors a literary usage of one author by a previous author. While this still begs the question as to whether the Gospels consulted each other or still earlier written materials consulted by all three, a literary overlap best explains this detail.

An additional hint for a literary correlation in the synoptics arises from material about the death of John the Baptist. Chronologically, John the Baptist was killed earlier than the time it is mentioned within Mark 6:17-29 and Matthew 14:3-12. In both Gospels, Herod hears of Jesus' power and fears He may be the murdered "ghost" of John the Baptist. Then the story of John's martyrdom is mentioned as a flashback to an earlier time. This order of material is more likely due to literary dependence than coincidence. Furthermore, Daniel Wallace in *"The Synoptic Problem"* on www.bible.org mentions that several parallel editorial comments within the Gospels point to a literary dependence rather than common oral traditions, e.g., Matthew 27:18 and Mark 15:10. Also, Wallace gives statistics about the word "immediately" indicating a more frequent usage within material common to Matthew and Mark (17 times) but rarity in the portions in Matthew not paralleled in Mark (only once). This is better explained by Matthew following Mark than by coincidence. He makes a similar argument about the word "for" used to give an explanation. Matthew uses an explanation "for" in ten places that overlap with Mark but only once in sections that do not parallel Mark. This is better explained by thinking Matthew consulted Mark than complete independence or that Matthew wrote first. A slight edge should be given to literary dependence without (again), being totally dogmatic.

While the synoptic problem might be explained as only common oral traditions or personal contacts (See Reicke pp. 130, 168, 170; Ellis 252ff.) with agreement on general order, some kind of literary dependence does better explain the details. The next issue is the order of Matthew, Mark, and Luke.

If we grant some kind of literary dependence, there are basically two options. The Greek Gospel of Matthew and Luke are expansions of Mark, or Mark arises from a transcript of Peter's sermons which delete some aspects in Matthew and Luke while elaborating on other subjects. The view that Mark abbreviates material from the other Gospels is possible. Following David Alan Black's hypothetical scenario, assume Peter is preaching following a text of say, Matthew. He could follow the basic order and sometimes the wording but delete some material not pertinent to his oral presentation but elaborate on other topics that fit the needs and interest of the audience. As a transcript, the data in Mark could be a collation of Matthew. However this is only a "could" be, a possibility. It is more likely there is some sort of literary dependence among the synoptic Gospels. In addition, it is more likely Mark was written first (except for proto-Matthew an Aramaic source connected to our Greek Matthew). Pages 29-33 above argue that Mark's material goes back to the earliest times. Perhaps Caiaphas is still high priest as there is no need to name him. Also, some characters who are not named in the text of Mark could be examples of protective anonymity because the text was written early enough for it still to be dangerous if Mark named those liable to prosecution. Also, the naming of witnesses such as Bartimaus may indicate they were still alive when Mark was written. Omission of such names in Matthew and Luke may indicate dates after the death of the participants. Finally, it is unlikely that Mark followed Matthew or Luke but omitted the Lord's Prayer or the Sermon on the Mount. Markan priority is a better explanation with Matthew and Luke expanding information such as the Lord's Prayer and the Sermon on the Mount.

It is still possible to explain that Mark is a transcript of Peter's lectures. Orchard and Black maintain Peter gave his own recollections while unrolling scrolls of Matthew and Luke before him. One suggestion has been that Peter only commented on aspects where he was an eyewitness. However, this fails because Peter was present at the "Sermon on the Plain" in Luke 6:12-17. It would be foolish to be dogmatic on such matters and attack other Christians with alternative explanations. Yet, because opinions on the synoptic problem overlap with the dates and provenance for the synoptic Gospels, such studies are not useless.

Stronger and clearer lines of evidence (explained in the chapters above), point to the A.D. 60's as being a safe date for Matthew, Mark, and Luke. The Gospel we select as the first one written may be pushed back to the late 50's. The early church believed Matthew was written first. However, this Matthew source was Aramaic, which somehow related (without the church fathers seeing any inconsistency) to the Greek canonical Gospel of Matthew. This Aramaic material related to Matthew may be seen as written first. Next it is probable that Mark was the first fully completed Gospel. Most think that

Greek Matthew would precede Luke says Bock in *Rethinking the Synoptic Problem*, p. 43 fn.2. Thus, a reasonable order would be: Aramaic proto-Matthew, Mark, Greek Matthew, Luke.

The relative order of Greek Matthew and Luke is the most conjectural. Hengel (pp. 169-207, especially 197ff.) and Bowker (pp. 307 and 311) are not among Bock's majority. They conclude Luke wrote before the Greek Gospel of Matthew. Both give later dates than adopted in this study. Hengel pp. 170 and 208 dates Luke at 75-80 and Matthew even later at 90-100. Bowker gives 80 for Luke and 85-90 for Matthew.

The book of Acts gives a better basis for conclusions on the dates of the synoptic Gospels. Acts closes with Paul in prison in Rome at about A.D. 61-62. There is no mention of James' death in about A.D. 62. This means Luke was composed no later than A.D. 60 or 61, then Mark may be dated no later than the late 50's with Aramaic or proto-Matthew still earlier in the mid to late 50's. The argument to this point remains neutral as to provenance for the books.

If one accepts as probable that Luke researched or even began to write in Israel, while Paul was in prison in Caesarea, then the dates can be pushed back a few more years. We would have Luke's composition in A.D. 58-60 with Mark around A.D. 55-58 and Matthew's source no later than the early to mid 50's.

Furthermore, if one adopts Reicke's and Ellis's view that the prison epistles were written from Caesarea (not Rome) and that Mark and Luke collaborated together there (Colossians 4:10, 14; Philemon 24), then the dates in the preceding paragraph are on more solid footing.

Also, remember that regardless of the final dates for composition, the information contained in biblical books pre-dates the time of composition. The epistles contain embedded doctrinal and historical facts within hymns and creeds. It is also likely the Gospels give clues as to eyewitness sources and time references that pre-date their time of composition (see chapters on Mark and John especially).

Chapter 5 - The Gospel of John

85. See also references to time that indicate an eyewitness: John 4:6, "the sixth hour" or John 13:30, "It was night."

86. "Indeed, John's Gospel is unique among the evangelists for two early papyri (p^{66} and p^{75} dated c. 200) attest to Johannine authorship. Since these two MSS were not closely related to each other, this common tradition must precede them by at least three or four generations of copying. Furthermore, although B and p^{75} are closely related, textual studies have demonstrated that p^{75} is not the ancestor of B - in fact, B's ancestor was, in many respects, more primitive than p^{75}. Hence, the combined testimony of B and p^{75} on Johannine authorship points to a *textual* tradition that must be at least two generations earlier than p^{75}. All of this is to say that from the beginning of the second century, the fourth Gospel was strongly attached to the Apostle John. Daniel B. Wallace, *"The Gospel of John: Introduction, Argument, Outline,"* (www.bible.org), accessed 02/03/2009. See also Hengel p. 48ff. and Reicke, *Roots*, p.150.

87. David A. DeSilva, *An Introduction to the New Testament*, p. 393.

88. Ben Witherington III, *What Have They Done with Jesus?*, p. 158. Footnote 168 traces the textual work to M. Oberweis, *Das Papias-Zeugnis, vom Tode des Johannes Zebedia, Novum Testamentum* 38 (1996): 227-295. The opposing view seems to be in E. Schnabel, *Early Christian Mission* vol. 1 (Downer's Grove: InterVarsity Press, 2005), pp. 820-21. Witherington also argues for Apostle John's martyrdom in *Biblical Archaeology Review* May/June 2007, p. 26.

89. Daniel Wallace, *"The Gospel of John: Introduction, Argument, Outline,"* on (www.bible.org), accessed 02/03/2009.

90. Bauckham, p. 14.

91. Reicke, pp. 161-162.

92. Ibid., p. 162.

93. Carson and Moo, pp. 233-235.

94. Ibid., 234 and Guthrie, pp. 266-267.

95. Orchard, pp. 172-184; Zahn, 2:435-438, 451-453; Gundry says, "Both times that the name John appears, it appears with both the designations 'elder'

and 'Lord's disciple.' By contrast, Aristion – even though designated a 'Lord's disciple'— lacks the title 'elder' when mentioned alongside John. This contrast points toward a single individual named John. Papias wanted to make plain the single identity of John by repeating the designation 'elder,' just used for the apostles but omitted with Aristion; and Papias mentioned John a second time because John was the only one of the Lord's disciples still living and speaking who was also an apostle. Admittedly, Eusebius interpreted Papias as referring to two different men named John and even claimed a tradition of two men named John and having different memorials in Ephesus. But one and the same person may have more than one memorial and sometimes does. Because Eusebius disliked the book of Revelation, he wanted to find a way around its apostolic authorship. So he conjured up an Elder John allegedly distinct from the Apostle John to enable an ascription of Revelation to someone lacking apostolic authority." Gundry, Robert H. *A Survey of the New Testament.* 4th ed. Grand Rapids: Zondervan, p. 257.

96. Bauckham, p. 452ff.

97. *The Ante-Nicene Fathers*, 1:414.

98. Ibid., 1:329.

99. Ibid., 1:416.

100. Ibid., 1:417.

101. Ibid., 1:392.

102. *The Nicene and Post-Nicene Fathers*, 1:244. Eusebius often quotes Irenaeus: Eusebius, *HE* 3.23.3-4 quotes Irenaeus, *AH* 2.22.5 and 3.3.4. He calls John "the Apostle" (see Nicene and Post-Nicene Fathers 1:150). *HE* 5.8.4. quotes Irenaeus *AH* 3.1.1 (see 1:222). *HE* 5.20.4-8 quotes *The Letter to Florinus* (see 1:238-239). *HE* 4.14.3-8 (see 1:187) quotes the story about John running from the bath-house because he spotted the heretic Cerinthus inside. This section also claims Irenaeus knew Polycarp and that Polycarp knew the eyewitnesses of Christ (see also *AH* 3.3.4). *HE* 3.39.1 quotes *AH* 5.33.4 **that Papias knew John personally** (see *Nicene and Post-Nicene Fathers*, 1:170).

103. *The Ante-Nicene Fathers*, 1:426.

104. Ibid., 1.568.

105. Irenaeus not only knew Polycarp who in turn knew John, he was also likely the successor to Pothinus as bishop of Vienne and Lyons. Pothinus "died in A.D.177 when over ninety years old" (Guthrie p. 259).

106. Henry Thiessen called Hippolytus "a disciple of Irenaeus" (p. 317). F.F. Bruce writes, "This work [i.e., Hippolytus' work] evidently defended the **apostolic authorship of the Gospel** and Apocalypse of John . . ." (*Canon* p. 178, emphasis mine). *The Ante-Nicene Fathers* 5:3 also calls Hippolytus "the disciple of Irenaeus." Philip Schaff in *History of the Christian Church* (1910 reprinted by Eerdmans in 1985) says ". . . as he [Hippolytus] himself says, in a fragment preserved by Photius, heard the discourses of Irenaeus (in Lyons or in Rome). See Philip Schaff, *History of the Christian Church* 2.759.

107. See F.F. Bruce, *Canon*, for quote and date, p. 155. Bock dates the *Anti-Marcionite-Prologues* about this time in *Studying the Historical Jesus*, p. 35 (". . . The second part of the second century") and *Luke*, vol. 1, p. 5 (about A.D. 175).

108. F.F. Bruce, p. 156.

109. Ibid.

110. Bock, *Studying the Historical Jesus*, p. 35.

111. Guthrie, p. 260. See also Ellis p. 152 quoting *HE* 6.14.5-7 who cites Clement of Alexandria ". . .a tradition of the earliest elders. . . last of all [the Evangelists] John. . . being urged by his companions. . . composed a spiritual Gospel."

112. *Theophilus to Autolycus* 2.22. Translation from *The Ante-Nicene Fathers* 2.103.

113. Barnett, p. 57 gives A.D. 180-200.

114. F.F. Bruce, p. 159.

115. Bock, *Studying the Historical Jesus*, p. 35.

116. Bauckham, p. 439ff.

117. Guthrie, p. 258.

118. Guthrie, p. 264, emphasis mine.

119. DeSilva, p. 393.

120. Daniel B. Wallace, *"The Gospel of John: Introduction, Argument, Outline,"* (www.bible.org).

121. Ibid.

122. Barnett, p. 68.

123. Guthrie, p. 269. See also F.F. Bruce in *Canon* on Justin using John pp. 128-129 and an even larger patristic list in Henry Thiessen pp. 162-163. Hengel also says the Gospel of John was quoted in the longer ending of Mark not later than A.D. 120 (p. 134). Both Hengel (pp. 57-58) and F.F. Bruce (pp. 128-129) also include the heretic Basilides as quoting the Gospel of John. He wrote during the reign of Emperor Trajan (A.D. 117-138).

124. Wallace, *"The Gospel of John: Introduction, Argument, Outline,"* (www.bible.org). J.A.T. Robinson also argued for a date in the 60's, *The Priority of John*, J.F. Coakley, ed. (London: SCM, 1985).

125. A date in the 60's would still allow for an early martyrdom of the Apostle John. See Paul N. Anderson, *Jesus and Archaeology*, pp. 597-613 (especially 600-601) for examples in John of eyewitnesses or early tradition.

126. F.F. Bruce, p. 155. English Irenaeus citations from *ANF*, 1:414 and 1:392.

127. Justin Martyr writing later but referring to a debate that "apparently took place in A.D. 132-134 at Ephesus" claimed that "Among us also a certain John, one of the apostles" prophesied about the 1,000 year rule of Christ in Jerusalem (see Ellis 200-202, *Dialogue with Trypho* 81:3, *ANF* 1:240). Justin speaking in Ephesus said John had been "among us." Here is evidence that John the Apostle wrote Revelation in the Ephesus region. While not a direct reference to the Gospel of John, it is more logical to think the "John" who wrote the Gospel is also best identified as the Apostle John who had a ministry in the Ephesus region. The alternative (that the Apostle wrote Revelation but an otherwise obscure "John" wrote the Gospel) is less likely. Perhaps the Apostle John moved from Jerusalem to Ephesus upon the outbreak of the Jewish war with Rome (A.D. 66) or upon news of the martyrdoms of Peter (c. A.D. 65) or Paul (c. A.D. 68).

Chapter 6 - Conclusions on the Four Gospels

128. The opinions of the early church fathers are not infallible. Nevertheless, they were much closer to the time than anyone in modern times. They should

be given the benefit of the doubt unless there would be some stronger reason than just hostility or disbelief. All historical conclusions are within the domain of what is historically probable not just the "what ifs" or "what might have beens" of any view that has the slightest possibility. We must go in the direction of where the evidence lies, and not base conclusions contrary to the facts that do exist. Given a space of 2,000 years, the amount of evidence that remains is actually quite impressive. This is true both of the questions about authorship of the Gospels and the overall historicity of the life of Christ. Hyper-skepticism must not be confused with research or intelligence as if the skeptical view automatically is safely classified as superior. The evidence that does exist supports traditional views about the authorship and early dates of the Gospels. No evidence exists and, therefore, no case whatsoever can be made for different authors. Skepticism should be directed at those who come along 2,000 years later with contrary opinions based on little more than distaste for the Bible or Christianity.

Chapter 7 - Jesus and Gospel History from A.D. 30 – A.D. 60

129. Hoehner, *Chronological Aspects*, pp. 114 and 143; Ellis p. 251; Maier, *The Fullness of Time*, p. 153; and Bock *Jesus According to Scripture*, p. 379 fn. 89 and *Studying the Historical Jesus*, pp. 73 fn. 6 and 77; Paul Barnett, *The Birth of Christianity*, p. 8.

130. Randall Price, *The Original Bible*, pp. 64-68. The early church following the synagogue tradition may also have been text-based very early. Perhaps both reading the stories about Jesus and oral retelling occurred in worship gatherings. This would provide yet another guide to the transmission of information into the final form of the Gospels. (See Chapter three on the Gospel of Mark for discussion on possible earlier written texts, also Luke 1:1-4, and Paul Barnett, *The Birth of Christianity*, p. 117 and 117 fn. 27, 154ff.)

131. Sidney Collet, pp. 14-15. A more recent list can be found in McDowell, *Evidence That Demands a Verdict*, 1999 edition, p. 74ff.

132. Donald A. Hagner in the forward to the English translation of Gerhardsson's work which was done originally in German and Swedish. Birger Gerhardsson, in *The Reliability of the Gospel Tradition*, p. xi.

133. Ibid.

134. Bauckham, pp. 249-250.

135. Bailey's work originally appeared in "Informal Controlled Oral Tradition and the Synoptic Gospels," *Asia Journal of Theology* 5 (1991) 34-51. Here I follow Richard Bauckham's discussion, pp. 252ff.

136. Bailey quoted by Bauckham p. 256.

137. Richard Bauckham, *Jesus and the Eyewitnesses*, Chapters 11 and 12. See also Komoszewski, Sawyer, and Wallace, *Reinventing Jesus*, Chapter 2. In establishing that eyewitnesses to Jesus events helped supervise the retelling of stories about Jesus, Bauckham quotes Quadratus (Bauckham pp. 53-54). Quadratus wrote to Emperor Hadrian (about A.D. 117) but refers to a time earlier in his life when some whom Jesus healed were still alive to attest to what the Lord had done for them. It is unreasonable to think those who became Christians did not participate in retelling their own experience and serving as authoritative guardians of their traditions as told by others in the next generation. In many cases they outlived the dates for the writing of New Testament books. Quadratus was quoted by Eusebius on the topic of those Jesus healed surviving into his own life span: "[T]he works of our Savior were always present, for they were true: those who were healed, those who rose from the dead, those who were not only seen in the act of being healed or raised, but were also always present, not merely when the Savior was living on earth, but also for a considerable time after his departure, so that some of them survived even to our own times" (Eusebius, *Hist. Eccl.* 4.3.2)

138. Mark D. Roberts, *Can We Trust the Gospels?*, pp. 73 and 77.

139. Randall Price, *The Original Bible*, p. 104.

140. Carson and Moo, p. 85.

141. Revelation 1:13 uses the indefinite article "a" but not "**The** Son of Man" and also is giving a simile not a title.

142. Pope Benedict XVI, *Jesus of Nazareth,* pp. 344-345.

143. Craig A. Evans, *Fabricating Jesus*, p. 130. Evans' full argument is on pages 127-138. He includes many extra-biblical Jewish parables about Israel being a vineyard with wicked tenants. J.A.T. Robinson has the same conclusion on the Parable of the Tenants, p. 57ff.

144. See Evans, pp. 46-51 for further study.

145. Evans, pp. 125-126.

146. F.F. Bruce, *Jesus and Christian Origins Outside the New Testament*, pp. 55-56.

147. Evans, pp. 156-157. Originally, Hans Dieter Betz, ed., *The Greek Magical Papyri in Translation, Including Demotic Spells*, 2nd ed. (Chicago: University of Chicago Press, 1992), 1:96.

148. Ibid., 139.

149. See also the "house divided" passages in Matthew 12:25-29; Mark 3:23-27; and Luke 11:17-22.

150. Evans, p. 144.

151. Ibid., p. 146.

152. Ibid., p. 147.

153. Ibid., pp. 147-148.

154. Richard Bauckham, *Jesus and the Eyewitnesses*, Chapter 3, *"Names in the Gospel Traditions."*

155. Bauckham, pp. 42, 44-45. In footnote 24 he also lists non-canonical early Christian writing as resisting the addition of fictional names. "Note, e.g., that the man with a withered hand and the woman with a hemorrhage are both unnamed in *Epistle of the Apostles* 5, as well as, the wise men in *Protoevangelium of James* 21:1-4."

156. Bock, *Jesus Under Fire*, p. 77.

157. Ibid., p. 84.

158. Ibid., p. 86-87.

159. Ibid., 88.

160. Bauckham, p. 319.

161. ". . . it seems likely that they regarded the degree of variation in detail that they exhibit as justified in different performances of the tradition. The 'gist' of the story that they all preserve conveys the common significance of the story in all their versions. It is this that would have been consistent in Peter's own telling of the story on various occasions. It is what he would

certainly have remembered and would have taken the trouble to remember accurately. Whether he himself varied other details or whether this was done only by others who subsequently performed the oral tradition he transmitted to them is of no great importance. Some of the additional details may be accurate reminiscences of Peter, but were not treated as essential to the story . . . . The transition from the one [the eyewitness] to the other [the one retelling of the story] need not entail a significant decrease in reliability . . ." (Bauckham, p. 345).

162. Ibid., p. 334.

163. Ibid., p. 329.

164. Ibid., p. 346.

Chapter Eight - The Life of Jesus in the Epistles

165. See Brown 1 Thessalonians A.D. 50-51 (p. 457), Galatians A.D. 54-55 (p. 468), Philippians A.D. 56-63 (p. 484), Philemon A.D. 55-63 (p. 503), 1 Corinthians A.D. 56-57 (p. 512), 2 Corinthians A.D. 57 (p. 542), and Romans A.D. 57-58 (p. 560). Hengel gives a chart with 1 Thessalonians beginning the list in A.D. 50 (pp. 208-209). Johnson also accepts these seven as authentic (p. 271). See Bowker pp. 411, 415, 421, 425, 433, 439, 443 and Metzger (*The New Testament*, Chapter 10). Often these scholars also argue for early dates to other epistles such as Hebrews or James (e.g., Bowker dates Hebrews before A.D. 70 (p. 451), and Hengel dates Hebrews as "contemporaneous with Luke-Acts" (p. 143) and calls James a "perhaps authentic letter" (p. 278, fn. 469) which must then date before A.D. 62.

166. Barnett, pp. 139-141. Barnett suggests we consult F.F. Bruce, *The Apostle of the Heart Set Free* pp. 95-112 for additional reading on the historical life of Christ as contained in the epistles.

167. Ibid., p. 141.

168. "According to an inscription at Delphi, Gallio was proconsul during the twelfth year of Claudius' tribunical power. . . . This must have been before August 52..." (Guthrie, p. 566).

169. Terry L. Miethe and Gary R. Habermas, *Why Believe God Exists?*, p. 267ff. See also Gary R. Habermas, *The Verdict of History*, pp. 124ff. for additional research on this creed found in 1 Cor. 15:3ff. See also Bauckham pp. 307-308, Roberts p. 68ff., and also Acts 10:38-42.

170. Habermas, *The Verdict of History*, p. 124.

171. Miethe and Habermas, p. 268.

172. Earle Ellis believes that much material incorporated into the New Testament comes from earlier pre-formed creeds, hymns, and teaching traditions. His chart on page 116 gives the following estimates for Paul's epistles:

Large %	Considerable %	Small %
Ephesians c. 54%	Romans c. 27%	1 Cor. c. 17%
Colossians c. 42%	Galatians c. 32%	2 Cor. c. 11%
1 Thess. c. 37%	2 Thess. c. 24%	Phil. c. 7%
1 Tim. c. 43%		2 Tim. c. 16%
Titus c. 46%		

Raymond Brown lists possible embedded creeds on page 491 with asterisks by Philippians 2:6-11; Colossians 1:15-20; Ephesians 1:3-14, 5:14 and 1 Timothy 3:16 as the clearest examples. The best single source in my own personal library on this topic is Neufeld, Vernon H. *The Earliest Christian Creeds*. Grand Rapids: Wm. B. Eerdmans, 1963. This is a publication of Neufelds's 1957 doctoral dissertation at Princeton Seminary. He later became the president of Bethel College in Kansas. See also *Reinventing Jesus*, p. 184ff. and Gary Habermas, *The Verdict of History*, pp. 119-124.

173. Habermas, *The Verdict of History*, p. 123.

174. Brown, p. 491.

175. F.F. Bruce, *Paul:Apostle of the Heart Set Free*, p. 475.

Chapter 9 - Gospel People Also Mentioned in Non-Christian Sources: Jesus and Followers

176. Printed notes include *Evidence for the Christian Faith,* 1986 with updates in 2001 and 2007 and Israel Tour Study notes, 1998. Also, there are sermon files and recordings on these topics for 2007.

177. Along with efforts to study the past, I have also collected 2000 year old Jewish coins from the New Testament period. They were all purchased from David Hendin of Nyack, New York (www.amphoracoins.com). Ten New Testament characters produced coins: Herod the Great, Archelaus, Herod

Antipas, Herod Philip, Aretas, Pontius Pilate, Antonius Felix, Porcius Festus, Agrippa 1 and Agrippa 2. Mr. Hendin is considered the world expert on Bible coins. His *Guide to Biblical Coins* is in its 5th edition. A more popular work is Friedberg, Arthur L. *Coins of the Bible*. Atlanta: Whitman Publishing, 2004. Bible coins help establish that the New Testament arises from an historical not mythological foundation.

178. See pp. 12-13 in Paul Maier, *Josephus: The Essential Writings*, published in 1988. Dr. Maier's translation gives the best Josephus translation into contemporary English. A complete translation of all Josephus' writing (as opposed to Dr. Maier's abridgement) may be found in *Josephus Complete Work* by William Whiston who lived from 1667 to 1752. Whiston succeeded Isaac Newton in the math department at Cambridge. His translation includes all of Josephus' writings but in old style English. The standard Greek work is the Loeb edition by Harvard Loeb Classical Library (Cambridge: Harvard University Press), 1926. Two ways of documenting Josephus' quotes have been used down through the centuries. Whiston uses one model. Maier following the Loeb edition uses another. Readers should be aware that notations in this book will try to follow both but may only use one or the other, especially when quoting from modern scholars or from a Josephus text that is not included in Maier's abridgement. **I used Maier or Whiston primarily (as opposed to Loeb) believing most lay readers would have better access to them. Sometimes the references to Josephus in this book only follow the general notations given by Maier and/or Whiston in their margins.**

179. Paul Maier, pp. 266-267. See also Origen, *Contra Celsum,* 1.47 (*ANF* 4:416), and Eusebius, *The Nicene and Post Nicene Fathers,* 1:97.

180. Paul Maier, pp. 275-276. Eusebius, *HE 2:23* quotes this Josephus text (*The Nicene and Post-Nicene Fathers,* 1:127) and Origen (A.D. 185-254) knew of it, *Contra Celsum,* 1:47, 2:13 and *Commentary on Matthew* 10:17 (*ANF* 1:416, 437).

181. That James was Jesus' half-brother assumes Mary and Joseph had children after Jesus. He was born of the Virgin Mary and the firstborn in the family. Others conclude references to Jesus' brothers mean "cousins" or that Joseph was a widower with at least six children (four brothers named in Mark 6:3 and Matthew 13:55 with at least plural "sisters") before his later engagement to the Virgin Mary. For scholarly assessments of the options see Richard Bauckham, *Jude and the Relatives of Jesus in the Early Church,* (London and New York: T and T Clark, 2004), p. 19ff. and Hershel Shanks and Ben Witherington III, *The Brother of Jesus,* (San Francisco: Harper San Francisco, 2003), p. 23ff.

182. In 2002 the world was stunned by the announcement of the discovery of the ossuary (bone-box) of "James, son of Joseph, brother of Jesus." Such scholars as Andre Lemaire of the Sorbonne in Paris and Edward Keall of the Toronto Museum stood behind its authenticity. Hershel Shanks, editor of the *Biblical Archaeology Review*, and Ben Witherington III, professor of New Testament at Asbury Seminary (Methodist) wrote a book: *The Brother of Jesus*, San Francisco: Harper San Francisco, 2003. The Geological Survey of the State of Israel gave a report confirming that the ossuary and inscription were ancient. "No sign of the use of a modern tool or instrument was found. No evidence that might detract from the authenticity of the patina and the inscription was found" (see *The Brother of Jesus* p. 18).

Later the Israel Antiquities Authority declared the ossuary a modern fraud and indicted antiquities dealer Oded Golan, the owner of the James ossuary. It seems that the engraving of "James, son of Joseph" is in a different "hand" than the additional phrase "brother of Jesus." Furthermore, the ossuary may have residue of tap water and cleaning solvent.

Defenders of the authenticity of the ossuary maintain their original conclusion. A second engraver need not disprove the ossuary is ancient. Tap water and/or cleaning solvents available anywhere in Israel may have contacted the ossuary in an unprofessional cleaning process. This need not prove the box is modern as the geology experts had concluded the markings were ancient.

Andre Lemaire and Edward Keall "stand by their original findings." (See Witherington, *What Have They Done with Jesus?* p. 322, fn.191, also p. 173.) Witherington writes "I see, nothing, however, at this juncture to cause me to change my earlier conclusion that the James ossuary is what it purports to be – the burial box of James" (Ibid., p. 214).

A DVD of Hershel Shanks giving a lecture on the James ossuary at the Bible Lands Museum on September 1, 2004 is available from the Biblical Archaeology Society (www.biblicalarchaeology.org) . On the cover Shanks explains, "Many people now think it is a forgery simply because the IAA said so. But the IAA never really made its case—and scholars I have challenged on the matter have been unable to defend the IAA decision." The debate over this artifact can be followed further at the *Biblical Archaeology Review* website (www.biblearchaeology.org).

On January 16-18, 2007 BAR hosted the "Jerusalem Forgery Conference." Leading scholars assembled "to consider matters relating to the numerous inscriptions that have been recently alleged to be forgeries. Among these inscriptions are the James Ossuary Inscription . . ." Shanks' "understanding of the overall judgment of the conference" is that "The James Ossuary Inscription is very probably authentic" (pp. 3-5).

The report on the Jerusalem Forgery Conference is available for free download on the *BAR* website.

James K. Hoffmeier (Trinity International Divinity School, near Chicago) writes "Thus, while questions remain, the weight of scholarly opinion seems to be turning in favor of the antiquity of the bone box and its text" (*The Archaeology of the Bible*, p. 168).

The January/February 2009 issue of *Biblical Archaeology Review* contains an article "Forgery Case Collapses" (pp. 12-13). It includes this quote: ". . . on cross-examination Goren was forced to admit that after police had removed this covering, he could see original ancient patina in the critical word 'Jesus.' With that, the case blew up."

183. Paul Maier, p. 265 footnote.

184. F.F. Bruce, *The New Testament Documents: Are They Reliable*,? p. 108 says all extant copies of Josephus have this wording. Maier in his translation of Eusebius says this form of the Josephus text was known "probably before 300" (p. 378, see also Eusebius *HE* 1:11, Maier, p. 46).

185. Origen says Josephus "did not believe in Jesus as the Christ" in *Against Celsus,* 1:47 and in his commentary on Matthew 10:17 (*ANF* 4:416).

186. F.F. Bruce, *Jesus and Christian Origins Outside the New Testament*, p. 39.

187. For further study see F.F. Bruce, *New Testament History*, p. 166; F.F. Bruce, *Jesus and Christian Origins Outside the New Testament*, p. 36ff.; F.F. Bruce, *The New Testament Documents: Are They Reliable?*, p. 108ff.; Paul Barnett, *Is The New Testament Reliable?*, pp. 32-33; Josh McDowell, *He Walked Among Us*, pp. 40-45; *The Zondervan Pictorial Encyclopedia of the Bible*, 3:696-697; Mark D. Roberts, *Can We Trust the Gospels?*, pp. 143-144; Gary Habermas, *The Verdict of History*, pp. 90-93.

188. McDowell, *He Walked Among Us*, p. 45.

189. Paul Maier, *Josephus*, pp. 264-265. Maier also argues for this version in an appendix written at the end of his translation of Eusebius' *Church History*, pp. 377-379. With the final sentence of the Josephus quote Maier follows Jewish scholar Pines. Schlomo Pines, *An Arabic Version of the Testimonium*

Flavianum and Its Implications, (Jerusalem: Israel Academy of Sciences and Humanities, 1971).

190. Ibid.

191. Language from either the Greek or Arabic text of Josephus sometimes points to words used by non-Christians and consistency with Josephus' other writings. Josephus also calls Solomon and Daniel "wise men," but Christians typically claim more for Jesus of Nazareth. Early Christians do not call themselves a "tribe." A Jewish person could write the bare historical data contained in this quote, and it would not be unusual for a non-Christian writer to call Jesus "good" or "virtuous." See sources in endnote 187 for additional arguments that language in the Josephus material about Jesus can fit what is known of Josephus' views and writing style. This is certainly true of the Arabic version and also the Greek version if Bruce's emendations are adopted.

192. Roberts, p.143.

193. Bruce, *Jesus and Origins*, p. 55 dates this quote from the early period and p. 56 gives the quote.

194. The quote may be found in McDowell, *He Walked Among Us*, pp. 67-68.

195. Ibid., p. 68.

196. F.F. Bruce, *Jesus and Christian Origins Outside the New Testament*, pp. 60-61.

197. F.F. Bruce, *The New Testament Documents: Are They Reliable?*, p. 102.

198. Barnett, *Is the New Testament Reliable?*, p. 30.

199. date from Roberts, p. 142. English quote from Tacitus, translated by Michael Grant, *The Annals of Imperial Rome*, New York: Penguin Books, 1982.

200. English translation from F.F. Bruce, *Jesus and Origins,* pp. 25-27. Bruce dates this letter in A.D. 111. Habermas dates it to A.D. 112 (p. 94). Trajan's reply was:

"My dear Secundus: You have acted with perfect correctness in declaring the cases of those who have been charged before you with being Christians. Indeed, no general decision can be made by which a set form of dealing with them could be established. They must not be ferreted out; if they are charged and convicted, they must be punished, provided that anyone who denies that he is a Christian and gives practical proof of that by invoking our gods is to be pardoned on the strength of this repudiation, no matter what grounds for suspicion may have existed against him in the past. Anonymous documents which are laid before you should receive no attention in any case; they form a very bad precedent and are quite unworthy of the age in which we live" (Bruce, *Jesus and Origins*, p. 27).

201. Barnett, p. 27. See *ANF*, 3:45.

202. Suetonius, translated by Robert Graves, *The Twelve Caesers,* New York: Penguin Books, 1981, p. 202.

203. Roberts, p. 141.

204. F.F. Bruce, *Jesus and Origins*, p. 21.

205. Suetonius, translated by Robert Graves, p. 221.

206. Additional authors probably refer to Christ or to Gospel events. As these references often only exist in secondary quotes because the originals have not been preserved or are in documents with disputed dates, we will place them within an endnote.

Thallus in about A.D. 52 seems to have mentioned Jesus' crucifixion and the darkness that covered the land during that event. Julius Africanus in A.D. 221 claimed Thallus tried to give a natural explanation of this darkness, but Africanus objected to a naturalistic explanation of this darkness because an eclipse can not occur at the time of Passover (a full moon). See Bruce, *Jesus and Origins,* p. 30 and *The New Testament Documents*, p. 113.

Another author, Plegon, was born about A.D. 80 and wrote about A.D. 140. Julius Africanus said Plegon also reported a darkness in the afternoon. Origen adds that Plegon wrote of the earthquake at Jesus' crucifixion and that Jesus made predictions (*Against Celsus* 2.14, 2.33, 2.59), see *ANF* 4:437, 445, 455.

Paul Maier in his historical novel *Pontius Pilate* gives this footnote on page 366:

THE DARKNESS AT THE CRUCIFIXION: This phenomenon, evidently, was visible in Rome, Athens, and other Mediterranean cities. According to Tertullian, *Apologeticus*, XXI, 20, it was a "cosmic" or "world event." Phlegon, a Greek author from Caria writing a chronology soon after 137 A.D., reported that in the fourth year of the 202nd Olympiad (i.e., 33 A.D.) there was "the greatest eclipse of the sun," and that "it became night in the sixth hour of the day [i.e. noon] so that stars even appeared in the heavens. There was a great earthquake in Bithynia, and many things were overturned in Nicaea." – Fragment from the 13th book of Phlegon, *Olympiades he Chronika*, ed. By Otto Keller, *Rerum Naturalium Scriptores Graeci Minores* I, (Leipzig: Teubner, 1877), p. 101. Trans. Mine."

Church historian Eusebius in his *History of the Church* (*HE* 4.9) quotes a letter from Emperor Hadrian about the Christians. This letter was sent to yet another governor of the province of Asia (see Habermas, p. 97).

Two additional writers are often mentioned in Jesus studies from non-Christian sources. Lucian a Greek satirist wrote about A.D. 170. He mocked Christians but in the process refers to Jesus' crucifixion and Christian beliefs about the after-life, the worship of Christ, and that all Christians are brothers. His satire reminds us of the 3rd century graffiti where one in a crude picture worships a crucified man on a cross with an ass head (see *Eerdman's Handbook to the History of Christianity*, p. 57).

Mar Bar Serapion wrote a letter to his son that can be dated after the Romans destroyed Judea (after A.D. 73) but can also be dated as late as the 2nd or 3rd century. He was not a Christian but blames Jewish dispersion for "executing their wise king" (Habermas, p. 101). Early Christian writers assume that Pilate's official records still existed in Rome in the 2nd and early 3rd century, but we have no trace of them (see Justin Martyr, *First Apology* 35.7-9 and 48:3 (*ANF* 1:175 and 179); Tertullian *Apology*, V.2 (*ANF* 3:21-22); F.F. Bruce, *Origins*, pp. 19-20; or Habermas, p. 107.

For further research on the ancient writings mentioned either in the main text or this footnote see: F.F. Bruce, *Origins*, pp. 19-31 and pp. 54-65; F.F. Bruce, *New Testament Documents*, pp. 100-120; Gary Habermas, *The Verdict of History*, pp. 87-115; Mark Roberts, pp. 140-144; Paul Barnett, *Is the New Testament Reliable?*, pp. 22-34.

207. Barnett, *Is The New Testament Reliable?*, pp. 24-25. This square puzzle has also been found as far away as Dura-Europos in Mesopotamia and Cirencester, England. House walls in Pompeii show signs that a wooden cross had been nailed on the wall. (See *Eerdman's Handbook to the History of Christianity*, p. 55.)

208. Of course, leaders such as Peter, Paul, and John and many others are mentioned in the early church fathers from the very beginning of Christianity. *Biblical Archaeology Review*, January – February, 2000, p. 14 features a small and partial fragment from first or second century in Cyprus that may be reconstructed as "The Apostle Paul."

209. Barnett, p. 160; Craig A. Evans, in *Jesus and Archaeology*, edited by James H. Charlesworth (Princeton), p. 340.

210. Another relevant artifact to this time period may have been the Nazareth Decree. "The Nazareth Decree" was found in 1878. While the date and place are in dispute, some scholars argue for an origin in Nazareth and a date during Claudius' rule. E.M. Blaiklock, Professor of Classics, University of Auckland, concluded this decree is the first Imperial response to the story of the resurrection of Jesus. Based upon the charge of grave robbing, the emperor issued this prohibition and placed the slab in Nazareth. "It consists of a score of lines of irregular Greek, which had been set up at Nazareth, in all probability somewhere a little before the year A.D. 50. The text runs:

> Ordinance of Caesar. It is my pleasure that graves and tombs remain undisturbed in perpetuity for those who have made them for the cult of their ancestors, or children, or members of their house. If, however, any man lay information that another has either demolished them, or has in any way extracted the buried, or has maliciously transferred them to other places in order to wrong them, or has displaced the sealing or other stones, against such a one I order that a trial be instituted, as in respect of the gods, so in regard to the cult of mortals. For it shall be much more obligatory to honor the buried. Let it be absolutely forbidden for anyone to disturb them. In the case of contravention I desire that the offender be sentenced to capital punishment on charge of violation of sepulture."

See Blaicklock in *The Zondervan Pictorial Encyclopedia of the Bible* 4:391-392 and Blaicklock *The Dictionary of Biblical Archaeology*, pp. 330-331. See also Paul Maier, *The Flames of Rome*, (Wheaton: Tyndale House, 1987) p. 478 who agrees that this slab comes from Nazareth and dates from Claudius.

Chapter 10 - Gospel People Also Mentioned in Non-Christian Sources: Jewish and Roman Leaders

211. Maier, *Josephus*, p. 262.

212. Ibid., pp. 275-276, see also 266.

213. Hershel Shanks gives a picture of a tomb on page 188. "The high priest Annas (6-15 C.E.) was probably buried in this tomb" (Shanks, *Jerusalem,* p. 189).

214. Maier, *Josephus*, p. 262.

215. Ibid., p. 266.

216. Zvi Greenhut, "Burial Cave of the Caiaphas Family," *Biblical Archaeology Review* 18.5 (September/October 1992): 28-44, 76. See also Hershel Shanks, editor, *Where Christianity was Born*, pp. 146-163.

217. Hershel Shanks, *Jerusalem: An Archaeological Biography*, p. 189. The next two pages give pictures of this ossuary, pp. 190-191.

218. e.g. Tom Mueller, "The Holy Land's Visionary Builder." *National Geographic*, December 2008, vol. 214 no. 6, (Washington, D.C.: National Geographic Society), p. 42. "Herod is best known for slaughtering every male infant in Bethlehem in an attempt to kill Jesus. He is almost certainly innocent of this crime."

219. Peter Richardson's *Herod King of the Jews and Friend of the Romans* contains 318 pages of fine print. Shorter accounts may be found in Harold Hoehner's article on Herod in *The Zondervan Pictorial Encyclopedia of the Bible*, 3:126-145 and *Dictionary of Jesus and the Gospels*, 317-326.

220. Peter Richardson, pp. 197-202, for more research on Herod's buildings see Ritmeyer, Leen and Kathleen. *Secrets of Jerusalem's Temple Mount.* Washington, D.C.: Biblical Archaeology Society, 2006; *Archaeology and the Bible: The Best of BAR.* Volume Two. Washington D.C.; Biblical Archaeology Society, 1990; McRay, John. *Archaeology and the New Testament.* Grand Rapids: Baker Book House, 1991; Finegan, Jack. *The Archaeology of the New Testament.* Princeton: The Princeton University Press, 1992. These sources not only discuss New Testament places but also reveal some of the mysteries about how ancient people could build such structures as Herod's work on the Temple in Jerusalem.

221. Richardson, p. 248. Hoehner in *Dictionary of Jesus and the Gospels*, p. 320.

222. Richardson, p. 298 fn. 15.

223. David Hendin, *Guide to Biblical Coins*, p. 64.

224. Josephus, Whiston translation, pp. 364-365, Maier p. 252, Josephus, *Antiquities*, 17.146/17.6.2-3.

225. Richardson, pp. 203-211. At least 34 total inscriptions counting duplicates.

226. Ibid., 177.

227. Ibid.

228. Ibid., 166. See also Maier, *Josephus* p. 380. Josephus said Herod built Masada in part to protect himself from Cleopatra who wanted Anthony to kill him so she could rule Judea.

229. See Richardson, pp. 43-51.

230. Amarillo Globe News, *"Israelis: Herod's Tomb Discovered,"* May 9, 2007. For documentation of facts in the above section see Josephus in the Whiston translation, pp. 297-367, 439-470, especially 317, 318, 322, 326, 316, 355, 366, 305, 314, 316-319, 469. On Herod and Anthony/Cleopatra see 316-319, on surrender and switch of loyalty to Augustus see 324, on hatred by Jews for introduction of pagan customs into the land see 328, 329, 333-334, 343.

231. Maier, p. 252. Herod's death and funeral is described in Maier, pp. 252-254, Josephus, *Antiquities*, 17:146ff.

232. See also *Strabo* 16.2.46 and *Dio Cassius* 55.27.6. In the Maier translation Josephus refers to Archelaus on pp. 253, 255-259, 262. *The Dictionary of Biblical Archaeology*, p. 235 mentions that Archelaus' name also appears on an inscription.

233. Maier, p. 262. Josephus, *Antiquities*, 18.26.

234. Hoehner, *The Zondervan Pictorial Encyclopedia of the Bible*, 3:143.

235. Ibid., also Josephus *Antiquities*, 18.5.4/18.137.

236. Another "Herod-Philip" was the first husband to Herodias not to be confused with Philip the tetrarch. She left this Philip in order to marry Herod Antipas (Matthew 14:3; Mark 6:17-29; and Luke 3:19). For study on the these two Philips see Harold Hoehner, *Herod Antipas: A Contemporary of Jesus Christ*, pp. 131-136. For Salome being wife to Philip the tetrarch see Josephus

Antiquities 18.5.4, i.e. the Whiston translation, p. 383. See Richardson, *Herod,* p. 301 fn. 32 for classical references to Philip.

237. Agrippa the First's time extends past the time of the Gospels. He was Herodias' brother and had been a boyhood friend of Gaius (the future emperor Caligula). Overhearing Agrippa say Gaius would make a better emperor than Tiberius, Tiberius had Agrippa put in chains. Agrippa and Gaius waited on the island of Capri for Tiberius to die. Josephus records one of Gaius' (Caligula) first decisions as new emperor. "One of Gaius' early acts was to put a diadem on Agrippa's head and appoint him king over the tetrarchy of Philip. He also gave him a golden chain equal in weight to the iron one that had bound him and Agrippa returned home in triumph" (Josephus *Antiquities,* 18.143, Maier p. 268). Later the arrogant Agrippa made a speech in the Caesarean theater. Because he would not reject people flattering him as a god, he died. It is amazing that this speech and death are recorded both in Acts 12:20-23 and Josephus! (See Maier p. 272).

238. Josephus, *Antiquities* 18.106 (Maier p. 266) calls the first husband "Herod." He is "Philip" in Matthew 14:3 and Mark 6:17. Luke 3:19 just says brother.

239. See Hoehner's argument that Herodias' first husband's full name was Herod Philip (not to be identified with Philip the tetrarch) in *Herod Antipas,* pp. 131-136; The *Zondervan Pictorial Encyclopedia of the Bible,* 3:140-141; and *Dictionary of Jesus and the Gospels,* pp. 323-324. The Kregel edition of Whiston's *Josephus* also deals with this subject in the footnote on p. 382. The alternative conclusion would be to identify Herodias' first husband Philip with Philip the tetrarch, but we know the tetrarch was married to Herodias' daughter, Salome (Whiston's *Josephus,* p. 383). Thus, a differentiation of the Philips is preferable (though given the contemptable nature of the Herodian family tree we could wonder whether in such a family it would be possible for a man to marry both a mother and then a daughter). Hyphenated names in the Herodian family are reasonable as in Herod-Antipas or Herod-Agrippa. The first husband was likely a Herod-Philip.

240. Hoehner in *Dictionary of Jesus and the Gospels,* p. 323.

241. *Josephus,* Whiston translation, p. 383. (*Antiquities,* 18.5.4)

242. Ibid.

243. *Josephus,* Whiston, p. 382. (*Antiquities,* 18.5.1)

244. *Josephus,* Maier translation, pp. 256, 259.

245. Hoehner, *Dictionary of Jesus and the Gospels*, p. 323. See also Maier, p. 262 on Sepphoris, Josephus, *Antiquities,* 18.26.

246. on Tiberias, see also Maier's translation, p. 262.

247. *The Dictionary of Biblical Archaeology*, p. 235.

248. Hoehner, *Antipas*, pp. 303-306 and 303 fn. 2.

249. Hoehner discusses both Philo's information on the conflict between Pilate and the Herod family and the fall of Sejanus in *Herod Antipas*, pp. 176-183. Paul Maier also links the hatred between Antipas and Pilate to the incident of the golden shields mentioned by Philo and the need for Pilate to reconcile after the fall of Sejanus. Paul Maier, *In the Fullness of Time*, pp. 149, 157, 346 fn. 4, Maier, *Pontius Pilate*, p. 362.

250. See Hoehner, "*Pontius Pilate*," in *Dictionary of Jesus and the Gospels*, pp. 615-616.

"Philo, who extols Tiberius's liberal policy toward the Jews, records the episode when Pilate had set up gilded votive shields bearing the name, though not the image, of the emperor in the former palace of Herod in Jerusalem .... when he refused to hear their request, they wrote to the Emperor Tiberius. Upon receiving the letter, Tiberius was enraged and immediately replied, ordering Pilate to remove the shields from Jerusalem and place them in the temple of Augustus at Caesarea (*Leg. Gai.* 299-305). Unlike the previous incident of the standards, prominent Jews and Herod's sons were able now to write directly to Tiberius, an event made possible by Sejanus's execution by Tiberius on October 18, A.D. 31. Tiberius was now trying to reverse Sejanus's anti-Semitic policies and hence gave a quick response to the Jews' request.

But why would Pilate have done such a thing when he had already been defeated in the incident of the standards? It seems that with the removal of his mentor Sejanus, whose anti-Semitic policies he had followed, Pilate wanted to dissociate himself from Sejanus and ingratiate himself with Tiberius. Consequently, he brought into Jerusalem shields that had no image but bore the name of the emperor. But the plan backfired and Tiberius was sorely displeased. The most likely time for this incident to have occurred is at a Jewish festival when the sons of Herod would have been in Jerusalem, possibly the Feast of Tabernacles in A.D. 32."

On Sejanus and Pilate, see also F.F. Bruce, *New Testament History*, pp. 35-36, 201 fn. 30 and 226.

251. *Josephus*, Maier translation, pp. 268-269. Josephus, *Antiquities*, 18.143ff.

252. The Maier translation says Lyons, Gaul. Richardson says the original is Lugdunum in Gaul and agrees with the location of modern Lyon on the Rhone River. However, there was also a Lugdunum near the border with Spain. According to Josephus, *War*, 2.183 Antipas was banished to Spain. Richardson concedes this "might have been meant" (p. 313). Hoehner in *Dictionary of Jesus and the Gospels*, p. 325, opts for the alternative "Lugdunum Convenarum, now Saint-Bertrand de Comminges in southern France in the foothills of the Pyrenees."

253. For a brief but excellent study of other details on Quirinius' life see E.M. Blaiklock (University of Auckland, New Zealand) in *The Zondervan Pictorial Encyclopedia of the Bible*, 5:5-6; see also F.F. Bruce in *The New Bible Dictionary*, pp. 993-994; Ben Witherington III in *Dictionary of Jesus and the Gospels*, pp. 67-68; and Darrell Bock in Luke in the *Baker Exegetical Commentary on the New Testament*, 1:903-909.

254. See Maier translation pp. 260, 262, 273, 286, 377. See also *Antiquities*, 17.355 and *Wars*, 7.252.

255. Maier, p. 260.

256. Bock, *Luke*, 1:202.

257. Witherington, *Dictionary of Jesus and the Gospels*, p. 67.

258. See John McRay, *Archaeology of the New Testament*, p. 154-155. He further explains on p. 155:

"There is a form in the British Museum dated by George Milligan and Adolf Deissmann to A.D. 104. Although we have nothing as yet from the years 90 and 76, there is one from 62. Another is dated by Milligan to 48, and yet another dates to 34. A fifth census form, although it contains no date, is considered by its editor to have been produced in 20. Acts 5:37 and Josephus in *Antiquities* refer to another in the year 6, to which year B.P. Grenfell and A.S. Hunt date Oxyrhynchus papyrus 256. Finally, Tertullian records a census when Sentius Saturnius (9-6 B.C.) was governor of Syria, which would have been in the year 9 B.C. according to the fourteen-year cycle established by the dated papyri. This census suggests the possibility of an earlier date for the birth of

Jesus than is commonly assumed. Vardaman argues for 11 or 10 B.C. at the latest; however, a census begun in Syria in 9 B.C. may have taken a long time to be completed in Palestine. It is clear that Jesus was born during an official imperial decree of Caesar Augustus (see Luke 2:1), and the fourteen-year cycle for such censuses suggests a date around 9 B.C. What is not clear is whether the census noted by Luke was part of the cycle or was a special one. The archaeological data seems to indicate an ordinary imperial census."

259. The following are two quotes from McRay, p. 155:

"Two census orders that have been found show an interesting correlation with the wording of the birth narrative of Jesus. One, British Museum papyrus 904, is from the year A.D. 104.

'Gaius Vibius Maximus, Prefect of Egypt [says]: Seeing that the time has come for the house to house census, it is necessary to compel all those who for any cause whatsoever are residing out of their provinces to return to their own homes [emphasis added], that they may both carry out the regular order of the census and may also attend diligently to the cultivation of their allotments.'

The second, Oxyrhynchus papyrus 255, is a census return from the year A.D. 48, the ninth year of Claudius: 'I the above-mentioned Thermoutharion along with my guardian the said Apollonius swear by Tiberius Claudius Caesar Augustus Germanicus Emperor that assuredly the preceding document makes a sound and true return of those living with me [emphasis added], and that there is no one else living with me, neither a stranger, nor an Alexandrian citizen, nor a freedman, nor a Roman citizen, nor an Egyptian in addition to the aforesaid. If I am swearing truly, may it be well with me, but if falsely, the reverse. In the ninth year of Tiberius Claudius Caesar Augustus Germanicus Emperor.' "

I own a home in Texas but am heir to the family home in Michigan. Which is home? This type of issue explains a census in which those in Israel had to return home, especially during the transition when Galilee would remain Herodian but Judea would now be ruled by Roman governors.

260. F.F. Bruce, *New Bible Dictionary*, p. 994.

261. McRay, p. 154. Vardaman's work is also mentioned in Craig Blomberg, *The Historical Reliability of the Gospels*, pp. 195-196.

Endnotes

262. See Harold Hoehner, *Chronological Aspects of the Life of Christ*, pp. 21-22. Hoehner gives an excellent treatment of the Quirinius Census on pp. 13-23. In *New Testament History,* F.F. Bruce also favors this translation, p. 32 fn. 1.

263. Bruce, *New Bible Dictionary*, p.993; Barnett, *Is the New Testament Reliable?*, p. 101.

264. In *Dictionary of Jesus and the Gospels*, Witherington, pp. 67-68 writes. "We also know that Quirinius undertook more than one census during his governorship, and that he did not scruple to enroll a basically autonomous group such as the Apameans . . . . We know also that Quirinius had been made consul in 12 B.C., and a person of his rank serving in the East frequently had far-reaching authority and duties. It is thus not improbable that, acting as Caesar's agent, he had Herod take a census . . . the possibility also remains that Luke may be identifying him by his later and, to his audience, more familiar office." Barnett (p. 101) says, "There is a parallel example of a census in the kingdom of Cappadocia ruled by Archelaus, a relative of Herod's . . ." Tacitus' *Annals* 6.41 says that "a tribe subject to the Cappodocian prince Archelaus the younger, resisted compulsion to supply property-returns and taxes in Roman fashion by withdrawing to the heights of the Taurus mountains . . . " (English trans. in Penguin Classics, p. 221). The account continues to report that Roman general, Marcus Trebellius, either was called in by client-king Archelaus or else just acted on his own to force surrender and then taxation. This was A.D. 36 but illustrates that a Roman leader in the East would step in to collect taxes in client kingdoms. It is possible that Quirinius as a high ranking consul in the East ordered a census in the waning days of King Herod and only later served as governor of Syria for yet another census in A.D. 6.

265. See *New Bible Dictionary*, p. 708; Bock, *Luke*, 1:283.

266. Hiebert, in *The Zondervan Pictorial Encyclopedia of the Bible*, 3:1013. Also, *The New Bible Dictionary*, p. 708. "His name appears on an inscription of Abila dated between A.D. 14 and 29, recording a temple dedication by a freedman of Lysanias the tetrarch (*CIG*, 4521).

267. Harold Mare on p. 294 (*CIG*, 4523). It is significant that Mare has worked on excavations in the Decapolis. See also Bock, *Luke*, 1:283. ". . . other inscriptions . . . attest to a later Lysanias who lived at the time of Tiberius."

268. McRay, *Archaeology of the New Testament*, p. 160.

269. Hiebert, *The Zondervan Pictorial Encyclopedia of the Bible*, 3:1013.

270. Bock, *Luke*, 1:283. See also Josephus, *Antiquities*, 18.6, 10; and *War*, 2.11.5

271. Maier, translation of *Josephus*, p. 271 *Antiquities*, 19.212ff.

272. See Kenneth G. Holum, Robert L. Hohlfelder, Robert J. Bull, Avner Raban, *King Herod's Dream: Caesarea on the Sea*, p. 110; Paul L. Maier, *In the Fullness of Time*, p. 147; F.F. Bruce, *In the Steps of the Apostle Paul*, p. 54; Randall Price, *The Stones Cry Out*, p. 308.

273. See *The New Bible Dictionary* which shows how the Greek word for "governor" used in the Gospels equates with "prefect" and that the Gospels are more technically correct than Tacitus or Josephus, p. 929. Maier, *In the Fullness of Time*, p. 146 and Hoehner in *Dictionary of Jesus and the Gospels*, p. 615 both conclude "prefect" has more military duties. Maier says, "It was only later, under the emperor Claudius, that the title of Roman governors in Judea shifted to procurator."

274. I own both of these coins. For these conclusions, see *The New Bible Dictionary*, p. 929.

275. Maier, *In the Fullness of Time*, p. 146.

276. Maier, *In the Fullness of Time*, p. 159.

277. For evidence here are my own notes used in leading a tour to Israel, p. 56:

> "At His trial Jesus was led to the Praetorium to be judged by Pilate. The place for this trial shown to visitors today is usually the pavement under the sisters of Zion Convent thought to be the spot for the Fortress of Antonia. However, another site in Jerusalem was a better place for Jesus' trial. Today it is called the Citadel after the Turkish towers and walls, but in Jesus' time this was the site of Herod's Palace. In the Lord's time the palace of Herod the Great had been taken over by the Roman government. Philo, a Jewish historian, who lived the same time as Jesus, wrote that the Roman governors lived in Herod's palace. He said that the Jews protested because Pilate hung golden shields (with the emperor's name but not his image) in Herod's palace which he also called "the house of the governors" (*Delegation to Gaius* 38). Josephus writes of a later governor, Gessius Florus, who held his tribunal just outside Herod's palace (*War*, 2.14.8/301-302). Furthermore, Mark 15:16 states, 'And the soldiers took Him away into the **palace** (that is,

the Praetorium) . . .' Pilate's wife stayed with Pilate in Jerusalem for the fateful Passover season. Is it more likely she resided in Herod's Palace or the soldier's barracks in the Antonia Fortress? Herod's Palace was larger than the later Citadel. It had three towers, Hippicus (named for Herod's friend), Phasael (named for Herod's brother) and Mariamme (named for Herod's favorite wife whom he later executed). Archaeologists have found foundation walls from Herod's time beneath the Citadel. The most interesting feature of the citadel is the middle tower. To the east of the modern Jaffa gate stands a tower 66'x 66' square and 66' high. Josephus had said it was 40 cubits in all three dimensions. Authorities disagree as to whether this is Phasael or Hippicus, but all agree it is a tower still remaining from Herod's palace. Today, the Jews call it David's Tower. (See also Maier, *In the Fullness of Time*, p. 149.)

278. Philo as quoted in *The Zondervan Pictorial Encyclopedia of the Bible*, 4:791.

279. Maier, Josephus translation, pp. 263-264.

280. Maier, Ibid., gives a picture of ruins from Pilate's aqueduct. *Jerusalem An Archaeological Biography*, p. 124 has a picture of pools south of Bethlehem from which water was carried by gravity to Jerusalem to the Temple Mount.

281. Maier, Ibid., 264.

282. See above section on Herod Antipas and scholars from footnotes 249 and 250.

283. Hoehner, in *Dictionary of Jesus and the Gospels*, p. 615. On the next page, 616, Hoehner continues:

"If Jesus was crucified in A.D. 33, the removal of Pilate's mentor Sejanus, and his failure to ingratiate himself with the emperor, may have broken Pilate's backbone and left him fighting for political survival . . . . Hoehner continues: "If Jesus was crucified in A.D. 33, the reconciliation of the enmity between Pilate and Herod Antipas becomes more historically realistic. The Jews, having only recently received the news of Sejanus's death (possibly during the winter of 32/33 or early 33), threatened Pilate that if he did not release Jesus, he was not a friend of Caesar (Jn. 19:12). Pilate realized the reverse of this was that the Jews would regard him as still being a friend of Sejanus and/or friendly toward his policies which Tiberius had now repudiated. Hence

Pilate's compliance with the Jews during the trial of Jesus would be fully understandable in light of recent events that made him more cautious."

284. F.F. Bruce, *New Testament History*, p. 35. Also, on page 35 fn. 11, Bruce notes that Philo's comments about Sejanus' anti-Semitism are immediately followed by reference to Pilate's misdeeds regarding the Temple. On page 36, Bruce again, "Even so, Philo has probably some factual basis for attributing an anti-Jewish policy to Sejanus, and if he was indeed Pilate's patron, Pilate would have certainly felt defenseless after Sejanus' fall in A.D. 31. This situation would have made him particularly sensitive to the chief priest's scarcely veiled menace" (i.e., John 19:12). On page 201 fn. 20, we find "Pilate's position was perhaps the more delicate, as he may have owed his influence to Sejanus' influence." Again on page 226 Sejanus is called Pilate's "patron."

285. Hoehner, *Herod Antipas*, p. 178.

286. Maier, *In the Fullness of Time*, p. 149. See also p. 157 ". . . Antipas had brutally embarrassed Pilate by forwarding a letter of protest over his head to the emperor in the case of the golden shields." Paul Maier, *Harvard Theological Review*, 62, 1969, pp. 109ff.

287. Hoehner, in *Dictionary of Jesus and the Gospels*, pp. 615-616.

288. Vos in *The Zondervan Pictorial Encyclopedia of the Bible*, 4:792.

289. Maier, *Pontius Pilate*, p. 360.

290. Maier, Josephus translation, p. 266.

291. Maier, *In the Fullness of Time*, p.152., see pp. 152-153.

292. Ibid., Maier, translation of Eusebius, p. 65 and 65 fn. 9.

293. See Origen, *Contra Celsum*, 2.34 who does not mention suicide (*ANF* 4:445) and Tertullian who felt Pilate "was a Christian in his conscience" (Maier, *In the Fullness of Time*, p. 153). Greek orthodoxy canonized Procula, and the Ethiopian church thinks both were saints.

294. Maier, *In the Fullness of Time*, p. 153.

295. All existing documents purporting to be Pilate's reports to Emperor Tiberius are fictional though he probably did write such reports, and a few

church fathers assumed they could be read in Rome by government leaders. See *The Zondervan Pictorial Encyclopedia of the Bible*, 4:789-790.

Chapter 11 - Places in the Gospels

296. Excellent archaeology resources include:

Archaeology of the New Testament by John McRay; *The Archaeology of the New Testament* by Jack Finegan; *Where Christianity was Born* edited by Hershel Shanks and also *Archaeology in the World of Herod, Jesus, and Paul* edited by Shanks. Both contain important articles on the New Testament from the journal *Biblical Archaeology Review*. *The Zondervan Pictorial Encyclopedia of the Bible, The New Bible Dictionary,* and the *Wycliff Bible Encyclopedia* are all helpful references on Bible places. Also, good for Bible places are *In the Steps of Our Lord* and *In the Steps of the Apostle Paul* by F.F. Bruce, *In the Fullness of Time* by Paul Maier, and *Jerusalem: An Archaeological Biography* by Hershel Shanks. For studies on the Temple, see also Leen and Kathleen Ritmeyer, *Secrets of the Temple Mount.*

297. See Finegan pp. 29-42, especially pp. 32 and 35.

298. Justin Martyr, *Dialogue with the Jew Trypho*, 78. (*ANF* 1:237).

299. See Finegan p. 30, (*ANF* 4:418).

300. Maier, *In the Fullness of Time,* p. 38.

301. McRay, pp. 156-157.

302. McRay, p. 163; Finegan, p. 101, ". . . perhaps about the middle of the third century . . ." This town was identified as Capernaum only in 1865-1866 with the synagogue being excavated in 1905 (Finegan, p. 99).

303. McRay, pp. 163-164.

304. Shanks and Strange, *Where Christianity was Born*, p. 77.

305. Total count from Finegan, p. 108.

306. See Finegan, pp. 108-110; McRay 165; Maier, *Fullness*, p. 103; Shanks and Strange, *Archaeology in the World of Herod, Jesus, and Paul*, pp. 188-199 and also *Where Christianity was Born*, pp. 66-78. *Biblical Archaeology Review*, Nov.-Dec. 1982 and Nov.-Dec. 1983 also concern Capernaum.

307. Maier, *Fullness*, p. 103; Charlesworth *Jesus Within Judaism*, p. 112 cited by McRay, p. 164; Charlesworth, *Jesus and Archaeology*, p. 50; von Wahlde, *Jesus and Archaeology*, p. 546 (see also 528 fn. 8); Finegan, p. 109; Shanks and Strange, *Where Christianity was Born*, p. 78.

308. Finegan, p. 238.

309. Ibid., p. 233.

310. Rainer Riesner (Tubingen, Germany) in *Dictionary of Jesus and the Gospels*, p. 42.

311. McRay, *Archaeology and the New Testament,* p. 203.

312. McRay, p. 214.

313. See Finegan for details pp. 261-268. My tour notes simplify and condense pp. 58-62.

314. Shanks and Strange, *Where Christianity was Born*, p. 184; Maier, *In the Fullness of Time*, p. 169; Shanks, *Jerusalem*, p. 202; McRay pp. 214-215; von Wahlde, *Jesus and Archaeology,* pp. 576-582. For further study on the place of Jesus' cross and tomb see Finegan 261-268.

315. Shanks, *Jerusalem*, p. 202.

316. "This is consistent with the identification of the tomb [Nicodemus' tomb/then also Jesus' tomb] as hewn from rock . . . . The identification of the place as like a skull also reflects knowledge that the area where the crucifixion took place was a protruding, bare, and rocky area, probably a hillock not quarried because of the poor quality of the stone there" (von Wahlde, *Jesus and Archaeology*, p. 578).

317. Dan Bahat, *Holy Sepulchre – Jesus' Tomb* in *Where Chrisianity was Born*, p. 184. Of course, Bahat also says one can not be "absolutely certain." We should note here Bahat's material that El-Hakim's destruction of the church in 1009 still left the rotunda over Jesus' tomb preserved to "about five feet" (p. 189). Thus, original rock from Jesus' tomb may still be beneath the rebuilt rotunda (also called *Anastasis*).

318. Finegan, McRay, *The Zondervan Pictorial Encyclopedia of the Bible, The New Bible Dictionary* or good commentaries on John would also be helpful on these Bible places.

319. Urban C. von Wahlde, "Archaeology in John's Gospel" in *Jesus and Archaeology*, edited by James H. Charlesworth, p. 526. The complete study is pp. 523-586.

320. Ibid.

321. Ibid., pp. 533-538.

322. Ibid., pp. 538-542. According to von Wahlde, p. 540 fn. 41 the definitive study on the location of Cana is by Julian Herrojo who is with the Spanish Institute of the Bible and Archaeology in Jerusalem. The book was published in Paris in 1999.

323. Josephus, *Antiquities*, 18.3/38; *Life*, 85; and *War* 2.614.

324. Josephus in *War* 3.3.2 mentions many of the towns around the Sea of Galilee had far over 15,000 inhabitants. *The Zondervan Pictorial Encyclopedia of the Bible*, 2:646 concludes there were nine such cities; it identifies eight: Tiberius, Magdala, Chorazin, Bethsaida, Hippos, Capernaum, Gadara, and Kinneret.

325. von Wahlde, p. 557.

326. McRay, pp. 179-183.

327. von Wahlde, p. 571.

328. Shanks, *Jerusalem*, p. 155.

329. Ibid., p. 156.

330. Anderson in *Jesus and Archaeology*, pp. 591-592; see also Maier, *In the Fullness of Time*, p. 120 for stables under the Temple.

331. von Wahlde, p. 550.

332. Friedberg, *Coins of the Bible*, p. 40.

333. von Wahlde, p. 570.

334. See the appendix for a possible connection between abortion and the custom of regarding gentile houses as unclean (pp. 241).

335. von Wahlde, pp. 573-575, quote from p. 575.

336. McRay, p. 119.

337. See von Wahlde, p. 561 fn. 112.

338. Ibid., p. 562.

339. Ibid., fn. 115.

340. Ibid., p. 563.

341. Ibid., p. 564.

342. Ibid., p.566.

343. Ibid., p. 583. The other two sites which remain difficult to pinpoint are Bethany beyond the Jordan and Aenon near Salim. These have possible but not definitive locations.

344. Ibid., pp. 582-583.

345. Paul N. Anderson, "Aspects to Historicity in the Gospel of John" in *Jesus and Archaeology*, p. 599. Here we follow his work which may be consulted for even more details in John.

346. Nathaniel was from Cana (21:2), Judas from Kerioth (6:71, 12:4, 13:2), Mary from Magdala (19:25-26, 20:1, 18), Joseph from Arimathea (19:38).

347. Anderson, p. 614.

348. See Maier, *Josephus*, pp. 224, 274, 283, 341, 347, 376 for examples. See also Price, *The Stones Cry Out*, pp. 308, 423 fn. 25-28.

349. Barnett, *Is the New Testament Reliable?*, p. 161.

350. Shanks, *Where Christianity was Born*, p. 173.

351. See McRay, pp. 204-206; Anderson in *Jesus and Archaeology*, p.593. For pictures see *Where Christianity was Born*, pp.170-173; Price, *The Stones Cry Out*, p. 309.

352. See *The Zondervan Pictorial Encyclopedia of the Bible*; *The New Bible Dictionary*; or *Wycliff Bible Encyclopedia*; F.F. Bruce, *The New Testament Documents: Are They Reliable?*; or Barnett, *Is The New Testament Reliable?* Excellent commentaries on Acts include those by Darrell Bock, F.F. Bruce, or

Homer Kent. All the items in these lists are also referenced in my own Christian Evidences notes.

353. Ovid, *Metamorphoses*, VIII, 626ff.

354. Josephus, *Antiquities,* 20.2.5; 20.5.2; 19.8.2; Seutonius, *The Twelve Caesars*, *Claudius*, 25.

355. Homer Kent, *Jerusalem to Rome*, p. 116.

356. See F.F. Bruce, *New Testament Documents*, p. 85 on Cicero. For other details see references in endnote 352.

Chapter 12 – Jesus, History and Misracles

357. Dr. John Whitcomb told me that when he was a student at Princeton Albert Einstein attended all the showings and discussions of the Moody science films about creation.

358. John Warwick Montgomery, *Where Is History Going: A Christian Response to Secular Philosophies of History* (Minneapolis: Bethany Fellowship Inc., 1969) p. 71; see also John Warwick Montgomery, *Faith Founded Upon Fact: Essays in Evidential Apologetics*. Nashville: Thomas Nelson Publishers, 1978, pp. 43-73.

359. After this Jesus countered with the logic quoted by Abraham Lincoln, "A house divided against itself can not stand" (Matthew 12:25; Mark 3:25). Satan would not be the power source for exorcisms and healings.

360. Early extra-biblical sources often classify Jesus as a sorcerer or magician. At the very least, this means Jesus could dazzle people with wonders and tricks. Using the Gospels as a guide these may also be intended as hints that ancient non-Christian people conceded the point that Jesus had supernatural abilities. They still did not believe His power came from God. Believing Jesus' name has magic powers, one ancient pagan exorcism formula contained the phrase, ". . . I conjure you by the God of the Hebrews, Jesus . . ." (see Evans, *Fabricating Jesus*, p. 157). Josephus in the Greek textual tradition calls Jesus "the achiever of extraordinary deeds (*Antiquities*, 18.63, Maier translation, p. 265). If we adopt the Arabic textual tradition, then the same passage may still contain a reference to Jesus' ability to amaze people, ". . . concerning whom the prophets have reported wonders." This can easily mean that a comparison of Jesus' life to the "wonders" predicted by the prophets would make people think (including Josephus) "he was perhaps the Messiah." Several passages in the Talmud charge Jesus with sorcery. Jesus

". . . practiced sorcery and led Israel astray . . ." (*Sanhedrin* 43a). For this reason Jesus was executed on Passover Eve. Evans writes, "Finally, even in rabbinic tradition recorded in the Talmud, we find discussion over the legitimacy of being healed in the name of Jesus. Evidently, some rabbis believed it was better to die than to be healed in the name of Jesus. A discussion such as this attests to the ongoing reputation of Jesus as healer and exorcist" (p. 157). Pagan authors as well often placed Jesus in the category of magician. Seutonius in *The Twelve Caesars*, Nero 6.16 calls Christianity a "superstition" (*supertitionis novae ac maleficae*). This refers to those who work evil magic. In countering the Jew Trypho, Christian Justin Martyr (A.D. 110-165) gave the Jewish position regarding Jesus and miracles. "But though they saw such works, they asserted it was magic art. For they dared to call Him a magician, and a deceiver of the people" (*Dialogue with Trypho*, 69, *ANF* 1:233). In *The First Apology of Justin* 30, Justin counters the pagan view of Christ and miracles. This writing addressed to Roman Emperor Antonius Pius answers the critical question of the day. "What should prevent that He whom we call Christ, being a man born of men, **performed what we call His mighty works by magical art**, and by this appeared to be the Son of God?" (See *ANF* 1:172.) Justin then answers the false view that Jesus was a sorcerer.

Later Origen wrote a defense of Christianity in rebuttal to Celsus who had attacked Christianity in about A.D. 150. "And he [Celsus] next proceeds to bring a charge against the Savior Himself, **alleging that it was by means of sorcery that He was able to accomplish the wonders which He performed**" (*Contra Celsum*, 6, *ANF* 4:399). In Chapter 38 Origen quotes Celsus' book which had claimed Jesus learned magic arts while a boy in Egypt. ". . . that he (Jesus), having been brought up as an illegitimate child, and having served for hire in Egypt, and then coming to the knowledge of certain miraculous powers, returned from thence to his own country, and by means of these powers proclaimed himself a god." Origin goes on to argue that it is inconsistent to concede Christ and the apostles did miracles but attribute them to evil. "But if they indeed wrought miracles, then how can it be believed that magicians exposed themselves to such hazards to introduce a doctrine which forbade the practice of magic?" (Both quotes *ANF* 4:413) The same pagan view of miracles is given in Chapter 68 of *Contra Celsus*. Quoting the pagan Celsus, Origen writes, "And he asks, 'since, then, these persons can perform such feats, shall we of necessity conclude that they are 'sons of God' or must we admit that they are the proceedings of wicked men under the influence of an evil spirit?' " Origen continues his refutation that Jesus was a sorcerer, "You see that by these expressions he allows, as it were, the existence of magic . . . he compares the (miracles) related of Jesus to the results produced by magic" (*ANF* 4:427). Finally, in 2:68, Origen says, "Celsus, moreover, unable to resist the miracles which Jesus is recorded to have performed, has already on several occasions spoken of them slanderously as works of sorcery, and we also on several occasions have, to the best of our ability, replied to his statements" (*ANF* 4:449). In addition to the above, see notations on Lucian and Porphyry in Philip Schaff, *History of the Christian Church*, 1:95 and Lactanius, *Divine Institutes*, 5.3 (*ANF* 7:138-139). Schaff said, "The heathen opponents of Christianity, Lucian, Celsus, Porphyry and Julian the Apostate, etc. presupposed the principal facts of gospel history, even the miracles of Jesus, but they mostly derive them, like the Jewish adversaries from evil spirits."

It seems that the ancient enemies of Christ concede the point he could do magic and miracles. They just attribute it to a false and evil source of power. According to Quadratus, some healed by Jesus lived into his own times (see Eusebius, *HE*, 4.3.2., *Nicene and Post Nicene Fathers,* 1:175.). Their testimony would have countered denials of the miracles long after Jesus' earthly ministry.

361. For additional studies on this important subject see Josh McDowell, *The Resurrection Factor;* Paul Maier, *In the Fullness of Time,* Chapters 23 and 24; and Lee Strobel, *The Case for the Real Jesus*, pp. 101-155.

362. See endnote 206 for details on Thallus and Plegon admitting the darkness in the daytime.

363. *JAMA* 1986; 255: 1455-1463. Quote from page 1463.

364. Ibid.

365. Maier in *The Fullness of Time*, p. 194 comments:

"Admittedly, there was indeed a period of time when the sepulcher was unguarded: the approximately twelve or thirteen hours between the burial of Jesus on Friday evening and the priests' request for a guard from Pilate early Saturday morning. A raiding party *could* have removed the body Friday night while everyone was sleeping off wine from the Passover Seder. Although the New Testament does not record whether or not the guard first rolled back the stone on Saturday morning to make sure the body of Jesus was still inside before sealing it, the most primitive logic would have dictated that they do just that. They would hardly have sealed and guarded an empty tomb. That they did in fact open the grave can easily be concluded from the reaction of the priests when the shaken guards reported the missing body to them: 'You must say,' they were instructed, 'His disciples came by night and stole him away while we were asleep' (Matt. 28:13). Obviously they would have had a *much* better excuse had they found the tomb empty already on Saturday morning which would not have compromised the soldiers."

366. See Maier, *In the Fullness of Time*, pp. 202-203.

"Provincial governors in the Roman Empire had to dispatch *acta* annual reports of their activities – to the emperor, and Justin Martyr claims that Pilate mentioned the case of Jesus in his records prepared for Tiberius. But these have never been found, possibly due to the destruction of government archives in the great fire of Rome in 64 A.D.

Some scholars think that Pilate *may* have included in his *acta* a reference to the empty sepulcher along with a natural explanation for it — Jesus' body having been stolen – because a fascinating inscription was found in Nazareth on a 15 by 24 inch marble slab that might have been promoted by Tiberius' reply to Pilate. The inscription is an edict against grave robbery, and was written in Greek (italics added):

'Ordinance of Caesar. It is my pleasure that graves and tombs remain perpetually undisturbed for those who have made them for the cult of their ancestors or children or members of their house. If, however, anyone charges that another has either demolished them, or has in any other way *extracted the buried, or has maliciously transferred them to other places in order to wrong them, or has displaced the sealing or other stones,* against such a one I order that a trial be instituted, as in respect of the gods, so in regard to the cult of mortals. For it shall be much more obligatory to honor the buried. Let it be absolutely forbidden for any one to disturb them. In case of violation I desire that the offender be sentenced to capital punishment on charge of violation of sepulture.'

All previous Roman edicts concerning grave violation set only a large fine, and one wonders what presumed serious infraction could have led the Roman government to stiffen the penalty precisely in Palestine and to erect a notice regarding it specifically in Nazareth or vicinity. If only the "Caesar" had identified himself, but most scholars conclude – from the style of lettering in the inscription – that the edict derives from Tiberius or Claudius, either of whom *might* have reacted to tidings of the Easter enigma in Jerusalem. Nothing conclusive, however, has thus far been discovered from Roman sources."

367. See Josh McDowell, *The Resurrection Factor*, p. 69; or *New Evidence That Demands a Verdict,* pp. 235-240.

368. Ibid. Revelation 16:15 refers to a sleeping guard who has his clothes removed for shame. This seems to have been the Jewish penalty whereas the Roman army allowed the death penalty for failure on guard duty.

369. See McDowell, *The Resurrection Factor*, p. 67 or *New Evidence That Demands a Verdict*, pp. 231-235.

370. See Simon Greenleaf as quoted by John Warwick Montgomery in *The Law Above the Law* (Minneapolis: Bethany Fellowship, Inc., 1975) pp. 120-121. Greenleaf, 19th century professor at Harvard Law School, gave a lengthy analysis of the Gospel authors as to whether they would be credible witnesses in a court of law. The entire essay is valuable. We will be content with Greenleaf's conclusions:

"Yet their lives do show them to have been men like all others of our race; swayed by the same motives, animated by the same hopes, affected by the same joys, subdued by the same sorrows, agitated by the same fears, and subject to the same passions, temptations and infirmities, as ourselves. And their writings show them to have been men of vigorous understandings. If then their testimony was not true, here was no possible motive for this fabrication. It would also have been irreconcilable with the fact that they were good men. But it is impossible to read their writings, and not feel that we are conversing with men eminently holy, and of tender consciences, with men acting under an abiding sense of the presence and omniscience of God, and of their accountability to him, living in his fear, and walking in his ways. Now, though, in a single instance, a good man may fall, when under strong temptations, yet he is not found persisting, for years, in deliberate falsehood, asserted with the most solemn appeals to God, without the slightest temptation or motive, and against all the opposing interests which reign in the human breast. If, on the contrary, they are supposed to have been bad men, it is incredible that such men should have chosen this form of imposture; enjoining, as it does, unfeigned repentance, the utter forsaking and abhorrence of all falsehood and of every other sin, the practice of daily self-denial, self-abasement and self-sacrifice, the crucifixion of the flesh with all its earthly appetites and desires, indifference to the honors, and the hearty contempt of the vanities of the world; and inculcating perfect purity of heart and life, and intercourse of the soul with heaven. It is incredible, that bad men should invent falsehoods, to promote the religion of the God of truth. The supposition is suicidal. If they did believe in a future state of retribution, a heaven and a hell hereafter, they took the most certain course, if false witnesses, to secure the latter for their portion. And if, still being bad men, they did not believe in future punishment, how came they to invent falsehoods the direct and certain tendency of which was to destroy all their prospects of worldly honor and happiness, and to insure their misery in this life? From these absurdities there is no escape, but in the perfect conviction and admission that they were good men, testifying to that which they had carefully observed and considered, and well knew to be true."

371. For study on the sensational claim that Jesus' tomb has been discovered see Darrell L. Bock and Daniel B. Wallace, *Dethroning Jesus*, pp. 193-213; Lee Strobel, *The Case for the Real Jesus*, pp. 148-151; Paul L. Maier, *The Jesus Family Tomb*, an open letter on Dr. Maier's website dated, February 27, 2007; James K. Hoffmeier, *The Archaeology of the Bible*, pp. 164-165. Those who originally discovered the "Jesus" ossuary such as Amos Kloner and Joe Zias concluded that there is virtually no chance the "Jesus" name on the ossuary refers to the Jesus of Nazareth. Maier calls the documentary of this tomb "more junk on Jesus" and "media fraud."

Jesus or *Yeshua* in Hebrew (Joshua) was a very common name (one in eleven men were named Joshua, Strobel p. 148). Other names such as Mary (one in four or five) or Joseph (one in seven) were also common. Josephus' writings contain references to 21 different *Yeshuas*. This does not count all those thousands who lived without making the pages of a history book. Bock estimates more than 76,000 men named Jesus' lived during this time period (p. 207). There is no reason whatsoever to equate the Mariamme in this burial plot with Mary Magdalene.

Given the common occurrences of such names, they can not be identified with Bible characters. The important fact is that the tomb of Jesus being guarded by the soldiers after His death was undeniably empty on the first Easter morning. The best explanation is that Jesus rose from the dead.

Outside the Heavenly City:
Abortion in Rome and the Early Church's Response

The Old Testament contains the bulk of scriptural material relative to the unborn and the abortion issue. Nevertheless, the New Testament contains several passages that merit consideration. Some evidence exists to indicate that the Greek word *pharmakia* can be used of abortion-causing drugs. Therefore, the five New Testament occurrences of the *pharmakia* word group will be addressed.

A Study of *pharmakia*

Most theological studies about the unborn neglect the only New Testament texts that might be references to abortion, namely those texts that include the word *pharmakia* or one of its cognates. It is common knowledge that drugs are presently used to induce abortions. If it can be established that drug-induced abortions were also practiced in the Greco-Roman world and that the New Testament forbids such illicit usage of drugs, then the New Testament indirectly condemns the practice of abortion. In order to evaluate such a possibility, it will be necessary to establish that abortion, including abortion caused by drugs, was a common practice in the ancient world and that *pharmakia* can refer to abortifacient drugs, i.e. drugs that are used to induce abortion.

Abortion in the Ancient World

It is not difficult to demonstrate that abortion is an ancient custom. It was practiced in both Greece and Rome and was universally condemned by early Christians.

Abortion: a practice among the Greeks.

One of the most famous physicians in history, Hippocrates (460-359 B.C.), writes in his Hippocratic Oath: "Neither will I administer a poisen (sic) to anybody when asked to do so, nor will I suggest such a course. Similarly, I will not give to a woman a pessary to cause abortion."[1] Hippocrates was against abortion. However, the two great philosophical giants of the Greek world maintained that abortion was a necessary and proper means of eugenics and population control.

> But when, I take it, the men and the women have passed the age of lawful procreation, we shall leave the men free to form such relations with whomever they may please....first admonishing them preferably not even to bring to light anything whatever is thus conceived, but if they are unable to prevent a birth to dispose of it (Plato 427-347 B.C.). [2]

> There must be a limit fixed to the procreation of offspring, and if any people have a child as a result of intercourse in contravention of these regulations, abortion must be practiced on it before it has developed sensation and life (Aristotle 384-322 B.C.).[3]

Apparently, the views of Plato and Aristotle were shared by the majority of ancient Greeks. Durant writes, "The voluntary limitation of the family was the order of the day, whether by contraception, by abortion, or by infanticide,"

---

[1] Hippocrates *Oath*, in vol. 1 of 4 vols., *Loeb Classical Library*, p. 299 (*Oath* lines 18-20).

[2] Plato *The Republic*, vol. 1 of 2 vols., *Loeb Classical Library*, p. 467 (*The Republic* 5:461).

[3] Aristotle Politics, in *Loeb Classical Library*, pp. 623-24 (Politics 7:14:10).

and Bates mentions a French article in which the author lists twelve pages of abortifacient drugs used by the ancient Greeks.[4] The evidence points to a widespread practice of abortion (often involving drugs) in Greece, a practice which like so much of Hellenistic culture was absorbed by the Roman Empire.

Abortion: A practice in the Roman Empire

During the period in which Rome was both at the height of her military strength and the depth of her moral depravity, abortions became frequent. Notable families used abortion as a means of birth control, and physicians wrote manuals on abortion which "were popular among great ladies and prostitutes."[5]

Hermann Strack says that one of the reasons Jews believed entering a gentile house would make them impure was that the gentiles practiced abortion and threw their aborted babies into the drains:

> The dwelling of gentiles (in the land of Israel) are (levitically) unclean (because they are accustomed to bury their abortions therein).... The house is reputed as defiled by a corpse and renders ...the Israelite who enters there unclean for seven days.[6]

---

[4] Will Durant, *The Life of Greece*, in *The Story of Civilization* (New York: Simon and Schuster, 1939), p. 468; Jerome Bates and Edward S. Zawandzki, *Criminal Abortion* (Springfield, Illinois: Charles C. Thomas, 1964), p. 16; the French material is in Marcel Moissilles, "Contribution a l'Etude de l'Avortment dans l'Antiquite Grecque," *Janus*, 26 (1922): 129-145.

[5] Will Durant, *Caesar and Christ*, in *The Story of Civilization* (New York: Simon and Schuster, 1944), pp. 313 and 364.

[6] Hermann Strack and Paul Billerbeck, *Kommentar Zum Neuen Testament* (Munich: C. H. Becksche Verlagsbuchhandlung, 1924), 1:838-39. This is the interpretation of the German word

Similarly, Bates teaches that abortion in the empire was common and was practiced among all social classes:

> During the time of the Roman consuls abortion was a rarity....In the halcyon days of Imperial Rome, however, the practice burgeoned without restraint among all classes....Roman ladies as well as public women were to be found patronizing the abortionists, many of whom were Greek slaves. These slaves had brought their art with them into captivity and were often to be seen as attendant freed-women to Roman ladies of rank.[7]

The Romans themselves testify to the presence of abortion and abortifacient drugs in their society.[8] The Cornelian Law (c. 81 B.C.) was enacted against abortifacient drugs which threatened the life of the mother.[9] It is interesting that several great Roman moralists stood firm in their belief that abortion was wrong:

> If vicious ways like this had found favor with mothers of olden time, the race of mortal men would

---

fehlgeburtem, abortion or miscarriage, given by K. Marquart in "Killing with Kindness," *Concordia Theological Quarterly* 41 (January, 1977): 48. (John 18:28-29 illustrates Jewish views.)

[7] Jerome Bates, *Criminal Abortion*, p. 17.

[8] Two Greek authors, Soranus and Plutarch, who write during the Roman period are treated in a following section, (pp. 247-249).

[9] See Richard Hawks, "Abortion in History and the Bible," M. Div. thesis, Grace Theological Seminary, 1979, pp. 23; and Athenagoras, *Embassy for the Christians*, in *Ancient Christian Writers*, trans. by Joseph H. Crehan, edited by J. Quasten and Joseph Plumpe, 40 vols. (New York: Newman Press, 1955) p. 167 n. 305.

have perished from the earth....Why cheat the full vine of the growing cluster, and pluck with ruthless hand the fruit yet in the green? What is ripe will fall of itself - let grow what has once become quick; a life is no slight reward for a short delay. Ah, woman, why will you thrust and pierce with the instrument, and give dire poisens (sic) to your children yet unborn? (Ovid 43 B.C. - A.D. 17).[10]

Never have you in the manner of other women whose only recommendation lies in their beauty, tried to conceal your pregnancy as if an unseemly burden, nor have you ever crushed the hope of children that were being nurtured in your body (Seneca 4 B.C. - A.D. 65).[11]

So great is the skill so powerful the drugs of the abortionist, paid to murder mankind within the womb (Juvenal A.D. 60-140). [12]

These writers are direct testimony to the fact that women of the Roman Empire frequently resorted to abortion in order to resolve an unwanted pregnancy and that abortion was often induced by drugs. Like these pagan moralists, early Christians lived in a society that aborted its unwanted children. Also like them, the early Christians had much to say regarding the moral issues of their day.

Abortion: The response from the early Church.

---

[10] Ovid, *Heroides and Amores*, vol. 1 of 6 vols., *Loeb Classical Library*, p. 425 (Amores 2:14:9-10 and 23-28).

[11] Seneca *Moral Essays*, vol. 2 of 3 vols., *Loeb Classical Library*, pp. 471 and 473 (*To Helvia on Consolation* 16:3).

[12] Juvenal and Persius, *Loeb Classical Library*, p. 133 (*Satire* 6:592-97).

The number of references to abortion among the writings of the early church fathers is astounding. Judging from the frequency of their comments, abortion continued to be a common practice. Not only is the quantity of references to abortion remarkable, but also the unanimity of the church's condemnation of abortion and abortion-causing drugs is striking. These references provide additional evidence to demonstrate that abortion was an important moral issue in ancient times, and they lead one to wonder whether the early church's unanimous and uncertain condemnation of abortion lies in what she felt to be a scriptural basis. The following quotations give the early church's position on abortion.[13]

> Thou shalt not procure abortion, nor shalt thou kill that which is begotten (*Didache* A.D. 100-120).[14]

> And when we say that those women who use drugs to bring on abortion commit murder, and will have to give an account to God for the abortion, on what principle should we commit murder? (Athenagoras A.D. 175).[15]

---

[13] Other church fathers who mention abortion include: *The Epistle of Barnabas* 19:5, Tertullian in *Apology* 9:8, Cyprian in *Epistle 58*, *Constitutions* 7:3:2, Basil in *Letters* 188:2 and 8, *Diognetus* 5:6, Augustine in *On Marriage and Concupiscence* 1:15-17, and *The Apocalypse of Peter* 8 (26 in Akhmim). There are also possible references in Methodius *Concerning Chastity* 2:6, *Christian Sibyllines* 2:280-290, and *The Apocalypse of Paul* 784.

[14] "The Teaching of the Twelve Apostles," in *The Ante-Nicene Fathers*, ed. by Alexander Roberts and James Donaldson, reprint ed., 10 vols. (Grand Rapids: Wm. B. Eerdmans Publishing Co., 1970), 7:377 (*Didache* 2:2).

[15] Athenagoras, "A Plea for Christians", in *The Ante-Nicene Fathers*, 2:147 (*A Plea for Christians* 35).

If we should but control our lusts at the start and if we would not kill off the human race born and developing according to divine plan, then our whole lives would be lived according to nature. But women who resort to some sort of deadly abortion drug kill not only the embryo but, along with it, all human kindness (Clement of Alexandria A.D. 200-215).[16]

There are some women who, by drinking medical preparations, extinguish the source of the future man in their very bowels, and thus commit parricide before they bring forth (Minucius Felix A.D. 210).[17]

Some, when they find themselves with child through their sin, use drugs to procure abortion, and when (as often happens) they die with their offspring, they enter the lower world laden with the guilt not only of adultery against Christ but also of suicide and child murder (Jerome A.D. 384).[18]

You see how drunkenness leads to whoredom, whoredom to adultery, adultery to murder; or rather to a something even worse than murder. For I have no name to give it, since it does not take off the thing born, but prevent its being born. Why then dost thou abuse the gift of God.... and make the chamber of procreation a chamber for murder? .... For sorceries (or drugs) are applied not to the womb that is

---

[16] Clement of Alexandria, *Christ the Educator*, in *The Fathers of the Church*, ed. by Ludwig Schopp (Washington DC: The Catholic University of America Press, 1954) pp. 173-74.

[17] Minucius Felix, "The Octavius of Minucius Felix," in *The Ante-Nicene Fathers*, 4:191-92 (*Octavius* 30).

[18] Jerome, "Letters," in *The Nicene and Post-Nicene Fathers*, second series, 6:27 (Letter 22, *To Eustochium* 22:13).

prostituted, but to the injured wife, and there are plottings, without number, and invocations of devils, and necromancies, and daily wars, and truceless fightings, and home-cherished jealousies (Chrysostom A.D. 380-400).[19]

These patristic sources and the classical sources that were cited earlier provide more than ample proof that abortion, including abortion by means of drugs, was a means of eliminating an unwanted pregnancy during the apostolic period. However, a question remains as to whether the ancients used the word *pharmakia* in reference to drugs that induce abortion.

Classical uses of *pharmakia*

The *pharmakia* word group has the dual meaning of "medicine" and "sorcery." Ancient physicians were often a combination of physician and sorcerer similar to the "witchdoctor" of Africa or the "medicine man" of the American Indian. Noonan discusses this connection between medicine and sorcery and then adds a brief but important observation that pertains to abortion:

Writing in the second part of the 1st century, Plutarch said that Romulus in his original laws for Rome had enacted "a severe law" permitting a husband to divorce his wife, not only for adultery, but for "medicine in regard to children".... In both the tradition preserved by Plutarch and in Garius the key word is "medicine" - in Greek *pharmakia*: in Latin *veneficium*. In both languages the term means use of "magic drugs." The ambiguity of the term, which is preserved in each language, although

---

[19] John Chrysostom, "Homilies on Acts and Romans," in *The Nicene and Post-Nicene Fathers*, first series, 11:520 (*The Epistle to the Romans* 24:4).

different roots form the words, is deliberate, and reflects the attitude of the Greco-Roman culture. Drugs are intimately associated by this culture with magic; the users of Greek or Latin see no need to have two words to differentiate magic and the drugs. A univocal translation suppresses one of the two meanings suggested by the word in most contexts.... The term "medicine" in respect to children designates abortifacients.[20]

Noonan's comment that *pharmakia* can designate abortifacients is supported by Liddell and Scott, the standard lexicon for classical Greek literature.[21] Even more important than this, it is demonstrated by the word's usage in several classical and patristic references.

In classical literature the clearest reference of *pharmakia* referring to abortion-causing drugs is located in the *Gynecology* of Soranus. Soranus was a renowned Ephesian physician of the first century after Christ. In two passages he uses a member of the *pharmakia* word family to describe abortifacient drugs.

Natural waters which have relatively pungent qualities differ in no way from drugs (*pharmakon*) inserted for abortion. And an "expulsive," some people say is synonymous with an abortive; others, however, say that there is a difference because an

---

[20] John T. Noonan, *Contraception: A History of Its Treatment by Catholic Theologians and Canonists* (Cambridge, MA: Harvard University Press, 1965), p. 25.

[21] Henry George Liddell and Robert Scott, *A Greek-English Lexicon*, revised by Henry Stuart Jones with the assistance of Roderick McKenzie, with a supplement edited by E. A. Barber (Oxford: At the Clarendon Press, 1968), p. 1917.

expulsive does not mean drugs (*pharmakois*) but shaking and leaping.[22]

In the same paragraph Soranus discusses Hippocrates. He states that many in his day interpreted Hippocrates as saying he would not perform a drug-induced abortion but that he would allow a mother to "leap with the heels to the buttocks" in order to expel a child.[23] The passage in Hippocrates is not as clear as the two quotations above, but the word *homoios* (similiarly) indicates that Hippocrates may be discussing two methods of abortion, one of them involving *pharmakon*, "drugs."

Neither will I administer a poisen (sic) (*pharmakon*) to anybody when asked to do so, nor will I suggest such a course. Similarly (*homoios*), I will not give to a woman a pessary to cause abortion.[24]

Plutarch provides an additional classical reference where *pharmakia* seems to be used of abortifacients. In *Plutarch's Lives* he writes:

He (Romulus) also enacted certain laws and among them one of severity, which forbids a wife to leave her husband, but permits a husband to put away his

---

[22] Owsei Temkin, trans., *Soranus' Gynecology* (Baltimore: John Hopkins Press, 1956), pp. 57 and 62-63. (*Gynecology* 1:56 and 60.) The Greek interpolations are from *Soranai Gynaeciorum vetus translatios latina nunc primum edita cum additus graeci textus reliquiss a Deitzio repertis atque ad ipsum codicem parisiensem, nunc recognitis, a Valentio Rose,* (Lipsiae: In aedibus B. G. Teubneri, 1882), pp. 223 and 229.

[23] Ibid.

[24] Hippocrates, *Loeb Classical Library*, p. 299 (*Oath* 18-20).

wife for using poisens (sic) (*pharmakia*), for substituting children, and for adultery.[25]

Noonan's comment on this reference, which is given above, is logical.[26] The list of offenses, which are grounds for divorce, includes two offenses that are related to sexuality and reproduction. In all probability the usage of poison is meant as a parallel offense and refers to the wife aborting a child without her husband's consent. Cicero mentions a woman who had an abortion so she could retain a large share of her husband's property.[27] It is not difficult to understand how a case like this could give rise to legislation to make secret abortion a ground for divorce.

Patristic uses of *Pharmakia*

Patristic writings also yield several clear examples of the *pharmakia* word group referring to abortifacient drugs. In *Paedagogus* Clement of Alexandria says, "But women who resort to some sort of deadly abortion drug (*pharmakois*) ....kill not only the embryo but, along with it all human kindness."[28] Likewise, the great preacher John Chrysostom uses *pharmakeai* to mean abortifacient drugs in his *Homilies on Romans*. His comments show that medicine and witchcraft were closely related in the ancient

---

[25] Plutarch *Plutarch's Lives*, vol. 1 of 11 vols., *Loeb Classical Library*, pp. 161-163 (*Romulus* 22:3).

[26] See pages 246-247.

[27] Bates and Zawandzki, *Criminal Abortion*, p. 18.

[28] Clement of Alexandria, *Christ the Educator*, pp. 173-74; the Greek interpolation is from Clemens Alexandrinus, *Protrepticus and Paedagogus*, ed. by Otto Stahlin (Leipzig: J. C. Hinrichs' sche Buchhandlung, 1905), p. 215 (*Paedagogus* 2:10:96:5).

world and that the immorality that often leads to an abortion can also lead to idolatry.

> Wherefore, I beseech you flee fornication, and the mother of it, drunkenness....You see how drunkenness leads to whoredom, whoredom to adultery, adultery to murder....For with a view to drawing more money by being agreeable and an object of longing to her lovers, even this (abortion) she is not backward to do, so heaping upon thy head a great pile of fire....Hence too come idolatries, since many, with a view to become acceptable, devise incantations, and libations, and love-potions, and countless other plans. Yet, still after such great unseemliness, after slaughters, after idolatries, the thing seems to many to belong to things indifferent, aye, and to many that have wives too....For sorceries (*pharmakeai*) are applied not to the womb that is prostituted, but to the injured wife, and there are plottings without number, and invocations of devils, and necromancies, and daily wars, and truceless fightings, and home-cherished jealousies.[29]

Finally, the author of the *Didache* implies that performing abortions, doing magic and *pharmakeo* are closely related. The verb does not appear to be restricted to the use of abortifacients. However, this passage seems to reinforce the idea that the progression from illicit drug use to abortion was natural to the ancient mind.

---

[29] John Chrysostom, "Homilies on Acts and Romans," in *The Nicene and Post-Nicene Fathers*, first series, 11:520 (*The Epistle to the Romans*, homily 24). The Greek interpolation is from Joannis Chrysostomi, *Opera Omnia Quae Exstant*, in *Bibliothecae Cleri Universae*, 18 volumina, editorem J. P. Migne (Parisiorum: Opera Et Studion D. Bern, De Montaucon, Monachi Benedictini E. Congr. S. Mauri, 1862), 9:627-28.

"Thou shall not use witchcraft; thou shalt not practice sorcery (*pharmakeuseis*), thou shalt not procure abortion, nor shalt thou kill the newborn child."[30]

Classical and patristic references leave no doubt that *pharmakia* can refer to drugs that induce abortion, but does it have this meaning in the New Testament?

The New Testament usage of *pharmakia*

The preceding discussion has established that abortion, including drug-induced abortion, was common to the cultural setting of the New Testament writings. It has also presented evidence to indicate that the early readers of the New Testament could have connected *pharmakia* with abortifacient drugs if the context in which the word was found suggested such a meaning. The following sections examine the contexts of the five biblical usages of the *pharmakia* group.

Paul's usage of *pharmakia*

Paul uses *pharmakia* only once. In Gal. 5:19-21a it is listed in a series of vices:

But the works of the flesh are evident which are fornication, uncleanness, sensuality, idolatry, use of magical drugs (*pharmakia*), enmity, strife, envy, anger, disputes, disagreements, dissensions, jealousies, drunkenness, carousings, and the such ... [31]

---

[30] *The Teaching of the Twelve in the Original with Translations and Discussions of Post-Apostolic Teaching, Baptism, Worship and Discipline*, Trans. by Philip Schaff, 3rd ed. (New York: Funk and Wagnalls Publishers, 1890), pp. 168-69 (*Didache* 2:2).

[31] The author's translation.

The word *pharmakia* follows three words that indicate illicit sexual activity, *pornia* (fornication), *akatharsia* (uncleanness), and *aselgia* (sensuality), and one word that means idolatry, *idololatria*. Idolatrous worship during the New Testament period often included sexual impurity, and if Chrysostom is correct, harlots, as well as married women, used love-potions and invoked spirits in order to attract their men.[32] The sins in the middle of the list could possibly be expressions of the attitudes and actions of those offended by their unfaithful partners or of those lusting for the same mate. The list of evils concludes with drunken orgies.

How would the original readers have understood this reference to *pharmakia*? Paul appears to be condemning sexual impurity and illicit drug use that is somehow associated with it. Knowing that drug-induced abortion was a common practice of the period in which the epistle was written and that *pharmakia* can refer to abortifacient drugs, it is not unreasonable to believe that Paul intended to include abortifacient drugs in this denunciation of drug abuse as it is associated with sexual immorality.

John's usage of the *pharmakia* group

In the Book of The Revelation, John uses *pharmakia* and its cognates four times. As in Galatians, most of these references involve a list of sins.

And they did not repent of their murders, neither of their magical drugs (*pharmakon*), nor of their fornication, nor of their thefts [Rev. 9:21].

Because by your sorcery (*pharmakia*) all the nations were deceived [Rev. 18:23].

---

[32] See the quotation on pages 245-246.

But for the cowardly, and the unbelievers, and the abominable, and the murderers, and the fornicators, and the medicine men (*pharmakois*), and the idolaters, and for all deceivers their part is in the lake that burns with fire and sulpher (Rev. 21:8).

But outside are the dogs, and the medicine men (*pharmakoi*), and the fornicators, and the murderers, and the idolaters and everyone who loves and who practices falsehood (Rev. 22:15).[33]

In Rev. 18:23 sorcery best fits the context. However, in Rev. 9:21 *pharmakon* is placed between the sin of murder and the sin of fornication. In Rev. 21:8 *pharmakois* follows murderers and fornicators and precedes idolaters. Likewise, in Rev. 22:15 *pharmakoi* is followed by fornicators, murderers, and idolaters. If there is any one practice that would be related to these three sins and would involve drugs, it is abortion.

It is not necessary to argue that the drug abuse of which John speaks must be limited to abortion, or to maintain that the "medicine men" did not commit additional evils with their potions. Yet, the cultural practice of drug-induced abortion, the evidence that the *pharmakia* group can be related to drugs used in abortion, and the contexts of these three passages in Revelation should alert Bible students that early readers would have understood John to be including abortifacient drugs in his condemnations. The above quotations from the early church establish that it understood the biblical condemnation of sorcery to include the practice of abortion.[34] Hawks' statement on the subject deserves consideration:

---

[33] The author's translations.

[34] See pp. 244-246, 249-251.

It would be unfair to insist that every New Testament use of pharmakeia is specifically to be translated "abortion." The word is broad and comprehensive, including all illegitimate uses of drugs for sinful ends, of which abortion was a major practice. Abortion is one specific act of the general sin of pharmakeia.[35]

Conclusion to the study of *pharmakia*

Abortions were relatively frequent during the time in which the New Testament was written, and drugs were used as a means of inducing them. In several ancient writings the word *pharmakia*, or one of its cognates, is used of abortifacient drugs, and such a meaning would fit well in most of the New Testament passages that use the word. Based upon the cultural background of New Testament literature and the range of meanings for *pharmakia*, it is reasonable to conclude that the New Testament condemns abortion by its teachings on *pharmakia* and related terms. The New Testament warns that those who refuse to repent of their sorceries (including abortion doctors) will be outside the heavenly city (cf. Rev. 9:21 with 22:15). Nevertheless, the statement immediately before this stern warning promises, "Blessed are those who wash their robes so that they may have the right to the tree of life and may enter by the gates into the city" (Rev. 22:14). Immediately after follows an invitation to "come" in faith to Christ as Savior. By the power of His death and resurrection He offers grace and mercy for all sins, including past abortions.

---

[35] Richard Hawks, *Abortion in History and the Bible*, p. 47.

The Spirit and the bride [the Church] say, "Come!"
And let him who hears say, "Come!" Whoever is
thirsty, let him come, and whoever wishes, let him
take the free gift of the water of life" [Rev. 22:17].

Bibliography

Barnett, Paul. *Is the New Testament Reliable?* revised edition. Downers Grove, IL: InterVarsity Press, 2003. (Anglican Bishop of North Sydney, Macquarie University in Australia, Regent College in Canada)

Barnett, Paul. *The Birth of Christianity: The First Twenty Years.* After Jesus Series, vol. 1. Grand Rapids, MI and Cambridge, UK: Wm. B. Eerdmans, 2005.

Barrett, C.K. *The Gospel According to St. John.* second edition. Philadelphia: Westminster Press, 1978. (University of Durham, England)

Bauckham, Richard. *Jesus and the Eyewitnesses.* Grand Rapids, MI and Cambridge, United Kingdom: Wm. B. Eerdmans Publishing Co., 2006. (University of St. Andrews, Scotland)

Bennett, W.H. and Adeney, Walter F. *A Biblical Introduction.* 3rd edition. New York: Whittaker, 1906.

Black, David Alan and Beck, David R. editors. *Rethinking the Synoptic Problem.* Grand Rapids: Baker Academic, 2001.

Black, David Alan and Dockery, David S. editors. *New Testament Criticism and Interpretation.* Grand Rapids: Zondervan, 1991.

Black, David Alan. *Why Four Gospels?* Grand Rapids: Kregel Publications, 2001. (Southeastern Baptist Theological Seminary, Wake Forest, NC)

Blaiklock, E.M. *The Archaeology of the New Testament.* Grand Rapids: Zondervan, 1974. (University of Auckland, New Zealand)

Blaiklock, Edward M. and Harrison, R.K. editors. *The New International Dictionary of Biblical Archaeology.* Grand Rapids: Zondervan, 1983.

Blomberg, Craig L. *Jesus and the Gospels.* Nashville: Broadman and Holman, 1997. (Denver Seminary)

Blomberg, Craig. *The Historical Reliability of the Gospels.* Downers Grove, IL: InterVarsity Press, 1987.

Bock, Darrell L. and Herrick, Gregory J. *Jesus in Context: Background Readings for Gospel Study.* Grand Rapids: Baker Academic, 2005.

Bock, Darrell L. and Wallace, Daniel B. *Dethroning Jesus.* Nashville: Thomas Nelson, 2007. (Both Dallas Theological Seminary)

Bock, Darrell L. *Jesus According to Scripture.* Grand Rapids: Baker, 2002.

Bock, Darrell L. *Luke.* 2 vols. Baker Exegetical Commentary on the New Testament. Moises Silva, editor. Grand Rapids: Baker Books, 1994.

Bock, Darrell L. *Studying the Historical Jesus.* Grand Rapids: Baker, 2002.

Bock, Darrell L. *The Missing Gospels.* Nashville: Thomas Nelson 2006.

Bowker, John. *The Complete Bible Handbook.* New York: Barnes and Noble, 2005. (Trinity College, Cambridge, UK)

Brown, Raymond E. *An Introduction to the New Testament.* New York: Doubleday, 1997. (Union Seminary, New York City)

Bruce, F.F. *Paul: Apostle of the Heart Set Free.* Grand Rapids: Wm. B. Eerdmans, 1997. (University of Manchester, England)

Bruce, F.F. *In the Steps of Our Lord.* Grand Rapids: Kregel, 1997.

Bruce, F.F. *Jesus and Christian Origins Outside the New Testament.* Grand Rapids: Wm. B. Eerdmans, 1974.

Bruce, F.F. *New Testament History.* New York: Anchor Books, 1972.

Bruce. F.F. *The Book of Acts*: The New International Commentary of the New Testament. Grand Rapids: Wm. B. Eerdmans, 1979.

Bruce, F.F. *The Canon of Scripture.* Downers Grove, IL: InterVarsity Press, 1988.

Bruce, F.F. *The New Testament Documents: Are They Reliable?* 5th edition. Wm. B. Eerdmans Publishing Co., 1978.

Carson, D.A. and Moo, Douglas J. *An Introduction to the New Testament.* Grand Rapids: Zondervan, 2005. (Trinity Evangelical Divinity School and Wheaton College, both near Chicago)

Cartledge, Samuel A. *A Conservative Introduction to the New Testament.* Sixth edition. Grand Rapids: Zondervan, 1951. (Columbia Seminary, Decauter, Georgia)

Charlesworth, James H. editor. *Jesus and Archaeology.* Grand Rapids, MI and Cambridge, UK: Wm. B. Eerdmans, 2006. (Princeton Seminary)

Collett, Sidney. *All About the Bible.* New York, London, and Edinburgh: Fleming H. Revell. N.D.

DeSilva, David A. *An Introduction to the New Testament.* Downers Grove, IL and Leicester, England: InterVarsity Press, 2004. (Ashland Seminary, Ohio)

Dowley, Tim. editor. *Eerdman's Handbook to the History of Christianity.* Grand Rapids: Wm. B. Eerdmans, 1977.

Ellis, E. Earle. *The Making of the New Testament Documents.* Boston and Leiden: Brill Academic Publishers, Inc. 2002. (Southwestern Baptist Theological Seminary, Ft. Worth)

Elwell, Walter A. and Yarbrough, Robert W. *Encountering the New Testament.* Grand Rapids: Baker, 1998. (Wheaton College and Trinity International University, both near Chicago)

Eusebius. *The Church History.* translated by Paul L. Maier. Grand Rapids: Kregel, 1999.

Evans, Craig A. *Fabricating Jesus.* Downers Grove, IL: InterVarsity Press, 2006. (Acadia Divinity College, Nova Scotia)

Farmer, William R. ed. *New Synoptic Studies.* Macon, GA: Mercer University Press, 1983. (Southern Methodist University and University of Dallas)

Finegan, Jack. *The Archaeology of the New Testament.* rev. ed. Princeton: Princeton University Press, 1992. (Pacific School of Religion, Berkeley)

Friedberg, Arthur L. *Coins of the Bible.* Atlanta: Whitman Publishing, 2004.

Gaebelein, Frank E. editor. vol. 8. *The Expositor's Bible Commentary.* Grand Rapids: Zondervan, 1984.

Geisler, Norman L. and Nix, William E. *A General Introduction to the Bible.* revised ed. Chicago: Moody Press, 1986. (Southern Evangelical Seminary, Charlotte, NC)

Gerhardsson, Birger. *The Reliability of the Gospel Tradition.* Peabody, MA: Hendrickson Publishers, 2001. (Lund University, Sweden)

Green, Joel B.; McNight, Scot; and Marshall, I. Howard. editors. *Dictionary of Jesus and the Gospels.* Downers Grove, IL and Leicester, England: InterVarsity Press, 1992. (abbreviation *DJG*)

Gundry, Robert H. *A Survey of the New Testament.* 4th edition. Grand Rapids: Zondervan, 2003. (Westmont College, Santa Barbara, CA)

Guthrie, Donald. *New Testament Introduction.* Downers Grove, IL: InterVarsity Press, 1970.(London Bible College)

Habermas, Gary R. and Miethe, Terry L. *Why Believe God Exists?* Joplin, MO: College Press, 1993. (Emmanuel College, Oxford, UK)

Habermas, Gary R. *The Verdict of History.* Nashville: Thomas Nelson, 1988.

Harris, R. Laird. *Inspiration and Canonicity of the Bible.* Grand Rapids: Zondervan, 1969. (Covenant Seminary, St. Louis)

Harrison, Everett. F. *Introduction to the New Testament.* revised edition. Grand Rapids: Wm. B. Eerdmans, 1971.

Hendin, David. *Guide to Biblical Coins.* Nyack, NY: Amphora Books, 1987.

Hengel, Martin. *The Four Gospels and the One Gospel of Jesus Christ.* Harrisburg, PA: Trinity Press International, 2000. (Tubingen, Germany)

Hoehner, Harold W. *Chronological Aspects of the Life of Christ.* Grand Rapids: Zondervan, 1977. (Dallas Theolgoical Seminary)

Hoehner, Harold W. *Herod Antipas.* Grand Rapids: Zondervan, 1980.

Hoffmeier, James K. *The Archaeology of the Bible.* Oxford, England: Lion Hudson, 2008. (Trinity International University near Chicago)

Holum, Kenneth G.; Hohlfelder, Robert L.; Bull, Robert J.; and Raban, Avner. *King Herod's Dream: Caesarea on the Sea.* New York: W.W. Norton and Company, 1988.

Johnson, Luke Timothy. *The Writings of the New Testament.* revised edition. Minneapolis: Fortress Press, 1999. (Emory University, Atlanta)

Jones, Timothy Paul. *Misquoting Truth.* Downers Grove, IL: InterVarsity Press, 2007. (Southern Baptist Seminary, Louisville, Kentucky)

Josephus, Flavius. *Josephus: Complete Works.* translated by William Whiston. rev.ed. Grand Rapids: Kregel, 1960. (Whiston was Isaac Newton's successor in math at Cambridge.)

Josephus, Flavius. *Josephus: The Essential Writings.* translated by Paul L. Maier. Grand Rapids: Kregel, 1988.

Kent, Homer A., Jr. *Jerusalem to Rome.* Grand Rapids: Baker Book House, 1972.

Kent, Homer A., Jr. *Light in the Darkness: Studies in the Gospel of John.* Grand Rapids: Baker Book House, 1974. (Grace Seminary, Indiana)

Kent, Homer A., Jr. *The Beginnings of the Gospel of Jesus Christ: Studies in Mark.* Winona Lake, IN: BMH Books, 2005.

Kerr, John H. *An Introduction to the Study of the Books of the New Testament.* 12th edition. New York, London, and Edinburgh: Fleming H. Revell, 1892-1931.

Komoszewski, J. Ed.; Sawyer, M. James; Wallace, Daniel B. *Reinventing Jesus.* Grand Rapids: Kregel Publications, 2006.

Linnemann, Eta. *Is There A Synoptic Problem?* Grand Rapids: Baker, 1992. (Philipps University in Marburg, Germany; missionary Indonesia)

Maier, Paul L. *In the Fullness of Time.* San Francisco: Harper San Francisco, 1991. (Western Michigan University)

Maier, Paul L. *Pontius Pilate: A Biographical Novel.* Wheaton, IL: Tyndale House, 1970.

Marshall, I. Howard; Millard, A.R.; Packer, J.I.; Wiseman, D.J. *New Bible Dictionary.* Downers Grove, IL and Leicester, UK: InterVarsity Press, 1996.

Marshall, I. Howard. *I Believe in the Historical Jesus.* Grand Rapids: Wm. B. Eerdmans, 1977. (University of Aberdeen, Scotland)

McDowell, Josh. *He Walked Among Us.* San Bernardino, CA: Here's Life Publishers, 1988.

McDowell, Josh. *The New Evidence that Demands a Verdict.* Nashville: Thomas Nelson, 1999.

McDowell, Josh. *The Resurrection Factor.* San Bernadino, CA: Here's Live Publishers, 1981.

McRay, John. *Archaeology of the New Testament.* Grand Rapids: Baker, 1991.

Metzger, Bruce M. *The Canon of the New Testament.* Oxford: Clarendon Press, 1997. (Princeton Seminary)

Metzger, Bruce M. *The New Testament.* third ed. Nashville: Abingdon Press, 2003.

Montgomery, John Warwick. *Faith Founded on Fact.* Nashville: Thomas Nelson, 1978.

Montgomery, John Warwick. *The Law Above the Law.* Minneapolis: Bethany Fellowship, 1975.

Montgomery, John Warwick. *The Shape of the Past.* Minneapolis: Bethany Fellowship, 1975.

Montgomery, John Warwick. *Where Is History Going?* Minneapolis: Bethany Fellowship, 1972.

Morris, Leon. *Studies in the Fourth Gospel.* Grand Rapids: Wm. B. Eerdmans, 1969. (Ridley College, Melbourne, Australia)

Neufeld, Vernon, H. *The Earliest Christian Confessions.* vol. 5. New Testament Tools and Studies. Grand Rapids: Wm. B. Eerdmans, 1963.

Orchard, Bernard and Harold Riley. *The Order of the Synoptics: Why Three Synoptic Gospels?* Macon, GA: Mercer University Press, 1987. (Ealing Abbey, London)

Patzia, Arthur G. *The Making of the New Testament.* Downers Grove, IL: InterVarsity Press, 1995. (Fuller Seminary, Pasadena, CA)

Pheiffer, Charles F.; Vos, Howard F. and Rea, John. editors. *Wycliffe Bible Encyclopedia.* Chicago: Moody Press, 1975.

Price, Randall. *Searching for the Original Bible.* Eugene, OR: Harvest House Publishers, 2007.

Price, Randall. *The Stones Cry Out.* Eugene, OR: Harvest House Publishers, 1997.

Ratzinger, Joseph (Pope Benedict XVI). *Jesus of Nazareth.* translated by Adrian J. Walker. New York: Doubleday, 2007.

Reicke, Bo. *Re-examining Paul's Letters.* Harrisburg, PA: Trinity Press International, 2001. (University of Basel, Switzerland)

Reicke, Bo. *The Roots of the Synoptic Gospels.* Philadelphia: Fortress Press, 1986.

Richardson, Peter. *Herod: King of the Jews and Friend of the Romans.* Columbia, SC: University of South Carolina Press, 1996.

Ritmeyer, Leen and Kathleen. *Secrets of Jerusalem's Temple Mount.* revised edition. Washington, D.C.: Biblical Archaeology Society, 2006. (Leen is from Holland. Kathleen is Irish. They participated in the Temple Mount Excavation.)

Roberts, Mark D. *Can We Trust the Gospels?* Wheaton, IL: Crossway Books, 2007. (Ph.D. from Harvard. He blogs at www.markdroberts.com.)

Robinson, John A.T. *Can We Trust the New Testament?* Grand Rapids: Wm. B. Eerdmans, 1977. (Anglican bishop from the UK)

Rowe, Arthur. *The Essence of Jesus.* London: Arcturus Publishing, 2006. (Spurgeon's College, London)

Schaff, Philip. *History of the Christian Church.* volume 1. "Apostolic Christianity." reprint edition. Grand Rapids: Wm. B. Eerdmans, 1985. (Union Seminary, New York City, 1880's)

Shanks, Hershel and Cole Dan P. *Archaeology and the Bible: The Best of BAR.* volume 2. "Archaeology in the World of Herod, Jesus, and Paul." Washington, D.C.: Biblical Archaeology Society, 1990.

Shanks, Hershel and Witherington, Ben. *The Brother of Jesus: The Dramatic Story and Meaning of the First Archaeological Link to Jesus and His Family.* San Francisco: Harper San Francisco, 2003.

Shanks, Hershel. editor. *Biblical Archaeology Society Special Report: Jerusalem Forgery Conference.* 2007. www.biblicalarchaeology.org.

Shanks, Hershel. *"Case Not Closed: Hershel Shanks Speaks on the James Ossuary."* DVD. Washington, D.C.: Biblical Archaeology Society, 2004.

Shanks, Hershel. *Jerusalem An Archaeological Biography*. Random House, 1995.

Shanks, Hershel, editor. *Where Christianity Was Born.* Washington, D.C.: Biblical Archaeology Society, 2006.

Sherwin-White. *Roman Society and Roman Law In the New Testament.* reprint edition. Grand Rapids: Baker Book House, 1978.

Stein, Robert H. *Studying the Synoptic Gospels*. 2nd ed. Grand Rapids: Baker Academic, 2001. (Southern Baptist Theological Seminary, Louisville, KY)

Strobel, Lee. *The Case for Christ.* Grand Rapids: Zondervan, 1998.

Strobel, Lee. *The Case for the Real Jesus.* Grand Rapids: Zondervan, 2007.

Stulmacher, Peter, editor. *The Gospel and the Gospels.* Grand Rapids: Wm. B. Eerdmans, 1991. (Tubingen, Germany)

Suetonius. *The Twelve Caesars*. translated by Robert Graves. New York: Penguin Books, 1981.

Tacitius. *The Annals of Imperial Rome*. translated by Michael Grant. revised edition. New York: Penguin Books, 1982.

Tenney, Merrill C. editor. *The Zondervan Pictorial Encyclopedia of the Bible.* 5 vols. Grand Rapids: Zondervan, 1976.

The Ante-Nicene Fathers. edited by Alexander Roberts and James Donaldson. 10 vols. 1885-1887. reprint edition. Grand Rapids: Wm. B. Eerdmans, 1970. (Citations abbreviated by *ANF.*)

The Nicene and Post-Nicene Fathers. edited by Philip Schaff and Henry Ware. 14 vols. 1890-1900. reprint edition. second series. Grand Rapids: Wm. B. Eerdmans, 1976.

Theissen, Gerd and Merz, Annette. *The Historical Jesus.* Minneapolis: Fortress Press, 1998. (University of Heidelberg, Germany)

Thiessen, Henry. *Introduction to the New Testament.* Grand Rapids: Wm. B. Eerdmans, 1943. (Wheaton College)
Thomas, Robert L. and Farnell, David F. editors. *The Jesus Crisis.* Grand Rapids: Kregel, 1998. (The Master's Seminary, CA)

Thomas, Robert L. editor. *Three Views on the Origins of the Synoptic Gospels.* Grand Rapids: Kregel, 2002.

Unger, Merrill F. *Archaeology and the New Testament.* Grand Rapids: Zondervan, 1962.

Vos, Howard F. editor. *Can I Trust the Bible?* Chicago: Moody Press, 1963.

Wallace, Daniel. *"John 5:2 and the Date of the Fourth Gospel . . . again."* http://www.bible.org.

Wallace, Daniel B. *"Luke: Introduction, Outline, Argument."* http://www.bible.org.

Wallace, Daniel B. *"Mark: Introduction, Argument and Outline."* http://www.bible.org.

Wallace, Daniel B. *"Matthew: Introduction, Argument and Outline."* http://www.bible.org.

Wallace, Daniel B. *"The Gospel of John: Introduction, Argument, and Outline."* http://www.bible.org.

Wallace, Daniel B. *"The Synoptic Problem."* http://www.bible.org.

Waterhouse, Steven. *Evidences for the Christian Faith*. Amarillo: Westcliff Bible Church, 1986.

Waterhouse, Steven. *Israel Tour Notes*. Amarillo: Westcliff Bible Church, 1998.

Westcott, B.F. *The Gospel According to St. John.* reprint edition. Grand Rapids: Wm. B. Eerdmans, 1975.

Wilkins, Michael J. and Moreland, J.P. *Jesus Under Fire*. Grand Rapids: Zondervan, 1995. (Talbot School of Theology, near Los Angeles)

Williams, Matthew C. *Two Gospels From One*. Grand Rapids: Kregel, 2006.

Wilson, Ian. *The Bible Is History*. London: Weidenfeld and Nicolson, 1999.

Wiseman, Donald J. and Yamauchi, Edwin. *Archaeology and the Bible*. Grand Rapids: Zondervan, 1979.

Witherington, Ben. *What Have They Done with Jesus?* San Francisco: Harper San Francisco, 2006. (Asbury Seminary, KY)

Zahn, Theodor. *Introduction to the New Testament.* 3 vols. reprint edition. Minneapolis: Klock and Klock, 1977. (Erlangen University, Germany; German original 1897-1899, English translation 1909)

Index

Glossary

Antioch – Antioch, Syria was the third largest city in the Roman Empire and an early Christian center.

Anti-Marcionite Prologues – These prologues were introductory comments to some early Latin manuscripts opposing the heretic Marcion. These comments also contain early material on authorship.

Apostle – Apostle refers to one sent with a commission by the Lord Jesus Christ. In a technical sense there were twelve apostles with Paul becoming the apostle to the gentiles.

Aramaic – The Jews in Jesus' day spoke the Aramaic language that their ancestors had learned in exile in Babylon.

Augustine – Augustine was an influential author and Bishop of Hippo in North Africa in the 4th century.

Caesarea – This city was the Roman capital of the province of Judea during Jesus' lifetime.

Church Fathers – These were the Christian leaders in the early church but after the times of the apostles.

Clement of Rome – Clement was one of the earliest Bishops of Rome (died about A.D. 100) and an early Christian author.

Didache – This Greek word means "teaching" and was an early Christian manual of instructions on church life (written late first or early second century).

Eusebius – Eusebius (c. 236-339) was Bishop of Caesarea, friend of Emperor Constantine, and author of a major work on church history (abbreviated HE for the Latin of ecclesiastical history).

Gentile – A gentile is a non-Jewish person.

Hebrew – While Hebrew is often a synonym for a Jewish or Israelite person, it often stresses language or culture. In Jesus' time most Jews spoke Aramaic but the Old Testament language still in use among religious leaders was Hebrew.

Ignatius – Ignatius was the Bishop of Antioch, Syria and author of several early documents (death c. A.D. 107).

Irenaeus – Irenaeus was Bishop of Lyons in Gaul (France) and wrote important books which give information about the background to the Gospels. He wrote around A.D. 180.

Judea – The name for one of the Roman provinces in Israel at the time of Jesus. Galilee was the province to Judea's north.

Justin Martyr – Justin was a Christian leader from Israel who taught in Ephesus and Rome. He wrote books defending Christianity and was killed about A.D. 165.

Liberal – A liberal within the context of this book's subject matter often refers to one who denies that the Gospels give a trustworthy account of Jesus' life and teachings.

Muratorian Canon – The word "canon" (related to the word "cane" as a measuring stick) refers to the list of books that belong in the Bible by which we can measure truth. The Muratorian Canon was a Latin list of New Testament books and dates to the end of the second century. It is named after the Italian scholar, Muratori, who discovered this early list in 1740.

Papias – Papias was Bishop of Hierapolis in Roman Asia (now Turkey). His writings date from A.D. 100-130 and remain in quotes within Eusebius' book on church history.

Papyrus fragments – Early writings such as the New Testament have been discovered in incomplete often small portions. Papyrus 52 contains only a few verses of John 18, and its early date (A.D. 100-125) shows the Gospel of John was itself an early book.

Polycarp – Polycarp was Bishop of Smyrna (now Izmir, Turkey). He wrote several books which can be dated around A.D. 110. He was a student of the Apostle John and a teacher of Irenaeus.

Polycrates – Polycrates was born about A.D. 130 and became the eighth Bishop of Ephesus. He was probably a descendant of Philip the Evangelist in the book of Acts, and some of his writings were quoted by Eusebius.

Prison Epistles – These are letters by Paul that were written while he was in prison (Ephesians, Colossians, Philippians, Philemon).

Sadducees – The Sadducees were a religious party in Jesus' time from which came the high priest and the chief priests. They were liberal in theology (Matthew 22:23; Acts 23:8) and opposed by the rigid Pharisees who were mostly business men.

Synoptic Problem – "Synoptic" refers to the similar viewpoint, order, and wording of Matthew, Mark, and Luke. The "synoptic problem" is how to explain these similarities. In which order were these synoptic Gospels written? Did the later authors use previous Gospels as a guide?

The Temple – The Temple in Jesus' day had been enlarged and renovated by King Herod. The Romans destroyed it in A.D. 70.

Tertullian – Tertullian was the first major Christian author to write in Latin. He was from Carthage in North Africa and his books date from A.D. 196-212.